THE

# SECOND ADMINISTRATION

OF

# JAMES MADISON

1813—1817

# HISTORY OF THE UNITED STATES.

BY

# HENRY ADAMS.

# HISTORY

OF THE

# UNITED STATES OF AMERICA

DURING THE SECOND ADMINISTRATION OF

# JAMES MADISON

By HENRY ADAMS

Vol. II.

ANTIQUARIAN PRESS LTD.
New York
1962

First Published
1891-1896
by
Charles Scribner's Sons

———

Reprinted 1962
by
Antiquarian Press, Ltd.
New York, N.Y.

Edition Limited to 750 Sets

Library of Congress Catalog Card Number: 61-8054

*Printed in the U.S.A.*

———

NOBLE OFFSET PRINTERS, INC.
NEW YORK 3, N.Y.

# CONTENTS OF VOL. II.

# HISTORY OF THE UNITED STATES.

## CHAPTER I.

At the beginning of the year 1814, the attitude of New England pleased no one, and perhaps annoyed most the New England people themselves, who were conscious of showing neither dignity, power, courage, nor intelligence. Nearly one half the people of the five New England States supported the war, but were paralyzed by the other half, which opposed it. Of the peace party, one half wished to stop the war, but was paralyzed by the other half, which threatened to desert their leaders at the first overt act of treason. In this dead-lock every one was dissatisfied, but no one seemed disposed to yield.

Such a situation could not last. In times of revolution treason might be necessary, but inert perversity could at no time serve a useful purpose. Yet the Massachusetts Federalists professed only a wish to remain inert. Josiah Quincy, who fretted at restraints, and whose instincts obliged him to act as energetically as he talked, committed his party to

the broad assertion that " a moral and religious people " could not express admiration for heroism displayed in a cause they disapproved.    They would
defend Massachusetts only by waiting to be invaded ;
and if their safety depended on their possessing the
outlet of Lake Champlain, they would refuse to seize
it if in doing so they should be obliged to cross the
Canadian line.    With one accord Massachusetts Federalists reiterated that until their territory should be
actually invaded, they would not take arms.    After
January 1, 1814, when news of the battle of Leipzig
arrived, the dreaded invasion of New England became imminent ; but the Federalists, officially and
privately, insisted on their doctrine of self-defence.

" In the tumult of arms," said Governor Strong in his
speech to the legislature, January 12, 1814, " the passions of men are easily inflamed by artful misrepresen-
tations ; they are apt to lose sight of the origin of a
contest, and to forget, either in the triumph of victory
or the mortification of defeat, that the whole weight of
guilt and wretchedness occasioned by war is chargeable
upon that government which unreasonably begins the
conflict, and upon those of its subjects who, voluntarily
and without legal obligation, encourage and support it."

The Massachusetts Senate echoed the sentiment
in language more emphatic : —

" Beyond that submission which laws enacted agree-
ably to the Constitution make necessary, and that self-
defence which the obligation to repel hostile invasions
justifies, a people can give no encouragement to a war

of such a character without becoming partakers in its guilt, and rendering themselves obnoxious to those just retributions of Divine vengeance by which, sooner or later, the authors and abettors of such a war will be assuredly overtaken."

The House of Representatives could see but one contingency that warranted Massachusetts in making voluntary exertion : —

"It is only after the failure of an attempt to negotiate, prosecuted with evidence of these dispositions on the part of our Administration, that any voluntary support of this unhappy war can be expected from our constituents."

In thus tempting blows from both sides, Massachusetts could hardly fail to suffer more than by choosing either alternative. Had she declared independence, England might have protected and rewarded her. Had she imitated New York in declaring for the Union, probably the Union would not have allowed her to suffer in the end. The attempt to resist both belligerents forfeited the forbearance of both. The displeasure of Great Britain was shown by a new proclamation, dated April 25, 1814, including the ports of New England in the blockade ; so that the whole coast of the Union, from New Brunswick to Texas, was declared to be closed to commerce by " a naval force adequate to maintain the said blockade in the most rigorous and effective manner." [1]

[1] Proclamation of Admiral Cochrane, April 25, 1814 ; Niles, vi. 182.

However annoying the blockade might be, it was a trifling evil compared with other impending dangers from Great Britain. Invasion might be expected, and its object was notorious. England was known to regret the great concessions she had made in the definitive treaty of 1783. She wished especially to exclude the Americans from the fisheries, and to rectify the Canadian boundary by recovering a portion of Maine, then a part of Massachusetts. If Massachusetts by her neutral attitude should compel President Madison to make peace on British terms, Massachusetts must lose the fisheries and part of the District of Maine; nor was it likely that any American outside of New England would greatly regret her punishment.

The extreme Federalists felt that their position could not be maintained, and they made little concealment of their wish to commit the State in open resistance to the Union. They represented as yet only a minority of their party; but in conspiracies, men who knew what they wanted commonly ended by controlling the men who did not. Pickering was not popular; but he had the advantage of following a definite plan, familiar for ten years to the party leaders, and founded on the historical idea of a New England Confederation.[1] For Pickering, disunion offered no terrors. "On the contrary," he wrote, July 4, 1813, "I believe an immediate separation

[1] Pickering to John Lowell, Nov. 7, 1814; New England Federalism, p. 404.

would be a real blessing to the 'good old thirteen States,' as John Randolph once called them."[1] His views on this subject were expressed with more or less fidelity and with much elaboration in a pamphlet published in 1813 by his literary representative, John Lowell.[2] His policy was as little disguised as his theoretical opinions; and in the early part of the year 1814, under the pressure of the embargo, he thought that the time had come for pressing his plan for a fourth time on the consideration of his party. Without consulting his old associates of the Essex Junto, he stimulated action among the people and in the State legislature.

The first step was, as usual, to hold town-meetings and adopt addresses to the General Court. Some forty towns followed this course, and voted addresses against the embargo and the war. Their spirit was fairly represented by one of the most outspoken, adopted by a town-meeting at Amherst, over which Noah Webster presided Jan. 3, 1814.[3] The people voted —

" That the representatives of this town in the General Court are desired to use their influence to induce that honorable body to take the most vigorous and decisive measures compatible with the Constitution to put an end

[1] Pickering to George Logan, July 4, 1813 ; New England Federalism, p. 391.

[2] Thoughts in Answer to a Question respecting the Division of the States; by a Massachusetts Farmer.

[3] The Palladium, Feb. 1, 1814.

to this hopeless war, and to restore to us the blessings of peace. What measures it will be proper to take, we pretend not to prescribe ; but whatever measures they shall think it expedient to adopt, either separately or in conjunction with the neighboring States, they may rely upon our faithful support."

The town of Newbury in Essex County made itself conspicuous by adopting, January 31, a memorial inviting bloodshed : —

" We remember the resistance of our fathers to oppressions which dwindle into insignificance when compared with those which we are called on to endure. The rights ' which we have received from God we will never yield to man.' We call on our State legislature to protect us in the enjoyment of those privileges to assert which our fathers died, and to defend which we profess ourselves ready to resist unto blood. We pray your honorable body to adopt measures immediately to secure to us especially our undoubted right of trade within our State. We are ourselves ready to aid you in securing it to us to the utmost of our power, ' peaceably if we can, forcibly if we must ; ' and we pledge to you the sacrifice of our lives and property in support of whatever measures the dignity and liberties of this free, sovereign, and independent State may seem to your wisdom to demand."

The voters of Newbury were constituents of Pickering. Their address could not have reached him at Washington when a few days afterward he wrote to Samuel Putnam, an active member of the General Court, then in session, urging that the time for remonstrances had passed, and the time for action had come : [1] —

" Declarations of this sort by Massachusetts, especially if concurred in by the other New England States, would settle the business at once. But though made now by Massachusetts alone, you surely may rely on the co-operation of New Hampshire, Rhode Island, and Connecticut, and I doubt not of Vermont and New York. With the executives and legislatures of most, and the representatives of all of them, you can freely communicate. Ought there not to be a proposal of a convention of delegates from those six States?"

The project of a New England convention was well understood to violate the Constitution, and for that reason alone the cautious Federalists disliked and opposed it. Doubtless a mere violence done to the law did not necessarily imply a wish for disunion. The Constitution was violated more frequently by its friends than by its enemies, and often the extent of such violations measured the increasing strength of the Union. In such matters intent was everything; and the intent of the proposed New England convention was made evident by the reluctance with which the leaders slowly yielded to the popular demand.

The addresses of the towns to the General Court were regularly referred to a committee, which reported February 18,[2] in a spirit not altogether satisfactory to the advocates of action : —

[1] Pickering to Putnam, Feb. 4, 1814; New England Federalism, p. 391.

[2] Report of Committee ; Niles, vi. 4–8.

" Whenever the national compact is violated and the
citizens of this State are oppressed by cruel and un-
authorized laws, the legislature is bound to interpose its
power and wrest from the oppressor his victim.    This
is the spirit of our Union, and thus it has been explained
by the very man who now sets at defiance all the principles of his early political life. . . . On the subject of
a convention, the committee observe that they entertain
no doubt of the right of the legislature to invite other
States to a convention and to join it themselves for the
great purposes of consulting for the general good, and
of procuring Amendments to the Constitution whenever
they find that the practical construction given to it by
the rulers for the time being is contrary to its true spirit
and injurious to their immediate constituents. . . . This
was the mode proposed by Mr. Madison [1] in answer to
objections made as to the tendency of the general government to usurp upon that of the States."

The *argumentum ad personam* commonly proved
only weakness.    Madison's authority on these points
had always been rejected by the Federalists when
in power; and even he had never asserted the right
of States to combine in convention for resistance to
measures of the national government, as the General
Court was asked to do.    So revolutionary was the
step that the committee of both Houses shrank from
it: " They have considered that there are reasons
which render it inexpedient at the present moment
to exercise this power."    They advised that the subject should not be immediately decided, but should

[1] Federalist, no. 46.

be referred to the representatives soon to be returned for the next General Court, who would " come from the people still more fully possessed of their views and wishes as to the all-important subject of obtaining by future compact, engrafted into the present Constitution, a permanent security against future abuses of power, and of seeking effectual redress for the grievances and oppressions now endured."

To the people, therefore, the subject of a New England convention was expressly referred. The issue was well understood, and excluded all others in the coming April election. So serious was the emergency, and so vital to the Administration and the war was the defeat of a New England convention, that the Republicans put forward no party candidate, but declared their intention to vote for Samuel Dexter, a Federalist, — although Dexter, in a letter dated February 14, reiterated his old opinions hostile to the embargo, and professed to be no further a Republican than that he offered no indiscriminate opposition to the war. His Federalism was that of Rufus King and Bayard.

" What good is to be expected," he asked,[1] " from creating division when engaged in war with a powerful nation that has not yet explicitly shown that she is willing to agree to reasonable terms of peace? Why make publications and speeches to prove that we are absolved from allegiance to the national government, and hint

[1] Dexter to the Electors of Massachusetts, Feb. 14, 1814; Niles, vi. 9.

that an attempt to divide the empire might be justified?
. . . The ferocious contest that would be the effect of
attempting to skulk from a participation of the burdens
of war would not be the greatest calamity."

Under such circumstances the load of the embargo
became too heavy for the Massachusetts Republicans
to carry. They tried in every manner to throw it off,
as persistently as President Madison tried to hold it
on. Their candidate, Dexter, argued strongly against
the restrictive system in his letter consenting to
stand. They drew a distinction between the restrictive system and the war; but even in regard to the
war they required not active support, but only absti-
nence from active resistance. The Federalists used
the embargo to stimulate resistance to the war, and
advocated a New England convention under cover of
the unpopularity of commercial restrictions.

With the pertinacity which was his most remarkable trait, Madison clung to the embargo all winter
in face of overwhelming motives to withdraw it. A
large majority in Congress disliked it. England having recovered her other markets could afford to conquer the American as she had conquered the Euro-
pean, and to wait a few months for her opportunity.
The embargo bankrupted the Treasury, threatened to
stop the operations of war, and was as certain as any
ordinary antecedent of a consequent result to produce a New England convention. Yet the President
maintained it until the news from Europe caused a
panic in Congress.

The Massachusetts election took place in the first days of April, while Congress was engaged in repealing the embargo and the system of commercial restrictions.   The result showed that Dexter might have carried the State and defeated the project of a New England convention, had the embargo been repealed a few weeks earlier.   A very large vote, about one hundred and two thousand in aggregate, was cast.   The Federalists, whose official vote in 1813 was 56,754, threw 56,374 votes ; while the Republicans, who cast 42,789 votes in 1813, numbered 45,359 in 1814.

The reduction of the Federalist majority from fourteen thousand to eleven thousand was not the only reason for believing that Dexter might have carried Massachusetts but for the embargo.   At the same time William Plumer, supported like Dexter by the Republicans, very nearly carried New Hampshire, and by gaining a majority of the executive council, precluded the possibility that New Hampshire as a State could take part in a New England convention. The President's Message recommending a repeal of the embargo was sent to Congress March 31, and the Act of Repeal was signed April 14.   Two weeks later, April 28, the New York election took place.   To this election both parties anxiously looked.   The Administration press admitted that all was lost if New York joined Massachusetts,[1] and the New England Federalists knew that a decisive defeat in New York would

[1] National Intelligencer, May 5, 1814.

leave them to act alone. The returns were watched
with such anxiety as had seldom attended a New
York election, although no general State officer was
to be chosen.

In May, 1813, Governor Tompkins carried the
State by a majority of only 3,506, and the Federal-
ists in the House of Assembly numbered sixty, while
the Republicans numbered fifty-two. The city of
New York and the counties of Queens, Westchester,
Dutchess, Columbia, Rensselaer, and Washington —
the entire range of counties on the east shore of the
Hudson — were then Federalist. The counties of
Albany, Montgomery, Oneida, Otsego, Madison, and
Ontario in the centre of the State were also Federalist. At the congressional election of 1812, twenty
Federalists and six Republicans had been chosen.
The May election of 1814 was for the State Assembly and for Congress. No opportunity was given for
testing the general opinion of the State on a single
issue, but no one could mistake what the general
opinion was. City and State reversed their political
character. The Republicans recovered possession of
the Assembly with a large majority of seventy-four
to thirty-eight, and the Congressional delegation
numbered twenty-one Republicans and only six
Federalists.

The result was supposed to be largely due to a dislike of the New England scheme and to a wish among
New York Federalists that it should be stopped. The
energy of the demonstration in New York marked

the beginning of an epoch in national character; yet the change came too late to save Massachusetts from falling for the first time into the hands of the extreme Federalists. The towns of Massachusetts chose as their representatives to the General Court a majority bent on taking decisive action against the war. Connecticut and Rhode Island were controlled by the same impulse, and the discouraged Republicans could interpose no further resistance. A New England convention could be prevented only by a treaty of peace.

The effect of the attitude of New England was felt throughout the Union, and, combined with the news from Europe, brought a general conviction that peace must be made. No man in the Union was more loyal to the war than Governor Shelby of Kentucky, but Shelby already admitted that peace had become necessary.

"I may in confidence confess to you," wrote Shelby, April 8,[1] "that I lament over my country that she has in her very bosom a faction as relentless as the fire that is unquenchable, capable of thwarting her best interests, and whose poisonous breath is extending to every corner of the Union. There is but one way to cure the evil, and that is an awful and desperate one; and in the choice of evils we had better take the least. Were we unanimous I should feel it less humiliating to be conquered, as I verily believe that the Administration will be driven to peace *on any terms* by the opposition to the war."

[1] Shelby to J. J. Crittenden, April 8, 1814; Life of Crittenden, p. 31.

If Governor Shelby had reached this conclusion before he knew the result of the Massachusetts election, the great mass of citizens who had been from the first indifferent to the war felt that peace on any terms could no longer be postponed. Mere disunion was not the result chiefly to be feared. That disunion might follow a collapse of the national government was possible; but for the time, Massachusetts seemed rather disposed to sacrifice the rest of the Union for her own power than to insist on a separation. Had the Eastern States suffered from the hardships of war they might have demanded disunion in despair; but in truth New England was pleased at the contrast between her own prosperity and the sufferings of her neighbors. The blockade and the embargo brought wealth to her alone. The farming and manufacturing industries of New England never grew more rapidly than in the midst of war and commercial restrictions.[1] "Machinery for manufactures, etc., and the fruits of household industry increase beyond calculation," said a writer in the "Connecticut Herald" in July, 1813. "Wheels roll, spindles whirl, shuttles fly. We shall export to other States many more productions of industry than ever were exported in any one former season." Manufactures were supposed to amount in value to fifteen or twenty million dollars a year. The Federalists estimated the balance due by the Southern States to New England at six million dollars a

[1] Letter of Jan. 15, 1814; "National Intelligencer," Jan. 27, 1814.

year.[1]  The New England banks were believed to draw not less than half a million dollars every month from the South.

" We are far from rejoicing at this state of things," wrote a Connecticut Federalist; [2] " and yet we cannot but acknowledge the hand of retributive justice in inflicting the calamities of war with so much more severity on that section of the Union which has so rashly and so unmercifully persisted in their determination to commence hostilities.  The pressure of this balance is sensibly felt, and will continue to increase as long as the war continues."

John Lowell declared [3] that " the banks are at their wits' end to lend their capital, and money is such a drug . . . that men against their consciences, their honor, their duty, their professions and promises, are willing to lend it secretly to support the very measures which are intended and calculated for their ruin."  To avoid the temptation of lending money to support Madison's measures, many investors bought British government bills of exchange at twenty to twenty-two per cent discount.  These bills were offered for sale in quantities at Boston; and perhaps the most legitimate reason for their presence there was that they were taken by New England contractors in payment for beef and flour furnished to the British commissariat in Canada.

[1] The Palladium, July 15, 1814.
[2] The Palladium, July 15, 1814.
[3] Road to Ruin, No. 5; The Examiner, Jan. 8, 1814.

While New England thus made profits from both sides, and knew not what to do with the specie that flowed into her banks, the rest of the country was already insolvent, and seemed bent on bankruptcy. In March, 1814, the legislature of Pennsylvania passed a bill for the creation of forty-one new banks. March 19 Governor Snyder vetoed it.[1]

" It is a fact well ascertained," said Governor Snyder, " that immense sums of specie have been withdrawn from the banks in Pennsylvania and certain other States to pay balances for British goods which Eastern mercantile cupidity has smuggled into the United States. The demand for specie has in consequence been and is still so great that the banks in Philadelphia and in some other parts have stopped discounting any new paper. I ask a patriotic legislature, Is this an auspicious era to try so vast an experiment? Shall we indirectly aid our internal and external enemies to destroy our funds and embarrass the government by the creating of forty-one new banks which must have recourse for specie to that already much exhausted source? Is there at this time an intelligent man in Pennsylvania who believes that a bank-note of any description is the representative of specie?"

The Pennsylvania legislature instantly overrode Governor Snyder's veto and chartered the new banks, which were, according to the governor, insolvent before they had legal existence. In ordinary times such follies punished and corrected themselves in regular course; but in 1814 the follies and illusions

[1] Niles, vi. 94.

of many years concentrated their mischiefs on the national government, which was already unequal to the burden of its own. The war was practically at an end as far as the government conducted it. The army could not show a regiment with ranks more than half full.[1] The first three months of the year produced less than six thousand recruits.[2] The government could defend the frontier only at three or four fortified points. On the ocean, government vessels were scarcely to be seen. The Treasury was as insolvent as the banks, and must soon cease even the pretence of meeting its obligations.

The Secretary of the Treasury, authorized by law to borrow twenty-five millions and needing forty, offered a loan for only ten millions shortly before Congress adjourned. In Boston the government brokers advertised that the names of subscribers should be kept secret,[3] while the Boston " Gazette " of April 14 declared that " any man who lends his money to the government at the present time will forfeit all claim to common honesty and common courtesy among all true friends to the country." The offers, received May 2, amounted to thirteen millions, at rates varying from seventy-five to eighty-eight. Jacob Barker, a private banker of New York, offered five million dollars on his single account. The sec-

---

[1] Scott's Autobiography, pp. 114, 118, 121.

[2] Return, etc. ; State Papers, Military Affairs, i. 521.

[3] Advertisement of Gilbert & Deane, Boston " Chronicle," April 14, 1814.

retary knew that Barker's bid was not substantial, but he told the President that if it had been refused " we could not have obtained the ten millions without allowing terms much less favorable to the government." [1]  The terms were bad at best.  The secretary obtained bids more or less substantial for about nine millions at eighty-eight, with the condition that if he should accept lower terms for any part of the sixteen millions still to be offered, the same terms should be conceded to Barker and his associates. The operation was equivalent to borrowing nine millions on an understanding that the terms should be fixed at the close of the campaign.  Of this loan Boston offered two millions, and was allotted about one million dollars.

The event proved that Campbell would have done better to accept all solid bids without regard to rate, for the government could have afforded to pay two dollars for one within a twelve-month, rather than stop payments ; but Campbell was earnest to effect his loan at eighty-eight, and accordingly accepted only four million dollars besides Barker's offer.  With these four millions, with whatever part of five millions could be obtained from Barker, with interest-bearing Treasury notes limited to ten million dollars,[2] and with the receipts from taxes, the Treasury was to meet demands aggregating about forty millions

---

[1] Secretary Campbell to Madison, May 4, 1814; Madison MSS., State Department Archives.

[2] Act of March 4, 1814 ; Annals, 1813–1814, p. 2795.

for the year; for the chance was small that another loan could succeed, no matter what rate should be offered.

For this desperate situation of the government New England was chiefly responsible. In pursuing their avowed object of putting an end to the war the Federalists obtained a degree of success surprising even to themselves, and explained only by general indifference toward the war and the government. No one could suppose that the New England Federalists, after seeing their object within their grasp, would desist from effecting it. They had good reason to think that between Madison's obstinacy and their own, the national government must cease its functions, — that the States must resume their sovereign powers, provide for their own welfare, and enter into some other political compact; but they could not suppose that England would forego her advantages, or consent to any peace which should not involve the overthrow of Madison and his party.

In such conditions of society morbid excitement was natural. Many examples in all periods of history could be found to illustrate every stage of a mania so common. The excitement of the time was not confined to New England. A typical American man-of-the-world was Gouverneur Morris. Cool, easy-tempered, incredulous, with convictions chiefly practical, and illusions largely rhetorical, Morris delivered an oration on the overthrow of Napoleon to a New York audience, June 29, 1814.

" And thou too, Democracy! savage and wild!" began Morris's peroration, — "thou who wouldst bring
down the virtuous and wise to the level of folly and
guilt! thou child of squinting envy and self-tormenting
spleen! thou persecutor of the great and good! — see!
though it blast thine eyeballs, — see the objects of thy
deadly hate!    See lawful princes surrounded by loyal
subjects! . . . Let those who would know the idol of
thy devotion seek him in the island of Elba!"

The idea that American democracy was savage
and wild stood in flagrant contrast to the tameness
of its behavior; but the belief was a part of conservative faith, and Gouverneur Morris was not ridiculed, even for bad taste, by the society to which he
belonged, because he called by inappropriate epithets
the form of society which most of his fellow-citizens
preferred.    In New England, where democracy was
equally reviled, kings and emperors were not equally
admired.    The austere virtue of the Congregational
Church viewed the subject in a severer light, and
however extreme might be the difference of conviction between clergymen and democrats, it was not
a subject for ridicule.

To men who believed that every calamity was a
Divine judgment, politics and religion could not be
made to accord.    Practical politics, being commonly
an affair of compromise and relative truth, — a human
attempt to modify the severity of Nature's processes,
— could not expect sympathy from the absolute and
abstract behests of religion.    Least of all could war,

even in its most necessary form, be applauded or encouraged by any clergyman who followed the precepts of Christ. The War of 1812 was not even a necessary war. Only in a metaphysical or dishonest sense could any clergyman affirm that war was more necessary in 1812 than in any former year since the peace of 1783. Diplomacy had so confused its causes that no one could say for what object Americans had intended to fight, — still less, after the peace in Europe, for what object they continued their war. Assuming the conquest of Canada and of Indian Territory to be the motive most natural to the depraved instincts of human nature, the clergy saw every reason for expecting a judgment.

In general, the New England clergy did not publicly or violently press these ideas. The spirit of their class was grave and restrained rather than noisy. Yet a few eccentric or exceptional clergymen preached and published Fast-day sermons that threw discredit upon the whole Congregational Church. The chief offenders were two, — David Osgood, of the church at Medford, and Elijah Parish, a graduate of Dartmouth College, settled over the parish of Byfield in the town of Newbury, where political feeling was strong. Parish's Fast-day sermon of April 7, 1814, immediately after the election which decided a New England convention, was probably the most extreme made from the pulpit : —

" Israel's woes in Egypt terminated in giving them the fruits of their own labors. This was a powerful motive for them to dissolve their connection with the Ancient Dominion. Though their fathers had found their union with Egypt pleasant and profitable, though they had been the most opulent section in Egypt, yet since the change of the administration their schemes had been reversed, their employments changed, their prosperity destroyed, their vexations increased beyond all sufferance. They were tortured to madness at seeing the fruit of their labors torn from them to support a profligate administration. . . . They became discouraged; they were perplexed. Moses and others exhorted them not to despair, and assured them that *one* mode of relief would prove effectual. Timid, trembling, alarmed, they hardly dared to make the experiment. Finally they dissolved the Union: they marched; the sea opened; Jordan stopped his current; Canaan received their triumphant banners; the trees of the field clapped their hands; the hills broke forth into songs of joy; they feasted on the fruits of their own labors. Such success awaits a resolute and pious people."

Although Parish's rhetoric was hardly in worse taste than that of Gouverneur Morris, such exhortations were not held in high esteem by the great body of the Congregational clergy, whose teachings were studiously free from irreverence or extravagance in the treatment of political subjects.[1]  A poor and straitened but educated class, of whom not one in four obtained his living wholly from his salary, the New England ministers had long ceased to speak with the authority of their predecessors,

[1] Defence of the Clergy; Concord, July, 1814.

and were sustained even in their moderate protest against moral wrong rather by pride of class and sincerity of conviction than by sense of power. Some supported the war; many deprecated disunion; nearly all confined their opposition within the limits of non-resistance. They held that as the war was unnecessary and unjust, no one could give it voluntary aid without incurring the guilt of blood.

The attitude was clerical, and from that point of view commanded a degree of respect such as was yielded to the similar conscientiousness of the Friends; but it was fatal to government and ruinous to New England. Nothing but confusion could result from it if the war should continue, while the New England church was certain to be the first victim if peace should invigorate the Union.

## CHAPTER II.

AFTER the close of the campaign on the St. Lawrence, in November, 1813, General Wilkinson's army, numbering about eight thousand men, sick and well, went into winter-quarters at French Mills, on the Canada line, about eight miles south of the St. Lawrence. Wilkinson was unfit for service, and asked leave to remove to Albany, leaving Izard in command; but Armstrong was not yet ready to make the new arrangements, and Wilkinson remained with the army during the winter. His force seemed to stand in a good position for annoying the enemy and interrupting communications between Upper and Lower Canada; but it lay idle between November 13 and February 1, when, under orders from Armstrong, it was broken up.[1] Brigadier-General Brown, with two thousand men, was sent to Sackett's Harbor. The rest of the army was ordered to fall back to Plattsburg, — a point believed most likely to attract the enemy's notice in the spring.[2]

[1] Armstrong to Wilkinson, Jan. 20, 1814; Wilkinson's Memoirs, i 625.

[2] Armstrong's Notices, ii. 64.

Wilkinson obeyed, and found himself, in March, at Plattsburg with about four thousand effectives. He was at enmity with superiors and subordinates alike; but the chief object of his antipathy was the Secretary of War. From Plattsburg, March 27, he wrote a private letter to Major-General Dearborn,[1] whose hostility to the secretary was also pronounced: " I know of his [Armstrong's] secret underworkings, and have therefore, to take the bull by the horns, demanded an arrest and a court-martial. . . . Good God! I am astonished at the man's audacity, when he must be sensible of the power I have over him." Pending the reply to his request for a court-martial, Wilkinson determined to make a military effort. " My advanced post is at Champlain on this side. I move to-day; and the day after to-morrow, if the ice, snow, and frost should not disappear, we shall visit the Lacolle, and take possession of that place. This is imperiously enjoined to check the reinforcements he [Prevost] continues to send to the Upper Province." [2]

The Lacolle was a small river, or creek, emptying into the Sorel four or five miles beyond the boundary. According to the monthly return of the troops commanded by Major-General de Rottenburg, the British forces stationed about Montreal numbered, Jan. 22, 1814, eight thousand rank-and-file present for duty. Of these, eight hundred and eighty-five

[1] Wilkinson to Dearborn, March 27, 1814; Dearborn MSS.
[2] Wilkinson to Dearborn, March 27, 1814; Dearborn MSS.

were at St. John's ; six hundred and ninety were at
Isle aux Noix, with outposts at Lacadie and Lacolle
of three hundred and thirty-two men.[1]

Wilkinson knew that the British outpost at the
crossing of Lacolle Creek, numbering two hundred
men all told,[2] was without support nearer than Isle
aux Noix ten miles away ; but it was stationed in a
stone mill, with thick walls and a solid front.    He
took two twelve-pound field-guns to batter the mill,
and crossing the boundary, March 30, with his four
thousand men, advanced four or five miles to Lacolle
Creek.    The roads were obstructed and impassable,
but his troops made their way in deep snow through
the woods until they came within sight of the mill.
The guns were then placed in position and opened
fire ; but Wilkinson was disconcerted to find that
after two hours the mill was unharmed.    He ventured neither to storm it nor flank it; and after
losing more than two hundred men by the fire of
the garrison, he ordered a retreat, and marched his
army back to Champlain.

With this last example of his military capacity
Wilkinson disappeared from the scene of active life,
where he had performed so long and extraordinary a
part.    Orders arrived, dated March 24, relieving him
from duty under the form of granting his request for
a court of inquiry.    Once more he passed the ordeal

[1] State of the Left Division, Jan. 22, 1814 ; MSS. Canadian
Archives.    Freer Papers, 1814, p. 17.

[2] James, ii. 82, 83.

of a severe investigation, and received the verdict of acquittal; but he never was again permitted to resume his command in the army.

The force Wilkinson had brought from Lake Ontario, though united with that which Wade Hampton had organized, was reduced by sickness, expiration of enlistments, and other modes of depletion to a mere handful when Major-General Izard arrived at Plattsburg on the first day of May. Izard's experience formed a separate narrative, and made a part of the autumn campaign. During the early summer the war took a different and unexpected direction, following the steps of the new Major-General Brown; for wherever Brown went, fighting followed.

General Brown marched from French Mills, February 13, with two thousand men. February 28, Secretary Armstrong wrote him a letter suggesting an attack on Kingston, to be covered by a feint on Niagara.[1] Brown, on arriving at Sackett's Harbor, consulted Chauncey, and allowed himself to be dissuaded from attacking Kingston. " By some extraordinary mental process," Armstrong thought,[2] Brown and Chauncey " arrived at the same conclusion, — that the main action, an attack on Kingston, being impracticable, the *ruse*, intended merely to mask it, might do as well." Brown immediately marched with two thousand men for Niagara.

When the secretary learned of this movement, al-

[1] Armstrong to Brown, Feb. 28, 1814; Notices, ii. 213.

[2] Armstrong's Notices, ii. 66.

though it was contrary to his ideas of strategy, he wrote an encouraging letter to Brown, March 20 : [1]

" You have mistaken my meaning. . . . If you hazard anything by this mistake, correct it promptly by return-ing to your post. If on the other hand you left the Har-bor with a competent force for its defence, go on and prosper. Good consequences are sometimes the result of mistakes."

The correspondence showed chiefly that neither the secretary nor the general had a distinct idea, and that Brown's campaign, like Dearborn's the year be-fore, received its direction from Chauncey, whose repugnance to attacking Kingston was invincible.

Brown was shown his mistake by Gaines, before reaching Buffalo March 24, and leaving his troops, he hurried back to Sackett's Harbor, " the most un-happy man alive." [2]   He resumed charge of such troops as remained at the Harbor, while Winfield Scott formed a camp of instruction at Buffalo, and, waiting for recruits who never came, personally drilled the officers of all grades. Scott's energy threw into the little army a spirit and an organization strange to the service. Three months of instruction con-verted the raw troops into soldiers.

Meanwhile Brown could do nothing at Sackett's Harbor. The British held control of the Lake, while Commodore Chauncey and the contractor Eckford were engaged in building a new ship which was to

[1] Lossing, p. 793.
[2] Brown to Armstrong, March 24, 1814; Lossing, p. 793.

be ready in July. The British nearly succeeded in preventing Chauncey from appearing on the Lake during the entire season, for no sooner did Sir James Yeo sail from Kingston in the spring than he attempted to destroy the American magazines. Owing to the remote situation of Sackett's Harbor in the extreme northern corner of the State, all supplies and war material were brought first from the Hudson River to Oswego by way of the Mohawk River and Oneida Lake. About twelve miles above Oswego the American magazines were established, and there the stores were kept until they could be shipped on schooners, and forwarded fifty miles along the Lake-shore to Sackett's Harbor, — always a hazardous operation in the face of an enemy's fleet. The destruction of the magazines would have been fatal to Chauncey, and even the capture or destruction of the schooners with stores was no trifling addition to his difficulties.

Sir James Yeo left Kingston May 4, and appeared off Oswego the next day, bringing a large body of troops, numbering more than a thousand rank-and-file.[1] They found only about three hundred men to oppose them, and having landed May 6, they gained possession of the fort which protected the harbor of Oswego. The Americans made a resistance which caused a loss of seventy-two men killed and wounded to the British, among the rest Captain Mulcaster of the Royal Navy, an active officer, who was danger-

[1] James, ii. 100.

ously wounded.    The result was hardly worth the
loss.    Four schooners were captured or destroyed,
and some twenty-four hundred barrels of flour, pork,
and salt, but nothing of serious importance.[1]    Yeo
made no attempt to ascend the river, and retired to
Kingston after destroying whatever property he could
not take away.

Although the chief American depot escaped destruction, the disgrace and discouragement remained,
that after two years of war the Americans, though
enjoying every advantage, were weaker than ever
on Lake Ontario, and could not defend even so important a point as Oswego from the attack of barely
a thousand men.    Their coastwise supply of stores
to Sackett's Harbor became a difficult and dangerous undertaking, to be performed mostly by night.[2]
Chauncey remained practically blockaded in Sackett's Harbor; and without his fleet in control of the
Lake the army could do nothing effectual against
Kingston.

In this helplessness, Armstrong was obliged to seek
some other line on which the army could be employed against Upper Canada; and the idea occurred
to him that although he had no fleet on Lake Ontario he had one on Lake Erie, which by a little in-
genuity might enable the army to approach the heart
of Upper Canada at the extreme western end of Lake
Ontario.    "Eight or even six thousand men," Arm-

[1] Report of Sir James Yeo; James, ii. 428–430.
[2] M. T. Woolsey to Chauncey, June 1, 1814; Niles, vi. 266.

strong wrote [1] to the President, April 30, "landed in the bay between Point Abino and Fort Erie, and operating either on the line of the Niagara, or more directly if a more direct route is found, against the British post at the head of Burlington Bay, cannot be resisted with effect without compelling the enemy so to weaken his more eastern posts as to bring them within reach of our means at Sackett's Harbor and Plattsburg."

Armstrong's suggestion was made to the President April 30. Already time was short. The allies had entered Paris March 31; the citadel of Bayonne capitulated to Wellington April 28. In a confidential despatch dated June 3, Lord Bathurst notified the governor-general of Canada that ten thousand men had been ordered to be shipped immediately for Quebec.[2] July 5, Major-General Torrens at the Horse-guards informed Prevost that four brigades, — Brisbane's, Kempt's, Power's, and Robinson's; fourteen regiments of Wellington's best troops, — had sailed from Bordeaux for Canada.[3] Prevost could afford in July to send westward every regular soldier in Lower Canada, sure of replacing them at Montreal by the month of August.

"A discrepancy in the opinions of the Cabinet," according to Armstrong,[4] delayed adoption of a plan

[1] Armstrong's Notices, ii. 216.
[2] Prevost to Bathurst, Aug. 27, 1814; MSS. British Archives.
[3] Torrens to Prevost, July 5, 1805; MSS. Canadian Archives.
[4] Armstrong's Notices, ii. 74, 82.

till June, when a compromise scheme was accepted,[1] but not carried out.

"Two causes prevented its being acted upon *in extenso*," Armstrong afterward explained,[2] — "the one, a total failure in getting together by militia calls and volunteer overtures a force deemed competent to a campaign of demonstration and manœuvre on the peninsula; the other, an apprehension that the fleet, which had been long inactive, would not yet be found in condition to sustain projects requiring from it a vigorous co-operation with the army."

Brown might have been greatly strengthened at Niagara by drawing from Detroit the men that could be spared there; but the Cabinet obliged Armstrong to send the Detroit force — about nine hundred in number — against Mackinaw. Early in July the Mackinaw expedition, commanded by Lieutenant-Colonel Croghan, started from Detroit, and August 4 it was defeated and returned. Croghan's expedition did not even arrive in time to prevent a British expedition from Mackinaw crossing Wisconsin and capturing, July 19, the distant American post at Prairie du Chien.[3]

Armstrong did not favor Croghan's expedition, wishing to bring him and his two batteries to reinforce Brown, but yielded to the Secretary of the Navy,

[1] Armstrong to Izard, June 11, 1814; Izard's Correspondence, p. 33.

[2] Armstrong's Notices, ii. 82.

[3] Colonel McKay to Colonel McDouall, July 27, 1814; Report on Canadian Archives by Douglas Brymner, 1887, p. cv.

who wished to capture Mackinaw,[1] and to the promises of Commodore Chauncey that on or before July 1
he would sail from Sackett's Harbor, and command
the Lake. In reliance on Chauncey, the Cabinet,
except Monroe, decided that Major-General Brown
should cross to the Canadian side, above the Falls
of Niagara, and march, with Chauncey's support, to
Burlington Heights and to York.[2]

This decision was made June 7, and Armstrong
wrote to Brown, June 10, describing the movement
intended.[3] The Secretary of the Navy, he said,
thought Chauncey could not be ready before July 15:

" To give, however, immediate occupation to your
troops, and to prevent their blood from stagnating, why
not take Fort Erie and its garrison, stated at three or
four hundred men? Land between Point Abino and Erie
in the night; assail the Fort by land and water; push
forward a corps to seize the bridge at Chippawa; and be
governed by circumstances in either stopping there or
going farther. Boats may follow and feed you. If the
enemy concentrates his whole force on this line, as I think
he will, it will not exceed two thousand men."

Brown had left Sackett's Harbor, and was at Buffalo
when these orders reached him. He took immediate
measures to carry them out. Besides his regular

[1] Madison to the Secretary of Navy, May 4, 1814; Madison's
Works, iii. 396.
[2] Madison's Cabinet Memorandum, June 7, 1814; Madison's
Works, iii. 403.
[3] Armstrong to Brown, June 10, 1814; MSS. War Department
Records.

force, he called for volunteers to be commanded by
Peter B. Porter; and he wrote to Chauncey, June 21,[1]
an irritating letter, complaining of having received
not a line from him, and giving a sort of challenge
to the navy to meet the army before Fort George, by
July 10. The letter showed that opinion in the army
ran against the navy, and particularly against Chauncey, whom Brown evidently regarded as a sort of
naval Wilkinson. In truth, Brown could depend
neither upon Chauncey nor upon volunteers. The
whole force he could collect was hardly enough to
cross the river, and little exceeded the three thousand
men on whose presence at once in the boats Alexander Smyth had insisted eighteen months before, in
order to capture Fort Erie.

So famous did Brown's little army become, that
the details of its force and organization retained an
interest equalled only by that which attached to the
frigates and sloops-of-war. Although the existence
of the regiments ceased with the peace, and their
achievements were limited to a single campaign of
three or four months, their fame would have insured
them in any other service extraordinary honors and
sedulous preservation of their identity. Two small
brigades of regular troops, and one still smaller brigade of Pennsylvania volunteers, with a corps of artillery, composed the entire force. The first brigade
was commanded by Brigadier-General Winfield Scott,

---

[1] Brown to Chauncey, June 21, 1814; enclosed in Brown to
Armstrong, June 22, 1814; MSS. War Department Archives.

and its monthly return of June 30, 1814, reported its organization and force as follows : [1] —

*Strength of the First, or Scott's, Brigade.*

| | PRESENT FOR DUTY. | | AGGREGATE. |
|---|---|---|---|
| | Non-com. Officers, rank-and-file. | Officers. | Present and absent. |
| Ninth Regiment . . . . . | 332 | 16 | 642 |
| Eleventh Regiment . . . . | 416 | 17 | 577 |
| Twenty-second Regiment . . | 217 | 12 | 287 |
| Twenty-fifth Regiment . . . | 354 | 16 | 619 |
| General Staff . . . . . . | | 4 | 4 |
| Total   . . . . . . . | 1319 | 65 | 2129 |

The Ninth regiment came from Massachusetts, and in this campaign was usually commanded by its lieutenant-colonel, Thomas Aspinwall, or by Major Henry Leavenworth.  The Eleventh was raised in Vermont, and was led by Major John McNeil.  The Twenty-second was a Pennsylvania regiment, commanded by its colonel, Hugh Brady.  The Twenty-fifth was enlisted in Connecticut, and identified by the name of T. S. Jesup, one of its majors.  The whole brigade, officers and privates, numbered thirteen hundred and eighty-four men present for duty on the first day of July, 1814.

The Second, or Ripley's, brigade was still smaller, and became even more famous.  Eleazar Wheelock Ripley was born in New Hampshire, in the year 1782. He became a resident of Portland in Maine, and was sent as a representative to the State legislature at

[1] Monthly Returns, etc., MSS. War Department Archives.

Boston, where he was chosen speaker of the Massachusetts House of Representatives, Jan. 17, 1812, on the retirement of Joseph Story to become a Justice of the Supreme Court of the United States. A few weeks afterward, March 12, 1812, Ripley took the commission of lieutenant-colonel of the Twenty-first regiment, to be enlisted in Massachusetts. A year afterward he became colonel of the same regiment, and took part in the battle of Chrystler's Field. Secretary Armstrong made him a brigadier-general April 15, 1814, his commission bearing date about a month after that of Winfield Scott. Both the new brigadiers were sent to Niagara, where Scott formed a brigade from regiments trained by himself; and Ripley was given a brigade composed of his old regiment, the Twenty-first, with detachments from the Seventeenth and Nineteenth and Twenty-third. The strength of the brigade, July 1, 1814, was reported in the monthly return as follows : —

*Strength of the Second, or Ripley's, Brigade.*

|  | PRESENT FOR DUTY. | | AGGREGATE. |
| --- | --- | --- | --- |
|  | Non-com. Officers, rank-and-file. | Officers. | Present and absent. |
| Twenty-first Regiment . . . | 651 | 25 | 917 |
| Twenty-third Regiment. . . | 341 | 8 | 496 |
| General staff  . . . . . . | | 2 | 2 |
| Total  . . . . . . . | 992 | 35 | 1415 |

Ripley's old regiment, the Twenty-first, was given to Colonel James Miller, who had served in the Tippecanoe campaign as major in the Fourth Infantry, and had shared the misfortune of that regiment at Detroit. The other regiment composing the brigade — the Twenty-third — was raised in New York, and was usually commanded by one or another of its majors, McFarland or Brooke. Ripley's brigade numbered one thousand and twenty-seven men present for duty, on the first day of July.

The artillery, under the command of Major Hindman, was composed of four companies.

*Strength of Hindman's Battalion of Artillery.*

|  | PRESENT FOR DUTY. | AGGREGATE. |
|---|---|---|
| Towson's Company . . . . . . | 89 | 101 |
| Biddle's Company . . . . . . | 80 | 104 |
| Ritchie's Company . . . . . | 96 | 133 |
| Williams's Company . . . . . | 62 | 73 |
| Total . . . . . . . . . . | 327 | 413 |

The militia brigade was commanded by Peter B. Porter, and consisted of six hundred Pennsylvania volunteer militia, with about the same number of Indians, comprising nearly the whole military strength of the Six Nations.[1]

*Strength of Major-General Brown's Army, Buffalo, July 1, 1814.*

|  | PRESENT FOR DUTY. | | AGGREGATE. |
|---|---|---|---|
|  | Non-com. Officers, rank-and-file. | Officers. | Present and absent. |
| Artillery . . . . . . . | 330 | 15 | 413 |
| Scott's Brigade . . . . . | 1312 | 65 | 2122 |
| Ripley's Brigade . . . . | 992 | 36 | 1415 |
| Porter's Brigade . . . . | 710 | 43 | 830 |
| Total . . . . . . . | 3344 | 159 | 4780 |

[1] Stone's Life of Red Jacket, p. 328.

Thus the whole of Brown's army consisted of half-a-dozen skeleton regiments, and including every officer, as well as all Porter's volunteers, numbered barely thirty-five hundred men present for duty. The aggregate, including sick and absent, did not reach five thousand.

The number of effectives varied slightly from week to week, as men joined or left their regiments; but the entire force never exceeded thirty-five hundred men, exclusive of Indians.

According to the weekly return of June 22, 1814, Major-General Riall, who commanded the right division of the British army, had a force of four thousand rank-and-file present for duty; but of this number the larger part were in garrison at York, Burlington Heights, and Fort Niagara. His headquarters were at Fort George, where he had nine hundred and twenty-seven rank-and-file present for duty. Opposite Fort George, in Fort Niagara on the American side, five hundred and seventy-eight rank-and-file were present for duty. At Queenston were two hundred and fifty-eight; at Chippawa, four hundred and twenty-eight; at Fort Erie, one hundred and forty-six. In all, on the Niagara River Riall commanded two thousand three hundred and thirty-seven rank-and-file present for duty. The officers, musicians, etc., numbered three hundred and thirty-two. At that time only about one hundred and seventy men were on the sick list. All told, sick and well, the regular force numbered two thousand eight hun-

dred and forty men.[1]  They belonged chiefly to the
First, or Royal Scots; the Eighth, or King's; the
Hundredth, the Hundred-and-third regiments, and
the Artillery, with a few dragoons.

As soon as Porter's volunteers were ready, the
whole American army was thrown across the river.
The operation was effected early in the morning of
July 3; and although the transport was altogether
insufficient, the movement was accomplished without
accident or delay.   Scott's brigade with the artillery
landed below Fort Erie; Ripley landed above; the
Indians gained the rear; and the Fort, which was an
open work, capitulated at five o'clock in the afternoon.   One hundred and seventy prisoners, including
officers of all ranks,[2] being two companies of the
Eighth and Hundredth British regiments were sur-
rendered by the major in command.

The next British position was at Chippawa, about
sixteen miles below.   To Chippawa Major-General
Riall hastened from Fort George, on hearing that
the American army had crossed the river above; and
there, within a few hours, he collected about fifteen
hundred regulars and six hundred militia and Indians, behind the Chippawa River, in a position not
to be assailed in front.   The American army also
hastened toward Chippawa.   On the morning of July
4 Scott's brigade led the way, and after an ex-

[1] Weekly Distribution Return, June 22, 1814 ; MSS. Canadian
Archives, Freer Papers, 1814, p. 53.

[2] James, ii. 117.

hausting march of twelve hours, the enemy tearing
up the bridges in retiring, Scott reached Chippawa
plain toward sunset, and found Riall's force in position beyond the Chippawa River. Scott could only
retire a mile or two, behind the nearest water, — a
creek, or broad ditch, called Street's Creek, — where
he went into camp.  Brown and Ripley, with the
second brigade and artillery, came up two or three
hours later, at eleven o'clock in the night.[1]  Porter
followed the next morning.

Brown, knowing his numbers to be about twice
those of Riall, was anxious to attack before Riall
could be reinforced; and on the morning of July
5, leaving Ripley and Porter's brigades encamped in
the rear, he reconnoitred the line of the Chippawa
River, and gave orders for constructing a bridge
above Riall's position. The bridge was likely to be
an affair of several days, and Riall showed a disposition to interfere with it.  His scouts and Indians crossed and occupied the woods on the American left, driving in the pickets and annoying the
reconnoitring party, and even the camp.  To dis-
lodge them, Porter's volunteers and Indians were
ordered forward to clear the woods; and at about
half-past four o'clock in the afternoon, Porter's advance began to drive the enemy's Indians back, pressing forward nearly to the Chippawa River.  There
the advancing volunteers and Indians suddenly became aware that the whole British army was in the

[1] Brown's Report of July 7, 1814; Official Letters, p. 368.

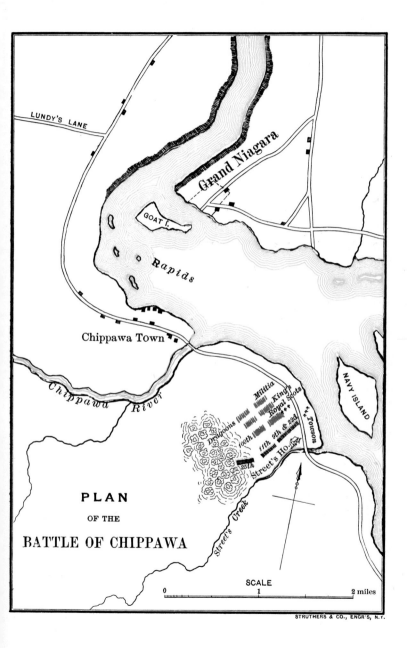

LUNDY'S LANE

Grand Niagara

GOAT I.

Rapids

Chippawa Town

Chippawa River

NAVY ISLAND

Dragoons
Militia
King's
Royal Scots
100th
11th 9th & 22d
25th
Street's Ho.
Towson

Street's Creek

PLAN

OF THE

BATTLE OF CHIPPAWA

SCALE

0          1          2 miles

STRUTHERS & CO., ENGR'S, N.Y.

act of crossing the Chippawa Bridge on their flank. The surprise was complete, and Porter's brigade naturally broke and fell back in confusion.[1]

No one could have been more surprised than Brown, or more incredulous than Scott, at Riall's extraordinary movement. The idea that a British force of two thousand men at most should venture to attack more than three thousand, with artillery, covered by a deep, miry creek, had not entered their minds. Riall drew up his little army in three columns on the Chippawa plain, — the King's regiment four hundred and eighty strong in advance, supported by the Royal Scots five hundred strong, and the Hundredth four hundred and fifty strong, with a troop of dragoons and artillerists ; in all about fifteen hundred regular troops, with two twenty-four-pound field-pieces and a five-and-a-half inch howitzer. Six hundred militia and Indians occupied the woods.[2] The whole force advanced in order of battle toward Street's Creek.

Brown was at the front when this movement was made. Porter was routed. Ripley with the second brigade was in the rear. Scott, having rested his brigade in the morning and given them a dinner to celebrate the Fourth of July, had ordered a grand parade " to keep his men in breath," as he said ; and while Riall's regular force, fifteen hundred strong, formed on the Chippawa plain a mile away, Scott's

[1] Stone's Life of Red Jacket, p. 352.
[2] Riall's Report of July 6, 1814 ; James, ii. 431.

brigade — which a week before had been reported as
containing thirteen hundred men present for duty,
and if all its details had been called in could hardly
have exceeded thirteen hundred men in the ranks
on the afternoon of July 5 — was forming, before
crossing the little bridge over Street's Creek to parade on the plain already occupied by the British.
Owing to the brushwood that lined the creek Scott
could not see the plain, and received no notice of
danger until he approached the bridge at the head
of his brigade.  At that moment General Brown in
full gallop from the front rode by, calling out in
passing, " You will have a battle ! " [1]  Scott remarked
that he did not believe he should find three hundred
British to fight, and crossed the bridge.

If Riall was unwise to attack, Scott tempted destruction by leaving his secure position behind the
creek ; but at that moment he was in his happiest
temper.  He meant to show what he and his brigade
could do.  As his thin column crossed the bridge, the
British twenty-four-pound guns opened upon it ; but
the American line moved on, steady as veterans, and
formed in order of battle beyond.  Towson's three
twelve-pounders were placed in position near the river
on the extreme right, and opened fire on the heavier
British battery opposite.  The infantry deployed in
three battalions, — the right, under Major Leavenworth of the Ninth ; the centre, under Major McNeil
of the Eleventh ; the left, under Major Jesup of the

[1] Scott's Autobiography, p. 128.

Twenty-fifth. Throwing the flanks obliquely forward, and extending Jesup's battalion into the woods on the left to prevent outflanking, Scott ordered an advance; and at the same time Riall directed the Royal Scots and the Hundredth to charge.[1] The two lines advanced, stopping alternately to fire and move forward, while Towson's guns, having blown up a British caisson, were turned on the British column. The converging American fire made havoc in the British ranks, and when the two lines came within some sixty or seventy paces of each other in the centre, the flanks were actually in contact. Then the whole British line broke and crumbled away.[2] Ripley's brigade, arriving soon afterward, found no enemy on the plain. The battle had lasted less than an hour.

Riall's report made no concealment of his defeat.[3]

" I placed two light twenty-four-pounders and a five-and-a-half inch howitzer," he said, " against the right of the enemy's position, and formed the Royal Scots and Hundredth regiment with the intention of making a movement upon his left, which deployed with the greatest regularity and opened a very heavy fire. I immediately moved up the King's regiment to the right, while the Royal Scots and Hundredth regiments were directed to charge the enemy in front, for which they advanced with the greatest gallantry under a most destructive fire. I am sorry to say, however, in this at-

[1] Riall's Report, July 6, 1814; James, ii. 432.

[2] Scott's Autobiography, p. 130. Jesup's Narrative; Ingersoll, ii. 90, 91. Mansfield's Scott, pp. 105–110.

[3] James, ii. 432.

tempt they suffered so severely that I was obliged to withdraw them, finding their further efforts against the superior numbers of the enemy would be unavailing."

For completeness, Scott's victory at Chippawa could be compared with that of Isaac Hull over the "Guerriere;" but in one respect Scott surpassed Hull. The "Constitution" was a much heavier ship than its enemy; but Scott's brigade was weaker, both in men and guns, than Riall's force. Even in regulars, man against man, Scott was certainly outnumbered. His brigade could not have contained, with artillerists, more than thirteen hundred men present on the field,[1] while Riall officially reported his regulars at fifteen hundred, and his irregular corps at six hundred. Scott's flank was exposed and turned by the rout of Porter. He fought with a creek in his rear, where retreat was destruction. He had three twelve-pound field-pieces, one of which was soon dismounted, against two twenty-four-pounders and a five-and-a-half inch howitzer. He crossed the bridge and deployed under the enemy's fire. Yet the relative losses showed that he was the superior of his enemy in every respect, and in none more than in the efficiency of his guns.

Riall reported a total loss in killed, wounded, and missing of five hundred and fifteen men,[2] not including Indians. Scott and Porter reported a total loss of two hundred and ninety-seven, not including Indians. Riall's regular regiments and artillery lost

[1] Mansfield's Scott, p. 112.　　[2] James ii. 434.

one hundred and thirty-seven killed, and three hundred and five wounded. Scott's brigade reported forty-eight killed and two hundred and twenty-seven wounded. The number of Riall's killed was nearly three times the number of Scott's killed, and proved that the battle was decided by the superior accuracy or rapidity of the musketry and artillery fire, other military qualities being assumed to be equal.

The battle of Chippawa was the only occasion during the war when equal bodies of regular troops met face to face, in extended lines on an open plain in broad daylight, without advantage of position; and never again after that combat was an army of American regulars beaten by British troops. Small as the affair was, and unimportant in military results, it gave to the United States army a character and pride it had never before possessed.

Riall regained the protection of his lines without further loss; but two days afterward Brown turned his position, and Riall abandoned it with the whole peninsula except Fort George.[1] Leaving garrisons in Fort George and Fort Niagara, he fell back toward Burlington Bay to await reinforcements. Brown followed as far as Queenston, where he camped July 10, doubtful what next to do. Fretting under the enforced delay, he wrote to Commodore Chauncey, July 13, a letter that led to much comment:[2] —

[1] Riall to Drummond, July 8, 1814; MSS. Canadian Archives.

[2] Brown to Chauncey, July 13, 1814; Niles, vii. 38.

" I have looked for your fleet with the greatest anxiety since the 10th. I do not doubt my ability to meet the enemy in the field, and to march in any direction over his country, your fleet carrying for me the necessary supplies. . . . There is not a doubt resting in my mind but that we have between us the command of sufficient means to conquer Upper Canada within two months, if there is a prompt and zealous co-operation and a vigorous application of these means."

Brown, like Andrew Jackson, with the virtues of a militia general, possessed some of the faults. His letter to Chauncey expressed his honest belief; but he was mistaken, and the letter tended to create a popular impression that Chauncey was wholly to blame. Brown could not, even with Chauncey's help, conquer Upper Canada. He was in danger of being himself destroyed; and even at Queenston he was not safe. Riall had already received, July 9, a reinforcement of seven hundred regulars;[1] at his camp, only thirteen miles from Brown, he had twenty-two hundred men; in garrison at Fort George and Niagara he left more than a thousand men; Lieutenant-General Drummond was on his way from Kingston with the Eighty-ninth regiment four hundred strong, under Colonel Morrison, who had won the battle of Chrystler's Field , while still another regiment, De-Watteville's, was on the march. Four thousand men were concentrating on Fort George, and Chauncey, although he might have delayed, could not have prevented their attacking Brown, or stopping his advance.

[1] James, ii. 132.

Brown was so well aware of his own weakness
that he neither tried to assault Fort George nor to
drive Riall farther away, although Ripley and the
two engineer officers McRee and Wood advised the
attempt.[1] After a fortnight passed below Queenston, he suddenly withdrew to Chippawa July 24,
and camped on the battle-field. Riall instantly left
his camp at eleven o'clock in the night of July 24,
and followed Brown's retreat with about a thousand
men, as far as Lundy's Lane, only a mile below the
Falls of Niagara. There he camped at seven o'clock
on the morning of July 25, waiting for the remainder of his force, about thirteen hundred men, who
marched at noon, and were to arrive at sunset.

The battle of Chippawa and three weeks of active
campaigning had told on the Americans. According
to the army returns of the last week in July, Brown's
army at Chippawa, July 25, numbered twenty-six
hundred effectives.[2]

### Strength of Major-General Brown's Army, Chippawa, July 25, 1814.

|  | PRESENT FOR DUTY. Non-com. Officers and Privates. | AGGREGATE Present and absent. |
|---|---|---|
| Scott's Brigade . . . . . . | 1072 | 1422 |
| Ripley's Brigade . . . . . | 895 | 1198 |
| Porter's Brigade. . . . . . | 441 | 538 |
| Artillery . . , . . . . . | 236 | 260 |
| Total . . . . . . . . | 2644 | 3418 |

[1] Ripley's "Facts relative to the Campaign on the Niagara,"
p. 8.  Jesup's Narrative ; Ingersoll, ii. 106.

[2] Ripley's "Facts," 1815.

Thus Brown at Chippawa bridge, on the morning of July 25, with twenty-six hundred men present for duty, had Riall within easy reach three miles away at Lundy's Lane, with only a thousand men; but Brown expected no such sudden movement from the enemy, and took no measures to obtain certain information. He was with reason anxious for his rear. His position was insecure and unsatisfactory except for attack. From the moment it became defensive, it was unsafe and needed to be abandoned.

The British generals were able to move on either bank of the river. While Riall at seven o'clock in the morning went into camp within a mile of Niagara Falls, Lieutenant-General Gordon Drummond with the Eighty-ninth regiment disembarked at Fort George, intending to carry out a long-prepared movement on the American side.[1]

Gordon Drummond, who succeeded Major-General de Rottenburg in the command of Upper Canada in December, 1813, and immediately distinguished himself by the brilliant capture of Fort Niagara and the destruction of Buffalo, was regarded as the ablest military officer in Canada. Isaac Brock's immediate successors in the civil and military government of Upper Canada were Major-Generals Sheaffe and De Rottenburg. Neither had won distinction; but Gordon Drummond was an officer of a different character. Born in 1772, he entered the army in 1789 as

[1] Harvey to Lieut.-Colonel Tucker, July 23, 1814; MSS. Canadian Archives.

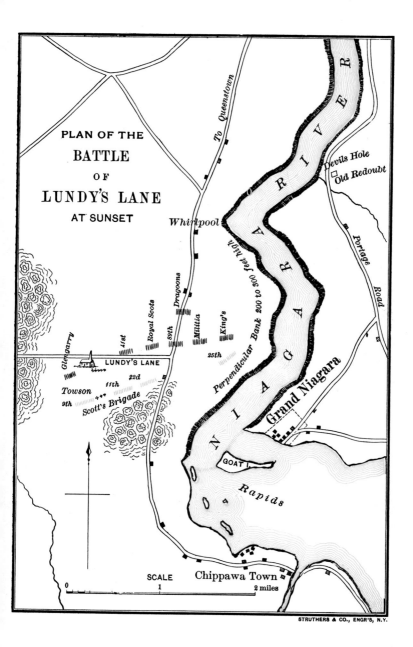

PLAN OF THE
BATTLE
OF
LUNDY'S LANE
AT SUNSET

To Queenstown

Whirlpool

Devils Hole
Old Redoubt

Portage Road

Glengarry
41st
Royal Scots
Dragoons
89th
Militia
King's
25th

LUNDY'S LANE

Towson
11th
22d
9th
Scott's Brigade

Perpendicular Bank 200 to 300 feet high

NIAGARA RIVER

Grand Niagara

GOAT I

Rapids

SCALE
0
1
2 miles

Chippawa Town

STRUTHERS & CO., ENGR'S, N.Y.

an ensign in the First regiment, or Royal Scots, and
rose in 1794 to be lieutenant-colonel of the Eighth,
or King's regiment. He served in the Netherlands,
the West Indies, and in Egypt, before being ordered
to Canada in 1808. In 1811 he became lieutenant-
general. He was at Kingston when his subordinate
officer, Major-General Riall, lost the battle of Chippawa and retired toward Burlington Heights. Having sent forward all the reinforcements he could
spare, Drummond followed as rapidly as possible to
take command in person.

No sooner did Drummond reach Fort George than,
in pursuance of orders previously given, he sent a
detachment of about six hundred men across the
river to Lewiston. Its appearance there was at once
made known to Brown at Chippawa, only six or
seven miles above, and greatly alarmed him for the
safety of his base at Fort Schlosser, Black Rock, and
Buffalo. Had Drummond advanced up the American side with fifteen hundred men, as he might have
done, he would have obliged Brown to recross the
river, and might perhaps have destroyed or paralyzed
him; but Drummond decided to join Riall, and accordingly, recalling the detachment from Lewiston
at four o'clock in the afternoon, he began his march
up the Canadian side with eight hundred and fifteen
rank-and-file to Lundy's Lane.[1]

At five o'clock, July 25, the British army was nearly concentrated. The advance under Riall at Lundy's

[1] James, ii. 142.

Lane numbered nine hundred and fifty rank-and-file, with the three field-pieces which had been in the battle of Chippawa, and either two or three six-pounders.[1] Drummond was three miles below with eight hundred and fifteen rank-and-file, marching up the river; and Colonel Scott of the One Hundred-and-third regiment, with twelve hundred and thirty rank-and-file and two more six-pound field-pieces, was a few miles behind Drummond.[2] By nine o'clock in the evening the three corps, numbering three thousand rank-and-file, with eight field-pieces, were to unite at Lundy's Lane.

At a loss to decide on which bank the British generals meant to move, Brown waited until afternoon, and then, in great anxiety for the American side of the river, ordered Winfield Scott to march his brigade down the road toward Queenston on the Canadian side, in the hope of recalling the enemy from the American side by alarming him for the safety of his rear. Scott, always glad to be in motion, crossed Chippawa bridge, with his brigade and Towson's battery, soon after five o'clock, and to his great surprise, in passing a house near the Falls, learned that a large body of British troops was in sight below. With his usual audacity he marched directly upon them, and reaching Lundy's Lane, deployed to the left in line of battle. Jesup, Brady, Leavenworth, and McNeil placed their little battalions, numbering at the utmost a thousand rank-and-

[1] James, ii. 139.        [2] James, ii. 144.

file, in position, and Towson opened with his three guns. The field suited their ambition. The sun was setting at the end of a long, hot, midsummer day. About a mile to their right the Niagara River flowed through its chasm, and the spray of the cataract rose in the distance behind them.

At the first report that the American army was approaching, Riall ordered a retreat, and his advance was already in march from the field when Drummond arrived with the Eighty-ninth regiment, and countermanded the order.[1] Drummond then formed his line, numbering according to his report sixteen hundred men, but in reality seventeen hundred and seventy rank-and-file,[2] — the left resting on the high road, his two twenty-four-pound brass field-pieces, two six-pounders, and a five-and-a-half-inch howitzer a little advanced in front of his centre on the summit of the low hill, and his right stretching forward so as to overlap Scott's position in attacking. Lundy's Lane, at right angles with the river, ran close behind the British position. Hardly had he completed his formation, when, in his own words, " the whole front was warmly and closely engaged."

With all the energy Scott could throw into his blow, he attacked the British left and centre. Drummond's left stopped slightly beyond the road, and was assailed by Jesup's battalion, the Twenty-fifth regiment, while Scott's other battalions attacked

[1] Drummond's Report of July 27, 1814 ; James, ii. 436.
[2] James, ii. 143.

in front. So vigorous was Jesup's assault that he forced back the Royal Scots and Eighty-ninth, and got into the British rear, where he captured Major-General Riall himself, as he left the field seriously wounded. "After repeated attacks," said Drummond's report, "the troops on the left were partially forced back, and the enemy gained a momentary possession of the road." In the centre also Scott attacked with obstinacy; but the British artillery was altogether too strong and posted too high for Towson's three guns, which at last ceased firing.[1] There the Americans made no impression, while they were overlapped and outnumbered by the British right.

From seven till nine o'clock Scott's brigade hung on the British left and centre, charging repeatedly close on the enemy's guns; and when at last with the darkness their firing ceased from sheer exhaustion, they were not yet beaten. Brady's battalion, the Ninth and Twenty-second, and McNeil's, the Eleventh, were broken up; their ammunition was exhausted, and most of their officers were killed or wounded. The Eleventh and Twenty-second regiments lost two hundred and thirty men killed, wounded, and missing, or more than half their number; many of the men left the field, and only with difficulty could a battalion be organized from the debris.[2] McNeil and Brady were wounded, and

[1] Letter of Major Leavenworth, Jan. 15, 1815; Ripley's "Facts," p. 21.

[2] Letter of Major Leavenworth, Jan. 15, 1815; Ripley's "Facts," pp. 18–27.

Major Leavenworth took command of the remnant.
With a small and exhausted force which could not
have numbered more than six hundred men, and
which Drummond by a vigorous movement might
have wholly destroyed, Scott clung to the enemy's
flank until in the darkness Ripley's brigade came
down on the run. The American line was also reinforced by Porter's brigade; by the First regiment,
one hundred and fifty strong, which crossed from
the American side of the river; and by Ritchie's
and Biddle's batteries.

At about the same time the rest of Riall's force,
twelve hundred and thirty rank-and-file, with two
more six-pound guns, appeared on the field, and were
placed in a second line or used to prolong the British right. If Scott had lost four hundred men from
the ranks Drummond had certainly lost no more,
for his men were less exposed. Brown was obliged
to leave details of men for camp duty; Drummond
brought three thousand rank-and-file on the field. At
nine o'clock Drummond could scarcely have had fewer
than twenty-six hundred men in Lundy's Lane, with
seven field-pieces, two of which were twenty-four-
pounders. Brown could scarcely have had nineteen
hundred, even allowing Porter to have brought five
hundred of his volunteers into battle.[1] He had also
Towson's, Ritchie's, and Biddle's batteries, — seven
twelve-pound field-pieces in all.

[1] Strength of the Army, July 25, 1814 ; Ripley's "Facts,"
Appendix.

As long as the British battery maintained its fire
in the centre, victory was impossible and escape difficult.[1]   Ripley's brigade alone could undertake the
task of capturing the British guns, and to it the order
was given.   Colonel Miller was to advance with the
Twenty-first regiment against the British battery in
front.[2]   Ripley himself took command of the Twenty-
third regiment on the right, to lead it by the road
to attack the enemy's left flank in Lundy's Lane.
According to the story that for the next fifty years
was told to every American school-boy as a model
of modest courage, General Brown gave to Miller
the order to carry the enemy's artillery, and Miller
answered, "I'll try!"[3]

The two regiments thus thrown on the enemy's
centre and left numbered probably about seven hundred men in the ranks, according to Ripley's belief.
The Twenty-first regiment was the stronger, and may
have contained four hundred and fifty men, including officers; the Twenty-third could scarcely have
brought three hundred into the field.   In a few minutes both battalions were in motion.   The Twenty-
third, advancing along the road on the right, instantly attracted the enemy's fire at about one hundred
and fifty yards from the hill, and was thrown back.
Ripley reformed the column, and in five minutes it

---

[1] Mansfield's Scott, p. 129 ; *note* 2.

[2] Miller's Letter in the Boston "Patriot," Sept. 4, 1814 ;
Ripley's "Facts," p. 27.

[3] Lossing, p. 820, *note.*

advanced again.[1]  While the Twenty-third was thus
engaged on the right, the Twenty-first silently advanced in front, covered by shrubbery and the darkness, within a few rods of the British battery undis-
covered, and with a sudden rush carried the guns,
bayoneting the artillery-men where they stood.

So superb a feat of arms might well startle the
British general, who could not see that less than
five hundred men were engaged in it; but according to the British account [2] the guns stood immediately in front of a British line numbering at least
twenty-six hundred men in ranks along Lundy's
Lane.  Drummond himself must have been near the
spot, for the whole line of battle was but five minutes'
walk; apparently he had but to order an advance,
to drive Miller's regiment back without trouble.  Yet
Miller maintained his ground until Ripley came up
on his right.  According to the evidence of Captain
McDonald of Ripley's staff, the battle was violent
during fifteen or twenty minutes : —

"Having passed the position where the artillery had
been planted, Colonel Miller again formed his line facing
the enemy, and engaged them within twenty paces distance.  There appeared a perfect sheet of fire between
the two lines.  While the Twenty-first was in this situation, the Twenty-third attacked the enemy's flank, and
advanced within twenty paces of it before the first volley
was discharged, — a measure adopted by command of
General Ripley, that the fire might be effectual and more

[1] Evidence of Captain McDonald ; Ripley's " Facts," p. 12.
[2] Drummond's Report, July 27, 1814; James, ii. 437.

completely destructive. The movement compelled the enemy's flank to fall back immediately by descending the hill out of sight, upon which the firing ceased." [1]

Perhaps this feat was more remarkable than the surprise of the battery. Ripley's Twenty-third regiment, about three hundred men, broke the British line, not in the centre but on its left, where the Eighty-ninth, the Royal Scots, King's, and the Forty-first were stationed,[2] and caused them to retire half a mile from the battle-field before they halted to reform.

When the firing ceased, Ripley's brigade held the hill-top, with the British guns, and the whole length of Lundy's Lane to the high-road. Porter then brought up his brigade on the left; Hindman brought up his guns, and placed Towson's battery on Ripley's right, Ritchie's on his left, while Biddle's two guns were put in position on the road near the corner of Lundy's Lane. Jesup with the Twenty-fifth regiment was put in line on the right of Towson's battery; Leavenworth with the remnants of the Ninth, Eleventh, and Twenty-second formed a second line in the rear of the captured artillery; and thus reversing the former British order of battle, the little army stood ranked along the edge of Lundy's Lane, with the British guns in their rear.

The British force was then in much confusion, a part of it marching into the American line by mis-

[1] Evidence of Captain McDonald ; Ripley's " Facts," p. 13.

[2] Drummond's Report ; James, ii. 143.

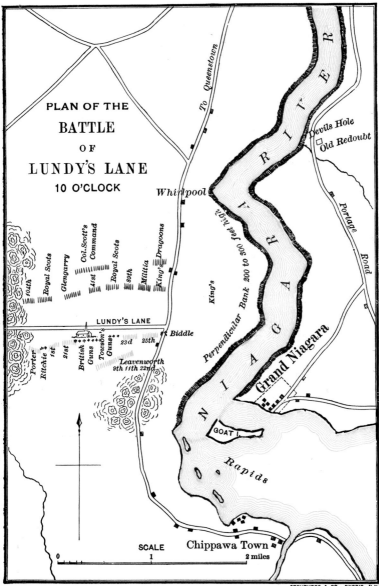

PLAN OF THE
## BATTLE
OF
## LUNDY'S LANE
### 10 O'CLOCK

To Queenstown

NIAGARA RIVER

Devils Hole
Old Redoubt

Whirlpool

Col.Scott's
Command

104th
Royal Scots
Glengarry
41st
Royal Scots
89th
Militia
King's Dragoons

King's

Perpendicular Bank 200 to 300 feet high

Portage Road

LUNDY'S LANE

Biddle

Porter
Ritchie
21st
1st
British
Guns
Towson's
Guns
23d
25th

Leavenworth
9th 11th 22nd

Grand Niagara

GOAT I.

Rapids

SCALE

0          1          2 miles

Chippawa Town

STRUTHERS & CO., ENGR'S, N.Y.

take, and suffering a destructive fire; a part of it
firing into the regiment on its own right, and keeping up the fire persistently.[1]   In order to recover
their artillery they must assault, without guns, a
steep hill held by an enemy with several field-pieces.
Had Brown been able to put a reserve of only a few
hundred men into the field, his victory was assured;
but the battle and exhaustion were rapidly reducing
his force.   He had at ten o'clock not more than
fifteen hundred men in the ranks, and almost every
officer was wounded.

After a long interval the British line was reformed,
and brought to the attack.   General Drummond's
report said nothing of this movement, but according
to the American account the two lines were closely
engaged their whole length at a distance of ten or
twelve yards.   In the darkness the troops could aim
only at the flash of the muskets.   " We having much
the advantage of the ground, the enemy generally
fired over our heads," said Captain McDonald of
Ripley's staff; " but the continual blaze of light was
such as to enable us distinctly to see their buttons."
After a sharp combat of some twenty minutes the
enemy retreated.   Three times, at intervals of half
an hour or more, the British line moved up the hill,
and after the exchange of a hot fire retired; between the attacks, for half an hour at a time, all was
darkness and silence, hardly interrupted by a breath
of air.   Brown and Scott were with Porter on the

[1] James, ii. 145.

extreme left. In the centre, by the captured cannon,
Ripley sat on his horse, ten or twelve paces in rear
of his line. Two bullets passed through his hat, but
he was unhurt. Captain Ritchie was killed at his
battery on the left; Jesup was wounded on the right.
Each attack sorely diminished the number of men in
the ranks, until at the close of the third about seven
hundred rank-and-file, with few officers, were believed
to remain in position.[1]

Scott, with Leavenworth's consolidated battalion,
after ranging somewhat wildly the entire length of
the line in the attempt to turn the enemy's flank,
and receiving the fire of both armies, joined Jesup's
Twenty-fifth regiment on the right, and was at last
severely wounded.[2] At about the same time Brown
was wounded on the extreme left,[3] where Porter's volunteers held the line. Major Leavenworth, with the
remnants of the first brigade, moving from the left
to reinforce Jesup on the right after the third repulse of the enemy, met Scott retiring from the field,
and soon afterward was hailed by General Brown,
who was also returning to camp severely wounded.
The time was then about eleven o'clock, and every
one felt that the army must soon retreat.[4] Farther
in the rear General Brown met Major Hindman of

[1] Evidence of Captain McDonald ; Ripley's " Facts," p. 16.

[2] Cf. Wilkinson's Memoirs, i. 712.

[3] Letter of Major Leavenworth, Jan. 15, 1815 ; Ripley's "Facts,"
p. 23.    Jesup's Narrative ; Ingersoll, ii. 107.

[4] Letter of Major Leavenworth, Jan. 15, 1815; Ripley's " Facts,"
p. 23.    Jesup's Narrative ; Ingersoll, ii. 107.

the artillery, who was bringing up his spare ammunition wagons. Brown ordered Hindman to collect his artillery as well as he could, and retire immediately ; " we shall all march to camp." He said that they had done as much as they could do ; that nearly all their officers were killed or wounded ; that he was himself wounded, and he thought it best to retire to camp. Hindman on arriving at the hill, firing having wholly ceased, immediately began to withdraw the guns. Ripley first learned the order to withdraw by discovering the artillery to be already gone.[1] Next came a peremptory order to collect the wounded and retire.[2] The order was literally obeyed. The enemy in no way molested the movement : and at about midnight the wearied troops marched for camp, in as good order and with as much regularity as they had marched to the battle-field.[3]

Hindman withdrew his own guns, and having with some difficulty procured horses to haul off the British pieces, on returning to the hill after Ripley's withdrawal found the enemy again in possession, and some men and wagons captured.[4] He left the field at once, with the British in possession of their guns, and followed the retreating column.

[1] Ripley's "Facts," Appendix.

[2] Letter of Captain Clarke, March 15, 1815 ; Ripley's " Facts," p. 30. Letter of Adjutant Livingston, March 6, 1815; Ripley's " Facts," p. 31.

[3] Letter of Major Leavenworth, Jan. 15, 1815 ; Ripley's " Facts," p. 25.

[4] Colonel Hindman's statement ; Ripley's " Facts," p. 43.

Lieutenant-General Drummond's report of the battle, though silent as to the repeated British repulses, declared that the Americans fought with uncommon gallantry : —

" In so determined a manner were the attacks directed against our guns that our artillery-men were bayoneted by the enemy in the act of loading, and the muzzles of the enemy's guns were advanced within a few yards of ours. The darkness of the night during this extraordinary conflict occasioned several uncommon incidents ; our troops having for a moment been pushed back, some of our guns remained for a few minutes in the enemy's hands."

Drummond's " few minutes " were three hours. According to the British account, the One-Hundred-and-third regiment, with its two field-pieces, arrived on the field just at nine, and " passed by mistake into the centre of the American army now posted upon the hill." [1] The regiment " fell back in confusion " and lost its two field-pieces, which were captured by Miller, with Riall's five pieces. By British report, Miller was at nine o'clock " in possession of the crest of the hill and of seven pieces of captured artillery." [2] Drummond admitted that in retiring " about midnight " the Americans carried away one of his light pieces, having limbered it up by mistake and leaving one of their own. During the entire action after nine o'clock Drummond did not fire a cannon, although, according to Canadian authority, the fighting was desperate : —

<hr>

[1] James, ii. 144–145.          [2] James, ii. 146.

" The officers of the army from Spain who have been engaged in Upper Canada have acknowledged that they never saw such determined charges as were made by the Americans in the late actions. . . . In the action on the 25th July the Americans charged to the very muzzles of our cannon, and actually bayoneted the artillery-men who were at their guns. Their charges were not once or twice only, but repeated and long, and the steadiness of British soldiers alone could have withstood them."[1]

[1] Letter in Halifax newspaper; Niles, vii. 410.

## CHAPTER III.

THE battle of Lundy's Lane lasted five hours, and Drummond believed the American force to be five thousand men. In truth, at no moment were two thousand American rank-and-file on the field.[1] "The loss sustained by the enemy in this severe action," reported Drummond,[2] "cannot be estimated at less than fifteen hundred men, including several hundred prisoners left in our hands." Drummond's estimate of American losses, as of American numbers, was double the reality. Brown reported a total loss, certainly severe enough, of eight hundred and fifty-three men,— one hundred and seventy-one killed, five hundred and seventy-two wounded, one hundred and ten missing. Drummond reported a total loss of eight hundred and seventy-eight men, — eighty-four killed, five hundred and fifty-nine wounded, one hundred and ninety-three missing, and forty-two prisoners. On both sides the battle was murderous. Brown and Scott were both badly wounded, the latter so severely that he could

[1] Strength of the American army; Ripley's "Facts," Appendix.

[2] Drummond's Report of July 27, 1814 ; James, ii. 438.

not resume his command during the war. Drummond and Riall were also wounded. On both sides, but especially on the American, the loss in officers was very great.

The effect of the British artillery on Scott's brigade, while daylight lasted, had been excessive, while at that period of the battle the British could have suffered comparatively little. Among Scott's battalions the severest loss was that of Brady's Twenty-second regiment, from Pennsylvania, — at the opening of the campaign two hundred and twenty-eight strong, officers and men. After Lundy's Lane the Twenty-second reported thirty-six killed, ninety wounded, and seventeen missing. The Ninth, Leavenworth's Massachusetts regiment, which was returned as numbering three hundred and forty-eight officers and men June 31, reported sixteen killed, ninety wounded, and fifteen missing at Lundy's Lane. The Eleventh, McNeil's Vermont battalion, which numbered three hundred and four officers and men June 31, returned twenty-eight killed, one hundred and two wounded, and three missing. The Twenty-fifth, Jesup's Connecticut corps, numbering three hundred and seventy officers and men at the outset, reported twenty-eight killed, sixty-six wounded, and fifteen missing. These four regiments, composing Scott's brigade, numbered thirteen hundred and eighty-eight officers and men June 31, and lost in killed, wounded, and missing at Lundy's Lane five hundred and six men, after losing two hundred and fifty-seven at Chippawa.

Ripley's brigade suffered less; but although, after the British guns were captured, the Americans were exposed only to musketry fire, the brigades of Ripley and Porter reported a loss of two hundred and fifty-eight men, killed, wounded, and missing. The three artillery companies suffered a loss of forty-five men, including Captain Ritchie. The total loss of eight hundred and fifty-three men was as nearly as possible one third of the entire army, including the unengaged pickets and other details.

When Ripley, following the artillery, arrived in camp toward one o'clock in the morning,[1] Brown sent for him, and gave him an order to return at day-break to the battle-field with all the force he could collect, " and there to meet and beat the enemy if he again appeared." [2]    The order was impossible to execute. The whole force capable of fighting another battle did not exceed fifteen or sixteen hundred effectives, almost without officers, and exhausted by the night battle.[3] The order was given at one o'clock in the morning; the army must employ the remainder of the night to reorganize its battalions and replace its officers, and was expected to march at four o'clock to regain a battle-field which Brown had felt himself unable to maintain at midnight, although he then

[1] Letter of Capt. McDonald, March 20, 1815 ; Ripley's " Facts," p. 29.

[2] Brown's Report of the battle of July 25 ; Niles, vi. 433.

[3] Letter of Major Leavenworth, Jan. 15, 1815 ; Ripley's " Facts," p. 27.

occupied it, and held all the enemy's artillery. The order was futile. Major Leavenworth of the Ninth regiment, who though wounded commanded the first brigade after the disability of Scott, Brady, Jesup, and McNeil, thought it "the most consummate folly to attempt to regain possession of the field of battle," and declared that every officer he met thought like himself.[1]

Yet Ripley at dawn began to collect the troops, and after the inevitable delay caused by the disorganization, marched at nine o'clock, with about fifteen hundred men, to reconnoitre the enemy. At about the same time Drummond advanced a mile, and took position in order of battle near the Falls, his artillery in the road, supported by a column of infantry. A month earlier Drummond, like Riall, would have attacked, and with a force greater by one half could hardly have failed to destroy Ripley's shattered regiments; but Chippawa and Lundy's Lane had already produced an effect on the British army. Drummond believed that the Americans numbered five thousand, and his own force in the ranks was about twenty-two hundred men. He allowed Ripley to retire unmolested, and remained at the Falls the whole day.

Ripley returned to camp at noon and made his report to Brown. The question requiring immediate decision was whether to maintain or abandon the line

[1] Letter of Major Leavenworth, Jan. 15, 1815; Ripley's "Facts," p. 27.

of the Chippawa River.  Much could be said on both
sides, and only officers on the spot could decide with
certainty how the enemy could be placed under most
disadvantage, and how the army could be saved from
needless dangers.  Ripley, cautious by nature, recommended a retreat to Fort Erie.  With the assent, as
he supposed, of Brown and Porter,[1] Ripley immediately broke up the camp at Chippawa, and began the
march to Fort Erie, sixteen miles in the rear.  Although complaint was made of the retreat as confused, hasty, and unnecessary, it was conducted with
no more loss or confusion than usual in such movements,[2] and its military propriety was to be judged
by its effects on the campaign.

The same evening, July 26, the army arrived at Fort
Erie and camped.  Brown was taken from Chippawa
across the river to recover from his wound.  Scott was
also removed to safe quarters.  Ripley was left with
the remains of the army camped on a plain, outside
the unfinished bastions of Fort Erie, where the destruction of his entire force was inevitable in case of
a reverse.  Ripley favored a withdrawal of the army
to the American side; but Brown, from his sick bed
at Buffalo, rejected the idea of a retreat, and fortunately Drummond's reinforcements arrived slowly.
The worst result of the difference in opinion was to
make Brown harsh toward Ripley, who — although

[1] Ripley's "Facts."  Cf. Brown's Narrative; Ingersoll, ii. 105.
[2] Letter of Major Leavenworth, **Jan. 15, 1815;** Ripley's
"Facts," p. 383.

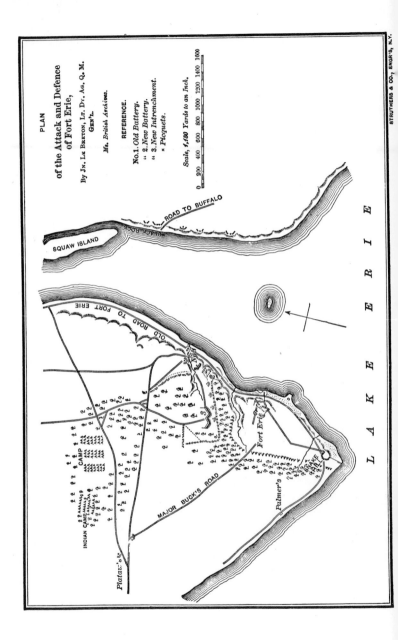

PLAN

of the Attack and Defence
of Fort Erie,

By JN. LE BRETON, LT. DV. AG. Q. M.
GENL.

*Ms. British Archives.*

REFERENCE.

No.1. *Old Battery.*
" 2. *New Battery.*
" 3. *New Intrenchment.*
× *Picquets.*

*Scale, 1,160 Yards to an Inch.*

0   200   400   600   800   1000   1200   1400   1600

ROAD TO BUFFALO

SQUAW ISLAND

BLACK ROCK

OLD ROAD TO FORT ERIE

CAMP

INDIAN CAMP

MAJOR BUCK'S ROAD

Platau

Palmer's

Fort Erie

L   A   K   E       E   R   I   E

STRUTHERS & CO., ENGR'S, N.Y.

his record was singular in showing only patient, excellent, and uniformly successful service — leaned toward caution, while Brown and Scott thought chiefly of fighting. The combination produced admirable results ; but either officer alone might have failed.

Distrusting Ripley, and angry at losing the British cannon at Lundy's Lane as well as at the retreat from Chippawa, Brown wrote, August 7, to the Secretary of War a report containing an improper implication, which he afterward withdrew, that Ripley was wanting either in courage or capacity.[1] He also summoned Brigadier-General Gaines from Sackett's Harbor to command the army.[2] Gaines arrived, and as senior brigadier assumed command at Fort Erie, August 4, while Ripley resumed command of his brigade. During the week that elapsed before Gaines's arrival, the army, under Ripley's orders, worked energetically to intrench itself in lines behind Fort Erie ; and after Gaines took command the same work was continued without interruption or change of plan, under the direction of Major McRee, Major Wood, and Lieutenant Douglass of the Engineers.

The result was chiefly decided by Drummond's errors. Had he followed Ripley closely, and had he attacked instantly on overtaking the retreating army at Fort Erie or elsewhere, he would have had the

[1] Report of Aug. 7, 1814; Niles, vi. 434. Brown to Dallas, May, 1815 ; Ripley's "Facts," p. 46.

[2] Brown's Diary; Ingersoll's History, ii. 105.

chances in his favor.  Had he crossed the river and
moved against Buffalo, he would have obliged Brown
to order the instant evacuation of Fort Erie, and
would have recovered all the British positions without
the loss of a man.  Drummond took neither course.
He waited two days at Chippawa before he moved up
the river within two miles of Fort Erie.  About August 1 his reinforcements arrived, — DeWatteville's
regiment from Kingston, and the Forty-first from
Fort George, — replacing his losses, and giving him
three thousand one hundred and fifty rank-and-file ; [1]
but he seemed still undecided what course to adopt.
The battles of Chippawa and Lundy's Lane had given
the British army respect for American troops, and
Drummond hesitated to assault the unfinished works
at Fort Erie, although he was fully one half stronger
in men than Gaines and Ripley, who had barely two
thousand rank-and-file after obtaining such reinforcements as were at hand.

*Strength of Scott's Brigade, Fort Erie, July 31, 1814.*

|  | PRESENT FOR DUTY. | | AGGREGATE. |
|  | Non-com. Officers, rank-and-file | Officers. | Present and absent. |
| --- | --- | --- | --- |
| Ninth Regiment . . . . . | 139 | 8 | 569 |
| Eleventh Regiment . . . . | 293 | 11 | 624 |
| Twenty-second Regiment . . | 218 | 10 | 408 |
| Twenty-fifth Regiment . . | 255 | 7 | 676 |
| General Staff . . . . . . | | 4 | 4 |
| Total  .  .  .  .  .  . | 905 | 40 | 2281 |

[1] James, ii. 161, 162.

*Strength of Ripley's Brigade.*

| | | | |
|---|---|---|---|
| First Regiment . . . . . | 141 | 6 | **220** |
| Twenty-first Regiment . . . | 441 | 20 | 849 |
| Twenty-third Regiment . . | 292 | 12 | 713 |
| General Staff . . . . . | | 4 | 4 |
| Total . . . . . . . | 874 | 42 | 1786 |

*Monthly return of troops under Major-General Brown, Fort Erie,*
*July* 31, 1814.

| | | | |
|---|---|---|---|
| Bombardiers, etc. . . . . | 58 | 2 | 69 |
| Light Dragoons . . . . . | 47 | 1 | 64 |
| Artillery Corps . . . . . | 241 | 12 | 364 |
| First Brigade . . . . . . | 905 | 40 | 2281 |
| Second Brigade . . . . . | 874 | 42 | 1786 |
| Total of Brown's army . | 2125 | 97 | 4564 |

Drummond began operations by ordering a detachment of six hundred men to cross the river and destroy the magazines at Black Rock and Buffalo.[1]
During the night of August 3 Colonel Tucker of the
Forty-first, with four hundred and sixty rank-and-file
of his own and other regiments,[2] landed two or three
miles below Black Rock, and advanced against it.
They were met at the crossing of a creek by two
hundred and forty men of Morgan's Rifles, then gar-
risoning Black Rock, with some volunteers. The
effect of the rifles was so deadly that the British
troops refused to face them, and Tucker returned
after losing twenty-five men. This repulse, as creditable in its way to the American army as the battles

[1] Drummond to Prevost, Aug. 4, 1814; MSS. Canadian
Archives.

[2] James, ii. 162, 163.

at Chippawa and Lundy's Lane, caused much annoyance to Drummond, who issued an order, August 5,
expressing " the indignation excited by discovering
that the failure of an expedition, the success of
which . . . would have compelled the enemy's forces
to surrender or . . . encounter certain defeat, was
attributable to the misbehavior of the troops employed." [1]    The only success achieved by British
detachments was the cutting out of two American
schooners which covered the approach to Fort Erie,
near the shore.

Drummond having decided not to assault the lines
of Fort Erie until he had made an impression on the
works, next sent for guns of heavy calibre.[2] Ten days
were passed in opening trenches and constructing batteries.   Gaines and Ripley employed the time in com-
pleting their defences.   Of these, the so-called Fort
Erie was the smallest part, and made only the salient
angle toward Drummond's approaches.   As the British had constructed the fort, it was a small, unfinished
work, about one hundred and fifty yards from the
Lake-shore, open in the rear, and mounting three
guns.   The American engineers completed its rear
bastions, and constructed an earthwork seven feet
high, with a ditch, to the shore, where a small stone-
work completed the defence on that side, and brought

[1] Ingersoll's History, ii. 145. Cf. Report of Major Morgan,
Aug. 5, 1814 ; Niles, vi. 437.
[2] Drummond to Prevost, Aug. 4, 1814 ; MSS. Canadian
Archives.

the lines to the water's edge. The stone-work was called the Douglass battery, after the lieutenant of engineers who built it. Fort Erie, Battery Douglass, and their connecting breastwork secured the camp on the right. A similar breastwork, nearly at right angles with the first, was extended three hundred and fifty yards westward parallel with the Lake-shore, then turning slightly ran three hundred and fifty yards farther till it neared the Lake-shore, where it was finished on Snake Hill by a projecting battery called Towson's. Traverses were constructed, and a strongly intrenched camp, about seven hundred yards by two hundred and fifty, was thus formed, open on its rear to the Lake.

Hindman had general charge of the artillery. Battery Douglass mounted one gun; another was mounted on the neighboring line; Fort Erie contained six,[1] under Captain Williams; Biddle's and Fanning's (Ritchie's) four guns were placed on the long line in the front; and Towson had six field-pieces at the extreme left.[2] Scott's brigade, commanded by Lieutenant-Colonel Aspinwall, was posted on the right; Porter's volunteers and the First Rifles occupied the centre; and Ripley with the Twenty-first and Twenty-third regiments defended the left.

Drummond opened with six guns, August 13, and prepared for assault the following day. His arrange-

---

[1] Charges of Lieutenant-Colonel Trimble against General Gaines; Niles, xi. 219.

[2] Report of General Gaines, August, 1814; Niles, vii. 19.

ments were somewhat complicated. He divided the
attacking force into three columns, retaining another
division in reserve. The strongest column, commanded by Lieutenant-Colonel Fischer of DeWatteville's regiment, was composed of portions of four
regular regiments, and numbered about thirteen hundred men; these were to assault Towson and Ripley
on Snake Hill. The centre column, commanded by
Lieutenant-Colonel Drummond of the One-Hundred-
and-fourth, numbered only one hundred and ninety
rank-and-file, including a party of seamen and marines;[1] these were to attack Fort Erie. The third
column, under Colonel Scott of the One-Hundred-
and-third regiment, numbered six hundred and fifty
rank-and-file; these were to assault the breastworks
between Fort Erie and Battery Douglass.[2] According to these numbers, Drummond meant to assault
with twenty-one hundred and forty rank-and-file, or
about twenty-four hundred men all told. His reserve
numbered one thousand men.[3] Some further number
must have been detailed in camp duty.

Drummond's instructions, dated August 14, to
Colonel Fischer were minute.[4] Fischer's column was
to march immediately, in order to pass through the
woods before dark, and halt for the night opposite

[1] James, ii. 170, 171.

[2] Drummond's orders of Aug. 14, 1814; Niles, vii. 21. James,
ii. 169–171.

[3] James, ii. 178.

[4] Instructions to Lieutenant-Colonel Fischer, Aug. 14, 1814;
MSS. Canadian Archives.

the point of attack, with every precaution against discovery : —

"You are to advance to the attack precisely at two o'clock. You are to enter the enemy's position betwixt Snake Hill and the Lake, which is represented to be sufficiently open ; but this is not to prevent your making your arrangements for assaulting any other part of the position by means of the short ladders and hay-bags with which you will be furnished. In order to *insure success*, the Lieutenant-General most strongly recommends that the flints be taken out of the firelocks, with the exception of a reserve of select and steady men who may be permitted to retain their flints, if you think it necessary or advisable, not exceeding one third of your force. This reserve, with the detachment of artillery, should take post on Snake Hill."

A demonstration was to be made a few minutes before two o'clock against the American pickets opposite the centre of the line.

Drummond's general orders concluded by encouraging his men to consider their task easy : [1] —

"The Lieutenant-General most strongly recommends a free use of the bayonet. The enemy's force does not exceed fifteen hundred fit for duty, and those are represented as much dispirited."

The British general underestimated Gaines's force, which probably contained at least two thousand rank-and-file fit for duty August 14, who though possibly overworked and inclined to grumble, were ready to

[1] Lieutenant-General Drummond's Order for attack [Secret]; Niles, vii. 21.

fight.   Neither Gaines nor Ripley, nor any of the excellent officers of engineers and artillery who defended the lines of Fort Erie, were likely to allow themselves to be surprised or even approached by a force no greater than their own without ample resistance.   They kept strong pickets far in advance of their lines, and were alive to every sign of attack. Soon after midnight of August 14 the fire of the British siege-guns slackened and ceased.   At the same moment Gaines left his quarters and Ripley ordered his brigade to turn out.   Both officers looked for an assault, and were not mistaken.   At two o'clock the pickets fired and fell back, and at half-past two o'clock Colonel Fischer's advancing column moved against Snake Hill.

There at the breastworks were Towson's guns and the Twenty-first regiment commanded by Major Wood of the Engineers, only two hundred and fifty strong, but as steady as at Lundy's Lane.[1]   A part of Fischer's brigade marched gallantly up to the abattis, bayonets charged and guns without flints, and approached within ten feet of the breastwork, but failed to reach it.   The other column, DeWatteville's regiment at its head, "marching too near the Lake," according to Colonel Fischer's report,[2] " found themselves entangled between the rocks and the

[1] Gaines's Report of Aug. 23, 1814; Niles, vii. 19.   Ripley's Report of Aug. 17, 1814; Niles, vii.   Supplement, p. 139.

[2] Report of Lieutenant-Colonel Fischer, Aug. 15, 1814; James, ii. 453.

water, and by the retreat of the flank companies were thrown in such confusion as to render it impossible to give them any kind of formation during the darkness of the night, at which time they were exposed to a most galling fire of the enemy's battery." A part of DeWatteville's regiment waded through the water round the American line, and came into the camp on the flank, but found there two companies posted to meet such an attempt, and were all captured, so that Colonel Fischer, writing his report the next day, seemed ignorant what had become of them.

The attack and repulse of Colonel Fischer on the extreme American left were soon over, and the story was easy to understand; but the attack on Fort Erie and the extreme right was neither quickly ended nor easily understood. There a column of more than seven hundred men, all told, under Colonel Scott of the One-Hundred-and-third, was to attack the Douglass battery. Another column, numbering somewhat more than two hundred men, all told, under Lieutenant-Colonel Drummond of the One-Hundred-and-fourth, was to assault Fort Erie. The American line between Battery Douglass and Fort Erie was held by the Ninth regiment and the volunteers, and was covered by the battery. Fort Erie was defended by about one hundred and eighteen men of the Nineteenth regiment under Major Trimble, and about sixty artillerists [1] under Captain Williams.

The most intelligible account of the battle at the

[1] Charges of Major Trimble; Niles, xi. 219.

eastern end of the lines was given neither in Gaines's nor Drummond's reports, but in some charges afterward brought against Gaines by Major Trimble, who was angry at the language of Gaines's report. Trimble's charges were judged to be frivolous, but his story of the battle was more precise than any other.

According to Major Trimble, Lieutenant-Colonel Drummond's column was directed against the north curtain of the fort, and was repulsed, but continued the assault. Colonel Scott's column at the same time advanced within about sixty yards of the Douglass battery, but deterred by the fire of the guns served under the direction of Major McRee and Lieutenant Douglass of the Engineers, and by the loss of its commanding officer Colonel Scott, who fell before the American line, the column moved quickly to the right, gained the ditch of the northeast bastion of Fort Erie, and under cover of the smoke and darkness entered the bastion. There they were joined by Drummond's men. They surprised the artillerists, and in the scuffle Captain Williams and his lieutenants — McDonough, Fontaine, and Watmough — were killed or disabled.

Without support the British columns could do no more, and Lieutenant-General Drummond did not come to their support. None of the reports mentioned the time at which the bastion was captured ; but the small British force, which could not have exceeded six or seven hundred men, remained for more than two hours in or about the bastion, exposed

to the American fire, to which they could not reply
with effect, and waiting for Drummond and the reserve, which the Americans also expected and trained
their guns to enfilade. The British in the bastion
repeatedly attempted to advance from the bastion
to gain possession of the Fort, and twice tried to
force the door of the stone mess-house from which
the men of the Nineteenth regiment kept up a destructive fire. They repulsed the attacks made by
reinforcements ordered by Gaines into the Fort to
recover the bastion; yet their destruction was inevitable as soon as the dawn should arrive, for they
could neither advance nor escape, nor remain where
they were, under the guns of the garrison.

After maintaining themselves till five o'clock in
this difficult position, the British soldiers and sailors
in the bastion were panic-struck by the explosion of
an ammunition-chest under the platform. According
to General Drummond's official report, " Some ammunition, which had been placed under the platform,
caught fire from the firing of guns in the rear, and
a most tremendous explosion followed, by which almost all the troops which had entered the place were
dreadfully mangled. Panic was instantly communi-
cated to the troops, who could not be persuaded
that the explosion was accidental; and the enemy at
the same time pressing forward and commencing a
heavy fire of musketry, the Fort was abandoned, and
our troops retreated toward the battery."

The explosion merely hastened the rout. Probably

the attacking columns would have fared still worse, had they remained. Even their panic-stricken flight saved only a remnant. Of Drummond's column, said to number one hundred and ninety rank-and-file, one hundred and eighty-eight officers and men were reported as missing, wounded, or killed. Of Scott's column, said to number six hundred and fifty rank-and-file, — the Royal Scots and the One-Hundred-and-third regiments, — four hundred and ninety-six officers and men were returned as killed, wounded, or missing. Of the whole rank-and-file engaged under Fischer, Scott, and Drummond, numbering two thousand one hundred and fifty men, if the British report was correct, seven hundred and eighty were officially reported among the casualties. The loss in officers was equally severe. Colonel Scott was killed before the lines. Lieutenant-Colonel Drummond was killed in the bastion. One major, ten captains, and fifteen lieutenants were killed, wounded, or missing. The total British loss was nine hundred and five among some twenty-four hundred engaged. The total American loss was eighty-four men.[1]

General Drummond was excessively mortified by his failure, in truth the severest blow that British arms could suffer at that moment. For the fourth time in six weeks a large body of British troops met a bloody and unparalleled check, if not rout, from an inferior force. In a private letter to Prevost, dated

[1] British Return; James, ii. 454. American Return; Niles, vii. 21.

August 16, Drummond attributed the disaster to the
misconduct of DeWatteville's regiment, a foreign
corps, which was struck by panic:[1] —

"It appears that part of the forlorn hope and about
half of Watteville's Light Company, by wading through
the water, though the footing was excessively rough and
rocky along the Lake-shore, turned the left flank of an
abattis which extended from the enemy's battery on
Snake Hill, the left of their position, to the Lake, and
part penetrated through the abattis itself, and thereby
gained the rear of the enemy's works. The fire of the
enemy at this time being extremely heavy both from artillery and musketry, it would seem as if a simultaneous
shock of panic pervaded the greater part of those not in
immediate advance; and the forlorn hope, not finding itself sufficiently supported, was reluctantly under the necessity of relinquishing the advantages they had gained,
and of retiring again through the water under a most
galling fire. They lost many men, and DeWatteville's
Light Company nearly half their number. The Light
Company of the Eighty-ninth, notwithstanding they were
almost overwhelmed by the grenadiers of DeWatteville in
the precipitancy of their retreat, was the only body that
preserved its order and remained firm upon its ground.
By this act of steadiness they fortunately lost scarcely
a man. The main body of DeWatteville's regiment retreated in such confusion that they carried the King's
regiment before them like a torrent. Thus by the misconduct of this foreign corps has the opportunity been
totally lost."

[1] Drummond to Prevost, Aug. 16, 1814; MSS. Canadian
Archives.

The mortification of Drummond was acute in having to charge both his attacking columns with being panic-stricken : " The agony of mind I suffer from the present disgraceful and unfortunate conduct of the troops committed to my superintendence, wounds me to the soul ! "    Yet he offered no evidence to show that his troops fled before they were beaten, nor did he explain why he had thought it useless to order the reserve to their support after they had captured the bastion.    In reality the battle of Fort Erie was more creditable to the British than the battles of Chippawa or Lundy's Lane, and the Americans could not admit that in either of the three the conduct of Drummond's troops was " disgraceful."

The defeat so much weakened Drummond that he could no longer keep the field without support, and immediately sent for two more regiments, — the Sixth and the Eighty-second from Burlington and York, — numbering about one thousand and forty rank-and-file, and making good his losses.[1]

At that time Chauncey was in control of Lake Ontario.    The anxieties and delays in fitting out his new ship had ended in a fever, under which he was still suffering when he received General Brown's challenge of July 13 to meet him opposite Fort George.    Chauncey did not immediately reply except by message through General Gaines.    July 31, everything being at last ready, he was carried on board his

[1] James, ii. 814.    Drummond to Prevost, Aug. 16, 1814 ; MSS. Canadian Archives.

ship, and the next day he sailed, arriving August 5 off Fort George. Brown's army was then besieged in Fort Erie, and could not approach the fleet. This situation gave to Chauncey the opportunity of writing a letter to Brown, repaying the harshness that Brown had shown to him.

" Was it friendly or just or honorable," asked Chauncey,[1] " not only to furnish an opening for the public, but thus to assist them to infer that I had pledged myself to meet you on a particular day at the head of the Lake, for the purpose of co-operation, and in case of disaster to your army, thus to turn their resentment from you, who are alone responsible, upon me, who could not by any possibility have prevented, or retarded even, your discomfiture? You well know, sir, that the fleet could not have rendered you the least service during your late incursion upon Upper Canada. You have not been able to approach Lake Ontario on any point nearer than Queenston."

Brown's quarrel with Chauncey made much noise in its day, and, like the less defensible quarrel with Ripley, proved that Brown was unnecessarily aggressive; but in the situation of the United States, aggressiveness was the most valuable quality in the service. That Brown might have become a great general was possible, had his experience been larger; but whatever was his merit as a general, his qualities as a fighter were more remarkable than those of any other general officer in the war. Except immediately

[1] Chauncey to Brown, Aug. 10, 1814 ; Niles, vii. 38.

after receiving his wound at Lundy's Lane, when his army was exhausted by four hours of extreme effort, he never seemed satiated with fighting. Among all the American major-generals, he alone made raw troops as steady as grenadiers, and caused militia to storm entrenched lines held by British regulars.

Brown might have been well satisfied to let Drummond exhaust his strength in attacking Fort Erie. From a military point of view, Fort Erie was worthless for any other purpose than to draw the enemy to the extreme end of their line, where they could with difficulty obtain supplies, and could take no part in the serious campaigning intended on Lake Champlain. For that object, no more pitched battles were needed. Drummond's force was wasting away by sickness and exposure.[1]

After the battle of August 15, the British continued to bombard Fort Erie. No great damage was done; but a shell exploded in Gaines's quarters August 29, injuring him severely and obliging him to relinquish command. Brown was still unfit for service, but was bent upon more fighting, and knew that Ripley preferred to abandon Fort Erie altogether. Accordingly he resumed command at Buffalo, September 2, and set himself to study the situation.

The situation was uncomfortable, but in no way perilous. The lines of Fort Erie were stronger than ever, and beyond danger of capture from any British force that could be brought to assault them,

[1] James, ii. 230.

until Drummond should discover some new means of supplying troops with subsistence. The army return of August **31** gave the precise strength of the garrison.

*Strength of the Army at Fort Erie, Aug. 31, 1814.*

| | PRESENT FOR DUTY. | | AGGREGATE. |
| --- | --- | --- | --- |
| | Non com. Officers, rank-and-file. | Officers. | Present and absent. |
| Dragoons . . . . . . . | 27 | 1 | 48 |
| Bombardiers, etc. . . . . . | 34 | | 51 |
| Artillery Corps . . . . . | 206 | 10 | 369 |
| First Brigade . . . . . . | 725 | 39 | 2311 |
| Second Brigade . . . . . | 698 | 42 | 1646 |
| Porter's Brigade . . . . . | 220 | 16 | 599 |
| First and Fourth Rifles . . | 217 | 11 | 504 |
| Total . . . . . . . | 2127 | 119 | 5528 |

The regular force in Fort Erie numbered two thousand and thirty-three effectives [1] September 4, and though annoyed by the enemy's fire and worn by hard work, they were in both these respects better situated than the besiegers. Sooner or later the British would be obliged to retreat; and Brown was informed by deserters that Drummond was then contemplating withdrawal.[2] Brown estimated the British force very loosely at three or four thousand;[3] and it was in fact about the smaller number.

Drummond's situation was told in his reports to

[1] Ripley to Armstrong, Sept. 4, 1814 ; MSS. War Department.

[2] Lossing, p. 837.

[3] Brown to Izard, Sept. 10, 1814; Izard's Correspondence, p. 86.

Sir George Prevost.    September 8 he wrote [1] that he should not fail to seize any favorable opportunity to attack ; " but should no such opportunity present itself, I feel it incumbent on me to prepare your Excellency for the possibility of my being compelled by sickness or suffering of the troops, exposed as they will be to the effects of the wet and unhealthy season which is fast approaching, to withdraw them from their present position to one which may afford them the means of cover.    Sickness has, I am sorry to say, already made its appearance in several of the corps." Three days afterward, September 11,[2] Drummond was warned by several signs that his lines were to be attacked by Brown, although " whether the account which is *invariably* given by deserters of his intention to act offensively . . . be correct, I have not yet been able accurately to ascertain."    Drummond's batteries had been almost silent for several days for want of ammunition, and he could do nothing till the arrival of reinforcements, — the Ninety-seventh regiment, — unaccountably delayed.    Rain had begun, and he dreaded its effect on the troops.    In his next despatch, dated September 14,[3] he said that the rain had been incessant, and " as the whole of the troops are without tents, and the huts in which they

[1] Drummond to Prevost, Sept. 8, 1814 ; MSS. Canadian Archives.

[2] Drummond to Prevost, Sept. 11, 1814 ; MSS. Canadian Archives.

[3] Drummond to Prevost, Sept. 14, 1814 ; MSS. Canadian Archives.

are placed are wholly incapable of affording shelter
against such severe weather, their situation is most
distressing." The roads were impassable ; the nearest depot of supplies was Fort George, and Drummond had not cattle enough to move a third of his
heavy ordnance if a sudden movement should be
necessary. The enemy seemed about to cross the
river in his rear, and the Ninety-seventh regiment
had not yet arrived : —

"In the mean time I have strong grounds for think-
ing that the enemy will risk an attack, — an event which
though from the necessity of defending my batteries in
the first instance with the pickets alone I shall have to
meet under every possible disadvantage, yet I am very
much disposed to hope may be the most fortunate circumstance which can happen, as it will bring us in contact with the enemy at a far cheaper rate than if we were
to be the assailants."

While Drummond struggled between the necessity
of retreat and the difficulty of retreating, Brown was
bent on attacking his lines. The plan was open to
grave objections, and a council of war, September 9,
discouraged the idea. Brown was much disappointed
and irritated at the result of the council, especially
with Ripley ; but while giving the impression that he
acquiesced, he brought over all the volunteers he could
obtain.[1] The number was never precisely given, but
according to the official reports of General Peter B.
Porter who commanded them, and of General Brown

[1] Jesup's Narrative; Lossing, p. 837, *note ;* Ingersoll, ii. **151.**

himself, they did not exceed one thousand.[1]    With
these, and an equal number of regular troops, Brown
undertook to assault Drummond's entrenchments.

The nearest British line was about six hundred
yards from old Fort Erie. From the first British
battery on the Lake-shore, to Battery No. 3 in the
woods, the line extended nearly half a mile, covered
by abattis, but defended only by the brigade of troops
on actual duty. If carried, the first line could not
be held without capturing the second line, about fifty
yards distant, and a third line, farther in the rear;
while the main British force was encamped, for reasons of health and comfort, a mile behind, and was
supposed to number at least three thousand six hundred men, or quite sufficient to recover their works.
Brown professed no intention of fighting the British
army.    He proposed only " to storm the batteries,
destroy the cannon, and roughly handle the brigade
upon duty, before those in reserve could be brought
into action." [2]

Although Drummond expected and wished to be
attacked, he kept no proper pickets or scouts in the
woods, and all day of September 16 American fatigue
parties were at work opening a path through the forest the distance of a mile, from Snake Hill on the
extreme left to the extremity of the British line in
the woods.    So little precaution had Drummond's

[1] Porter's Report of Sept. 22, 1814, and Brown's Report of
Sept. 29, 1814; Niles, vii. 100, 101.

[2] Brown's Report of Sept. 29, 1814; Niles, vii. 100.

engineers taken that they left the dense forest standing within pistol-shot of the flank and rear of their Battery No. 3 on their extreme right, and the American parties opened a path within one hundred and fifty yards of the flank of the British line without being discovered.

At noon, September 17, General Porter led a column of sixteen hundred men — of whom one thousand were militia volunteers, and a part were the Twenty-third regiment — along the path through the woods, in three divisions, commanded by Colonel Gibson of the Fourth Rifles, Colonel E. D. Wood of the Engineers, and Brigadier-General Davis of the New York militia. At three o'clock, under cover of heavy rain, the whole force fell suddenly on the blockhouse which covered the flank and rear of the British battery No. 3, and succeeded in capturing the blockhouse and mastering the battery held by DeWatteville's regiment. While detachments spiked the guns and blew up the magazine, the main column advanced on Battery No. 2, while at the same time General Miller, promoted to the command of Scott's old brigade, moved with " the remains of the Ninth and Eleventh Infantry and a detachment of the Nineteenth " from a ravine in front of Battery No. 3 to pierce the centre of the British line between Battery No. 3 and Battery No. 2.[1]

Within half an hour after the first gun was fired, Porter and Miller had effected their junction within

[1] Brown's Report of Oct. 1, 1814; Official Letters, p. 445.

the British lines, had captured Battery No. 2, and
moved on Battery No. 1, by the Lake-shore. There
the success ended. Battery No. 1 could not be carried. By that time the Royal Scots, the Eighty-ninth,
the Sixth, and the Eighty-second British regiments
had arrived, — probably about one thousand men.[1]
A sharp engagement followed before Brown, after
ordering his reserve under Ripley to the assistance
of Porter and Miller, could disengage his troops.
The three commanders of Porter's divisions — Gibson,
Wood, and Davis — were killed or mortally wounded,
— Gibson at the second battery, Davis and Wood in
assaulting the shore battery. Ripley was desperately
wounded at the same time. General Porter, Lieutenant-Colonel Aspinwall of the Ninth, and Major
Trimble of the Nineteenth, as well as a number of
other officers, were severely wounded. That the last
action was sharp was proved by the losses suffered
by the British reinforcements. According to the
British official return, the four regiments which came
last into the field — the Royal Scots, Sixth, Eighty-
second, and Eighty-ninth — lost thirty-six killed, one
hundred and nine wounded, and fifty-four missing, —
a total of two hundred men, in a short action of
half an hour at the utmost, without artillery.

The American forces were recalled by Brown and
Miller as soon as their progress was stopped, and they
retired without serious pursuit beyond the British

[1] James, ii. 232, 233. Report of Major-General DeWatteville,
Sept. 19, 1814; James, ii. 469.

lines.  Their losses were very severe, numbering five hundred and eleven killed, wounded, and missing, or about one fourth of their number.  Among them were several of the best officers in the United States service, including Ripley, Wood, and Gibson.  Drummond's loss was still more severe, numbering six hundred and nine,[1] probably almost one man in three of the number engaged.  The British killed numbered one hundred and fifteen.  The Americans reported seventy-nine killed, — sixty regulars, and nineteen militia.

The next day Drummond issued a general order claiming a victory over an American force of " not less than five thousand men, including militia ; " but his situation, untenable before the sortie, became impossible after it.  Three out of six battering cannon were disabled;[2] he had lost six hundred men in battle, and his losses by sickness were becoming enormous. " My effective numbers are reduced to considerably less than two thousand firelocks," he reported, September 21.  Immediately after the sortie, although reinforced by the Ninety-seventh regiment, he made his arrangements to retreat.

" Within the last few days," he wrote to Prevost, September 21,[3] " the sickness of the troops has increased to such an alarming degree, and their situation has really become one of such extreme wretchedness from the tor-

---

[1] James, ii. 234.    [2] James, ii. 236.

[3] Drummond to Prevost, Sept. 21, 1814; MSS. Canadian Archives.

rents of rain which have continued to fall for the last thirteen days, and from the circumstance of the Division being entirely destitute of camp-equipage, that I feel it my duty no longer to persevere in a vain attempt to maintain the blockade of so vastly superior and increasing a force of the enemy under such circumstances. I have therefore given orders for the troops to fall back toward the Chippawa, and shall commence my movement at eight o'clock this evening."

## CHAPTER IV.

WEAK as was the army at Niagara, it was relatively stronger than the defence at any other threatened point. Sackett's Harbor contained only seven hundred effectives.[1] On Lake Champlain, Major-General Izard tried to cover Plattsburg and Burlington with about five thousand regular troops.[2] Already Armstrong knew that large British reinforcements from Wellington's army were on their way to Canada;[3] and within a few weeks after the battle of Lundy's Lane eleven thousand of the best troops England ever put in the field were camped on or near the Sorel River, about to march against Izard's five thousand raw recruits.

They could march nowhere else. Not only was the line of Lake Champlain the natural and necessary path of an invading army, but the impossibility of supplying any large number of troops in Upper Canada made Lake Champlain the only region in

[1] Chauncey to Jones, Aug. 10, 1814; Niles, vii. 37.

[2] Izard to Armstrong, July 19, 1814; Izard's Correspondence, p. 54.

[3] Armstrong to Izard, July 2, 1814 ; Izard's Correspondence, p. 51.

which a large British force could exist. Sir George
Prevost had reached the limit of his powers in defending Upper Canada. His commissary-general,
W. H. Robinson, wrote to him, August 27, expressing "the greatest alarm" on account of deficient
supplies at Burlington Heights and Niagara, where
instead of nine thousand rations daily as he expected, he was required to furnish fourteen thousand,
half of them to Indians.[1]  Much as Prevost wanted
to attack Sackett's Harbor, and weak as he knew
that post to be, he could not attempt it, although
he had thirteen or fourteen thousand rank-and-file
idle at Montreal. In October he went to Kingston
expressly to arrange such an attack, and found it
impossible.

" An investigation of the state of the stores at this
post," he wrote to Lord Bathurst October 18,[2] " proved
that the articles for the armament and equipment for a
ship of the class of the 'St. Lawrence,' carrying upward
of one hundred guns, had absorbed almost the whole of
the summer transport-service from Montreal, leaving the
materials for an undertaking of the magnitude of the
destruction of Sackett's Harbor still at the extremity of
the line of communication ; and now, by giving prece-
dence to that supply of provisions and stores without
which an army is no longer to be maintained in Upper
Canada, its removal is inevitably postponed until the
winter roads are established."

[1] W. H. Robinson to Sir G. Prevost, Aug. 27, 1814; MSS.
British Archives.
[2] Prevost to Bathurst, Oct. 18, 1814 ; MSS. British Archives.

Not only were military operations on a large scale impossible in Upper Canada, but for the opposite reason occupation of Lake Champlain by a British force was necessary. Northern New York and Vermont furnished two thirds of the fresh beef consumed by the British armies. General Izard reported to Armstrong, July 31,[1] —

"From the St. Lawrence to the ocean, an open disregard prevails for the laws prohibiting intercourse with the enemy. The road to St. Regis is covered with droves of cattle, and the river with rafts, destined for the enemy. The revenue officers see these things, but acknowledge their inability to put a stop to such outrageous proceedings. On the eastern side of Lake Champlain the high roads are found insufficient for the supplies of cattle which are pouring into Canada. Like herds of buffaloes they press through the forest, making paths for themselves. . . . Nothing but a cordon of troops from the French Mills to Lake Memphramagog could effectually check the evil. Were it not for these supplies, the British forces in Canada would soon be suffering from famine, or their government be subjected to enormous expense for their maintenance."

After Chauncey, August 1, regained possession of Lake Ontario, any British campaign against Sackett's Harbor or Detroit became doubly impossible, and the occupation of Lake Champlain became doubly necessary. Prevost wrote to Bathurst, August 27,[2] —

[1] Izard's Correspondence, p. 57.
[2] Prevost to Bathurst, Aug. 27, 1814 ; MSS. British Archives.

" In fact, my Lord, two thirds of the army in Canada are at this moment eating beef provided by American contractors, drawn principally from the States of Vermont and New York. This circumstance, as well as that of the introduction of large sums in specie into this province, being notorious in the United States, it is to be expected that Congress will take steps to deprive us of those resources ; and under that apprehension large droves are daily crossing the lines coming into Lower Canada."

The fear that Izard might at any moment take efficient measures to cut off the British supplies gave double force to the reasons for occupying Lake Champlain, and forcing the military frontier back beyond Plattsburg and Burlington.

The political reasons were not less strong or less notorious than the military. England made no secret of her intention to rectify the Canadian frontier by lopping away such territory as she could conquer. July 5, the day of the battle of Chippawa, Lieutenant-Colonel Pilkington sailed from Halifax, and under the naval protection of Sir Thomas Hardy in the " Ramillies," landed at Eastport, July 11, with the One-Hundred-and-second regiment, some engineers and artillery, — a detachment of six hundred men, — and took possession of Moose Island.[1] Fort Sullivan, with six officers and eighty men, capitulated, and Great Britain took permanent possession of the place.

[1] Lieut.-Colonel Pilkington to Lieut.-General Sherbrooke, July 12, 1814 ; James, ii. 472.

Moose Island was disputed territory, and its occupation was not necessarily conquest; but the next step showed wider views. August 26, Lieutenant-General Sir J. C. Sherbrooke, the British governor of Nova Scotia, set sail from Halifax with a powerful fleet, carrying near two thousand troops, and arrived September 1 at the Penobscot.[1] At his approach, the American garrison of the small battery at Castine blew up their fort and dispersed. In all Massachusetts, only about six hundred regular troops were to be found, and beyond the Penobscot, in September, 1814, hardly a full company could have been collected. The able-bodied, voting, male population of the counties of Kennebeck and Hancock, on either side of the Penobscot River, capable of bearing arms, was at that time about twelve thousand, on an estimate of one in five of the total population; but they offered no resistance to the British troops.

One misfortune led to another. A few days before Sherbrooke's arrival at Castine the United States ship "Adams," a heavy corvette carrying twenty-eight guns, having escaped from Chesapeake Bay and cruised some months at sea struck on a reef on the Isle of Haut, and was brought into the Penobscot in a sinking condition. Captain Morris, who commanded her, took the ship up the river about twenty-five miles, as far as Hampden near Bangor, and removed her guns in order to repair her. Sherbrooke,

[1] Sherbrooke to Bathurst, Sept. 18, 1814; James, ii. 475.

on occupying Castine, sent a detachment of some
six hundred men in boats up the river to destroy
the ship, while he occupied Belfast with another
regiment.[1] Captain Morris hastily put his guns in
battery, and prepared to defend the ship with his
crew, numbering probably more than two hundred
men, relying on the militia to cover his flanks. On
the morning of September 3, in a thick fog, the
enemy's boats approached and landed their infantry,
which attacked and routed the militia, and obliged
Captain Morris to set fire to the "Adams," abandon
his guns, and disperse his men.[2] The British force
then marched to Bangor, which they occupied without opposition. Their entire loss was one man killed
and eight wounded.[3] At Bangor they remained
nearly a week, destroying vessels and cargoes; but
Sir John Sherbrooke had no orders to occupy the
country west of the Penobscot, and his troops returned September 9 to Castine.

At Castine the British remained, while another
detachment occupied Machias. All the province of
Maine east of the Penobscot was then in Sherbrooke's
hands. The people formally submitted. One hundred miles of Massachusetts sea-coast passed quietly
under the dominion of the King of England. The
male citizens were required to take, and took, the
oath of allegiance to King George,[4] and showed no

---

[1] Sherbrooke to Bathurst, Sept. 18, 1814 ; James, ii. 475.

[2] Morris to Jones, Sept. 20, 1814 ; Niles, vii. 63.

[3] James, ii. 482.          [4] Lossing, p. 903, *note*.

unwillingness to remain permanently British subjects. After September 1 the United States government had every reason to expect that Great Britain would require, as one condition of peace, a cession of the eastern and northern portions of Maine.

For this purpose the British needed also to occupy Lake Champlain, in order to make their conquests respectable. The British general might move on Plattsburg or on Burlington; but in order to maintain his position he must gain naval possession of the Lake. In such a case the difficulties of the American government would be vastly increased, and the British position would be impregnable. Armstrong knew these circumstances almost as well as they were known to Sir George Prevost.

In May the British flotilla entered Lake Champlain from the Sorel River, and cruised, May 9, as far southward as Otter Creek, terrifying Vermont for the safety of the American flotilla under Lieutenant Thomas Macdonough at Vergennes. Irritated and alarmed by this demonstration, Armstrong ordered Izard to seize and fortify Rouse's Point, or the mouth of Lacolle River, or Ash Island, and so close the entrance to the Lake.[1] Apparently Armstrong gave the order in ignorance that Lacolle River and Ash Island were strongly fortified British positions,[2]

[1] Armstrong to Izard, May 25 and June 30, 1814 ; Izard's Correspondence, pp. 23, 48.

[2] Izard to Armstrong, July 12, 1814; Izard's Correspondence, p. 52.

and that a battery established at Rouse's Point, in the relative situation of forces, must have fallen into British hands. On this point the opinion of Izard was more valuable than that of Armstrong; and Izard, after much study and inquiry, decided to erect his fortifications at Plattsburg. He preferred the task of taking a position which he could certainly hold, although it would not prevent the enemy from passing if they chose to leave it behind them. At Plattsburg, therefore, he collected his troops, amounting to five or six thousand men, and constructed strong forts, while Macdonough's fleet took position in the bay.

While thus occupied, Izard cast anxious glances westward, doubting whether, in case of a reverse at Niagara or Sackett's Harbor, he ought not to move on the St. Lawrence and threaten the British communications between Montreal and Kingston.[1] The same idea occurred to Armstrong, who in a letter dated July 27 recommended Izard to carry it out.[2] The letter reached Izard August 10, when he had advanced with his army to Chazy, and had learned enough of the concentration of British troops in his front to be assured that they meant to direct their serious attack against Lake Champlain. He wrote Armstrong a letter, August 11, which failed only in

[1] Izard to Armstrong, July 19, 1814; Izard's Correspondence, p. 54.

[2] Armstrong to Izard, July 27, 1814; Izard's Correspondence, p. 64.

saying too little, rather than too much, of the dangers
risked in obeying Armstrong's order : [1] —

" I will make the movement you direct, if possible ;
but I shall do it with the apprehension of risking the
force under my command, and with the certainty that
everything in this vicinity but the lately erected works
at Plattsburg and Cumberland Head will in less than
three days after my departure be in the possession of
the enemy. He is in force superior to mine in my front ;
he daily threatens an attack on my position at Champlain ; we are in hourly expectation of a serious conflict.
That he has not attacked us before this time is attributable to caution on his part, from exaggerated reports
of our numbers, and from his expectation of reinforcements. . . . It has always been my conviction that the
numerical force of the enemy has been under-rated. I
believe this to be the strong point of our frontier for
either attack or defence, and I know that a British force
has been kept in check in Lower Canada for many weeks
past, greatly superior to that which I could oppose to
it."

Izard was right. Every week new British forces
poured into Quebec and were forwarded to Montreal.
The arrival of the first division at Quebec was announced in the American newspapers early in August.
Within a few weeks three brigades arrived and were
sent to the front. When Izard wrote, he was probably faced by ten thousand veteran British troops
within twenty or thirty miles of his position, and more
were known to be on their way. At such a moment

[1] Izard to Armstrong, Aug. 11, 1814 ; Izard's Correspondence.

the danger of attempting a diversion was great; but Armstrong refused to believe it. Irritated by Izard's remonstrance, the secretary not only persisted in his own opinion, but, abandoning the idea of a movement against the British communications along the St. Lawrence, ordered Izard to march his army to Sackett's Harbor, and from there to operate either directly in force against Kingston,[1] or to go on to Niagara and assist Brown, then hard pressed at Fort Erie. "It is very distinctly my opinion," wrote the secretary August 12,[2] " that it has become good policy on our part to carry the war as far to the westward as possible, particularly while we have an ascendency on the Lakes."

Izard obeyed. His troops, numbering four thousand men, began their march August 29 for Sackett's Harbor, and for several weeks at the crisis of the campaign ceased to exist for military purposes. Within the fortifications at Plattsburg Izard left a miscellaneous body of three thousand, three hundred men,[3] without an organized battalion except four companies of the Sixth regiment. Brigadier-General Alexander Macomb, who as senior officer was left in command, reported his force as not exceeding fifteen hundred effectives.[4]

[1] Armstrong to Izard, July 27, 1814; Izard's Correspondence, p. 64.

[2] Armstrong to Izard, Aug. 12, 1814; Izard's Correspondence, p. 69.

[3] Izard's Correspondence, p. 144.

[4] Macomb to Armstrong, Sept. 15, 1814; Niles, vii. 60.

Armstrong's policy of meeting the enemy's main attack by annihilating the main defence never received explanation or excuse. At times Armstrong seemed to suggest that he meant to rely on the navy,[1] — and indeed nothing else, except Izard's forts, was left to rely upon; but in truth he rather invited the invasion of a British army into New York to " renew the scene of Saratoga." [2] As Izard predicted, the enemy crossed the frontier at once after his departure, occupying Chazy September 3, and approaching, September 5, within eight miles of Plattsburg.

Great Britain had never sent to America so formidable an armament. Neither Wolfe nor Amherst, neither Burgoyne nor Cornwallis, had led so large or so fine an army as was under the command of Sir George Prevost. According to his proposed arrangement, the light brigade, under Major-General Robinson, contained four battalions of the Twenty-seventh, Thirty-ninth, Seventy-sixth, and Eighty-eighth foot, with artillery, and numbered two thousand eight hundred and eighty-four rank-and-file. The second brigade, under Major-General Brisbane, contained battalions of the Eighth, Thirteenth, and Forty-ninth, De Meuron's regiment and Canadian voltigeurs and chasseurs, numbering four thousand and forty-eight rank-and-file. The third brigade, under Major-General Power, contained battalions of the Third, Fifth,

[1] Armstrong to Izard, Aug. 2, 1814; Izard's Correspondence, p. 61.

[2] See ante, vol. vii. p. 173.

Twenty-seventh, and Fifty-eighth, and numbered three
thousand eight hundred and one rank-and-file.    The
reserve, under Major-General Kempt, contained battalions of the Ninth, Thirty-seventh, Fifty-seventh,
and Eighty-first, numbering three thousand five hundred and forty-nine rank-and-file.    Finally, fourteen
hundred and eighty-eight men of the Sixteenth and
Seventieth regiments, under the command of Major-
General DeWatteville, were stationed between Coteau
du Lac and Gananoque on the St. Lawrence.[1]

Thus the left division of the British army in Canada
numbered fifteen thousand seven hundred and seventy
effectives, or, including officers, probably eighteen
thousand men, without reckoning the Canadian militia,
either incorporated or sedentary.    Two lieutenant-
generals and five major-generals were in command.
Amply provided with artillery and horses, every brigade well equipped, they came fresh from a long
service in which the troops had learned to regard
themselves as invincible.    As they were at last organized, four brigades crossed the border, numbering not
less than " eleven thousand men with a proportionate
and most excellent train of artillery, commanded in
chief by Sir George Prevost, and under him by officers of the first distinction in the service." [2]    A reserve of about five thousand men remained behind.

The fleet was almost as formidable as the army.

[1] Proposed Distribution of the Forces in the Left Division;
MSS. Canadian Archives, Freer Papers, 1812–1813, p. 107.

[2] James, ii. 206.

As the force of the flotilla was reported to Prevost, it consisted of a thirty-six-gun ship, the "Confiance;" an eighteen-gun brig, the "Linnet;" two ten-gun sloops and twelve gunboats, carrying sixteen guns,[1] — all commanded by Captain Downie, of the Royal Navy, detached by Sir James Yeo for the purpose.

Such an expedition was regarded with unhesitating confidence, as able to go where it pleased within the region of Lake Champlain. About every other undertaking in America the British entertained doubts, but in regard to this affair they entertained none.[2] Every movement of the British generals showed conviction of their irresistible strength. Had Prevost doubted the result of attacking Plattsburg, he could have advanced by St. Albans on Burlington,[3] which would have obliged Macomb and Macdonough to leave their positions. So little did his army apprehend difficulty, that in advancing to Plattsburg in face of Macomb's skirmishers they did not once form in line, or pay attention to the troops and militia who obstructed the road. "The British troops did not deign to fire on them except by their flankers and advanced patrols," reported Macomb.[4] "So undaunted was the enemy that he never deployed in his whole march, always pressing on in column."

[1] Comparative Force of the Flotillas; MSS. Canadian Archives. Prevost's Report ; James, ii. 462 ; Christie, ii. 211, *note*.

[2] Christie, ii. 221, 222.

[3] Montreal Herald, Sept. 24, 1814.

[4] Report of Sept. 15, 1814; Niles, vii. 50.

The fleet felt the same certainty. According to the best Canadian authority,[1] "the strongest confidence prevailed in the superiority of the British vessels, their weight of metal, and in the capacity and experience of their officers and crews." Captain Downie informed Sir George Prevost's staff-officer that he considered himself with the "Confiance" alone a match for the whole American squadron.[2] Taking the British account of the "Confiance" as correct, she was one hundred and forty-six feet long on the gundeck, and thirty-six feet broad; she carried a crew of three hundred officers and men;[3] her armament was thirty-seven guns, — twenty-seven long twenty-four-pounders, six thirty-two-pound carronades, and four twenty-four-pound carronades, — throwing in all nine hundred and thirty-six pounds.[4] The American account, which was more trustworthy because the "Confiance" became better known in the American than in the British service, gave her thirty-one long twenty-four-pounders and six carronades.[5]

Macdonough's best ship was the "Saratoga." Her dimensions were not recorded. Her regular complement of men was two hundred and ten, but she fought with two hundred and forty; she carried eight twenty-four-pounders, twelve thirty-two and six forty-two-pound carronades, — or twenty-six guns, throwing

---

[1] Christie, ii. 212.    [2] Christie, ii. 212.

[3] London Naval Chronicle, xxxii. 292. Niles, viii.; Supplement, p. 173.

[4] James, p. 413.    [5] Cooper's Naval History, ii. 429.

eight hundred and twenty-eight pounds. Her inferiority to the " Confiance " at long range was immense,
and within carronade range it was at least sufficient
to satisfy Captain Downie. He believed that a few
broadsides would dispose of the " Saratoga," and that
the other American vessels must then surrender.

Assuming Sir George Prevost's report to have been
correct, the two fleets compared as follows : [1] —

### Force of British Fleet.

| Vessels. | Guns. | Long. | Short. | Long metal. | Short metal | Weight of metal. |
|---|---|---|---|---|---|---|
| Confiance . . . | 37 | 31 | 6 | 744 | 192 | 936 |
| Linnet . . . . | 16 | 16 | | 192 | | 192 |
| Chubb . . . . | 11 | 1 | 10 | 6 | 180 | 186 |
| Finch . . . . | 10 | 4 | 6 | 24 | 108 | 132 |
| Twelve Gunboats | 16 | 8 | 8 | 162 | 256 | 418 |
| Total . . . | 90 | 60 | 30 | 1128 | 736 | 1864 |

### Force of American Fleet.

| Vessels. | Guns. | Long. | Short. | Long metal. | Short metal. | Weight of metal. |
|---|---|---|---|---|---|---|
| Saratoga . . . | 26 | 8 | 18 | 192 | 636 | 828 |
| Eagle . . . . | 20 | 8 | 12 | 144 | 384 | 528 |
| Ticonderoga . . | 17 | 12 | 5 | 168 | 146 | 314 |
| Preble . . . . | 7 | 7 | | 63 | | 63 |
| Ten Gunboats . | 16 | 10 | 6 | 192 | 108 | 300 |
| Total . . . | 86 | 45 | 41 | 759 | 1274 | 2033 |

In this calculation the possible error consists only
in one disputed eighteen-pound columbiad on the

[1] Macdonough's Report of Sept. 12, 1814; Niles, vii. 42.
Cooper's Naval History, chap. xxviii.  James's Naval Occurrences,
pp. 414, 415.  Roosevelt's Naval War of 1812, pp. 378–384.

" Finch," and three disputed guns — one long and two short — on the British gunboats. In one case the British would have thrown about nineteen hundred pounds of metal, — in the other, about eighteen hundred. A glance at the two tables shows that in one respect Downie held a decisive superiority in his guns. He had no less than sixty long-range pieces, while Macdonough had but forty-five. Downie's long-range guns threw at least eleven hundred pounds of metal ; Macdonough's threw but seven hundred and sixty. If Downie chose his own distance beyond range of the thirty-two-pound carronades, and fought only his long guns, nothing could save Macdonough except extreme good fortune, for he had but fourteen twenty-four-pound guns against Downie's thirty-four. Firing by broadsides, Downie could throw from his single ship, the " Confiance," sixteen twenty-four-pound shot, to which Macdonough could reply only with eight, even if he used all his long guns on the same side.

The Americans had a decided advantage only in their commander. Thomas Macdonough, born in Delaware in 1783, was thirty years old when this responsibility fell upon him. He had been educated, like most of the naval heroes, in the hard service of the Tripolitan war, and had been sent to construct and command the naval force on Lake Champlain in the spring of 1813. Macdonough's superiority over ordinary commanders consisted in the intelligent forethought with which he provided for the chances of

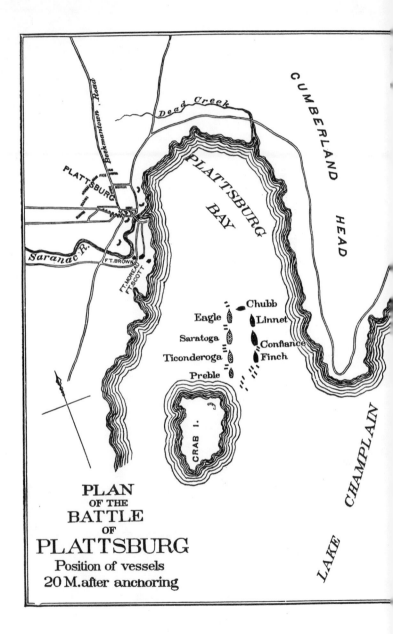

PLAN
OF THE
BATTLE
OF
PLATTSBURG
Position of vessels
20 M. after anchoring

battle. His arrangement showed that he foresaw, and as far as possible overcame in advance, every conceivable attack. He compelled the enemy to fight only as pleased himself.

Macdonough anchored his four large vessels across Plattsburg Bay, where it was a mile and a half wide, and placed his gunboats in their rear to fill the gaps. Cumberland Head on his left and front, and Crab Island on his right obliged the enemy to enter in a line so narrow that Downie would find no room to anchor on his broadside out of carronade range, but must sail into the harbor under the raking fire of the American long guns, and take a position within range of the American carronades.[1] As the battle was to be fought at anchor, both squadrons would as a matter of course be anchored with springs on their cables ; but Macdonough took the additional precaution of laying a kedge off each bow of the " Saratoga," bringing their hawsers in on the two quarters, and letting them hang in bights under water.[2] This arrangement enabled him to wind his ship at any time without fear of having his cables cut by the enemy's shot, and to use his larboard broadside if his starboard guns should be disabled. In effect, it doubled his fighting capacity.

Sir George Prevost and the army were ready to move before Downie's fleet could be prepared. Marching directly forward with the utmost confidence, Sir

---

[1] Cooper's Naval History, ii. 427, 431.

[2] Cooper's Naval History, ii. 432.

George turned the advanced American position at Dead Creek Bridge and drove away the gunboats that covered it. He reached the Saranac River September 6, and saw beyond it a ridge " crowned with three strong redoubts and other field-works, and block-houses armed with heavy ordnance, with their flotilla at anchor out of gunshot from the shore." [1] The description was not exaggerated. Izard was himself a trained engineer, and the works built by him, under the direction of Major Totten of the Engineer Corps, were believed capable of resisting for three weeks a combined attack by land and water, even if the British fleet were victorious.[2] Three good companies of artillery manned the guns. Excellent officers of every arm were in command.

Prevost properly halted, and declined to assault without the co-operation of the fleet. He waited five days impatiently for Downie to appear. Not till seven o'clock on the morning of September 11 did the British flotilla sail round Cumberland Head. At the same time Prevost ordered his troops to cross the Saranac and storm the American works.

Downie intended, without regarding his superiority in long-range guns, to sail in and to lay the " Confiance " alongside of the " Saratoga ; " but the wind was light and baffling, and his approach was so slow that he could not long bear the raking fire of the American guns. As he came within carronade range

[1] Prevost's Report of Sept. 11, 1814; James, ii. 461.
[2] Izard to Monroe, Oct. 7, 1814 ; Izard's Correspondence, p. 97.

the wind baffling, he was obliged to anchor at two cables' lengths,[1] or three hundred yards,[2] and begin action. With the same discipline that marked the movements of the troops on shore, Downie came to, anchored, made everything secure, and then poured a full broadside into Macdonough's ship. The " Saratoga " shivered under the shock of sixteen twenty-four-pound shot and canister charges striking her hull; almost one-fifth of her crew were disabled; but she stood stoutly to her work, and the whole line was soon hotly engaged.

Americans usually had a decided advantage in their better gunnery, but three hundred yards was a long range for thirty-two-pound carronades, which at point-blank carried less than two hundred and fifty yards, and lost accuracy in proportion to elevation.[3] Macdonough was slow to prove superiority. Early in the battle the British suffered a severe, and perhaps in the experience of this war a decisive, loss in their commander, Captain Downie, instantly killed by one of his own guns thrown off its carriage against him by a solid shot. Yet at the end of two hours' combat the British squadron was on the whole victorious, and the American on the point of capture. Of the three smaller American vessels, the " Preble " on the extreme right was driven out of the engagement, and

[1] Report of Captain Pring, Sept. 12, 1814 ; James, Appendix no. 90.

[2] Report of Commodore Macdonough, Sept. 13, 1814 ; Niles, vii. 41.

[3] Howard Douglas's Naval Gunnery, p. 115. (Fourth edition).

the British gunboats, turning the American flank, attacked the "Ticonderoga," which maintained a doubtful battle. The American left was also turned, the "Eagle" having been driven to take refuge between the "Saratoga" and "Ticonderoga," in the centre. Macdonough's ship was then exposed to the concentrated fire of the "Confiance" and "Linnet," and his battery was soon silenced. The "Saratoga" could no longer use a gun on the engaged side, and the battle was nearly lost.

Then Macdonough's forethought changed the impending defeat into victory. His fire had nearly silenced the "Confiance," and disregarding the "Linnet," he ceased attention to the battle in order to direct the operation of winding ship. Little by little hauling the ship about, he opened on the "Confiance" with one gun after another of the fresh broadside, as they bore; and the "Confiance," after trying in vain to effect the same operation, struck her colors. Then the British fleet was in the situation which Downie had anticipated for the Americans in the event of silencing the "Saratoga." The three smaller vessels were obliged to surrender, and the gunboats alone escaped. The battle had lasted from quarter past eight till quarter before eleven.

By land, the British attack was much less effective than by water. The troops were slow in reaching their positions, and had time to make no decisive movement. A column under Major-General Robinson was ordered to move round by the right flank to a

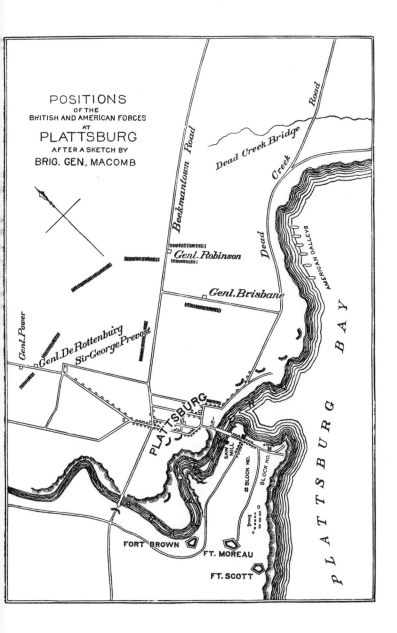

POSITIONS
OF THE
BRITISH AND AMERICAN FORCES
AT
PLATTSBURG
AFTER A SKETCH BY
BRIG. GEN. MACOMB

*Beekmantown Road*

*Dead Creek Bridge*

*Dead Creek*

*Genl. Robinson*

*Genl. Brisbane*

AMERICAN GALLEYS

*Genl. Power*

*Genl. De Rottenburg*

*Sir George Prevost*

PLATTSBURG

SAW MILL

BLOCK HO.

BLOCK HO.

P L A T T S B U R G   B A Y

FORT BROWN

FT. MOREAU

FT. SCOTT

ford previously reconnoitred, some distance up the Saranac, in order to gain a position whence they could reverse the American works and carry them by assault ; but Robinson's column missed its way, and before reaching the ford heard the cheers of the American troops, and halted to ascertain its cause.[1] The remainder of the army waited for Robinson's column to assault. The casualties showed that nothing like a serious engagement took place. The entire loss of the British army from September 6 to September 14 was officially reported as only thirty-seven killed and one hundred and fifty wounded, and of this loss a large part occurred previous to the battle of September 11. The entire American loss was thirty-seven killed and sixty-two wounded.

In the naval battle, Macdonough reported fifty-two killed and fifty-eight wounded, among about eight hundred and eighty men. The British reported fifty-seven killed and seventy-two wounded, in crews whose number was never precisely known, but was probably fully eight hundred. In neither case was the loss, though severe, as great relatively to the numbers as the severity of the action seemed to imply. The " Saratoga " lost twenty-eight killed in a crew of two hundred and forty. In Perry's battle on Lake Erie, the " Lawrence " lost twenty-two men killed in a crew of one hundred and thirty-one. About one man in eight was killed on Macdonough's ship ; about one man in six on Perry's.

[1] Christie, ii. 215, 216.

With needless precipitation, Prevost instantly retreated the next day to Champlain, sacrificing stores
to a very great amount, and losing many men by desertion.  The army was cruelly mortified, and Prevost
lost whatever military reputation he still preserved
in Canada.  In England the impression of disgrace
was equally strong.  " It is scarcely possible to conceive the degree of mortification and disappointment,"
said the " Annual Register," [1] " which the intelligence
of this defeat created in Great Britain."  Yeo brought
official charges of misconduct against Prevost, and
Prevost defended himself by unusual arguments.

" With whatever sorrow I may think of the unfortunate occurrences to which I allude," he wrote to Bathurst,
three weeks later,[2] " I consider them as light and trivial
when compared to the disastrous results which, I am solemnly persuaded, would have ensued had any considera-
tions of personal glory, or any unreflecting disregard of
the safety of the province, or of the honor of the army
committed to my charge, induced me to pursue those
offensive operations by land, independent of the fleet,
which it would appear by your Lordship's despatch were
expected of me.  Such operations, my Lord, have been
attempted before, and on the same ground.  The history
of our country records their failure ; and had they been
undertaken again with double the force placed under my
command, they would have issued in the discomfiture of
his Majesty's arms, and in a defeat not more disastrous
than inevitable."

[1] Annual Register for 1814, p. 332.
[2] Prevost to Bathurst, Oct. 6, 1814; Christie, ii. 395.

The Duke of Wellington was not so severe as other critics, and hesitated to say that Prevost was wrong; "though of this I am certain, he must equally have returned . . . after the fleet was beaten; and I am inclined to think he was right. I have told the ministers repeatedly that a naval superiority on the Lakes is a *sine qua non* of success in war on the frontier of Canada, even if our object should be wholly defensive." [1] Yet the Duke in conversation seemed to think that his army in Canada was also at fault. "He had sent them some of his best troops from Bordeaux," he said five-and-twenty years afterward,[2] "but they did not turn out quite right; they wanted this iron fist to command them."

Meanwhile Major-General Izard, by Armstrong's order, marched his four thousand men as far as possible from the points of attack. Starting from Champlain, August 29, the army reached Sackett's Harbor September 17, having marched about two hundred and eighty miles in twenty days. At Sackett's Harbor Izard found no orders from the government, for the government at that time had ceased to perform its functions; but he received an earnest appeal from General Brown to succor Fort Erie. "I will not conceal from you," wrote Brown, September 10,[3] "that I consider the fate of this army very doubtful

[1] Wellington to Sir George Murray, Dec. 22, 1814; Despatches, xii. 224.

[2] Stanhope's Conversations, p. 252.

[3] Brown to Izard, Sept. 10, 1814; Izard's Correspondence, p. 86.

unless speedy relief is afforded." Izard, who had
no means of testing the correctness of this opinion,
decided to follow Brown's wishes, and made, September 17, the necessary preparations. Violent storms
prevented Chauncey from embarking the troops until
September 21; but September 27 the troops reached
Batavia, and Izard met Brown by appointment. The
army had then been a month in movement. The distance was more than four hundred miles, and no
energy could have shortened the time so much as to
have affected the result of the campaign. At one
end of the line Sir George Prevost retreated from
Plattsburg September 12; at the other end, Lieutenant-General Drummond retreated from Fort Erie
September 21; and Izard's force, constituting the
largest body of regular troops in the field, had
been placed where it could possibly affect neither
result.

Izard was a friend of Monroe, and was therefore
an object of Armstrong's merciless criticism.[1] Brown
was a favorite of Armstrong, and shared his prejudices. The position of Izard at Buffalo was calculated to excite jealousy. He had implicitly obeyed the
wishes of Armstrong and Brown; in doing so, he had
sacrificed himself, — yielding to Macomb the credit
of repulsing Prevost, and to Brown, who did not wait
for his arrival, the credit of repulsing Drummond.
As far as could be seen, Izard had acted with loyalty
toward both Armstrong and Brown; yet both dis-

[1] Notices, ii. 102–107.

trusted him. Brown commonly inclined toward severity, and was the more sensitive because Izard, as the senior officer, necessarily took command.

Until that moment Izard had enjoyed no chance of showing his abilities in the field, but at Niagara he saw before him a great opportunity. Drummond lay at Chippawa, with an army reduced by battle and sickness to about twenty-five hundred men. Izard commanded fifty-five hundred regular troops and eight hundred militia.[1] He had time to capture or destroy Drummond's entire force before the winter should set in, and to gather the results of Brown's desperate fighting. Brown was eager for the attack, and Izard assented. October 13 the army moved on Chippawa, and stopped. October 16, Izard wrote to the War Department,[2] —

"I have just learned by express from Sackett's Harbor that Commodore Chauncey with the whole of his fleet has retired into port, and is throwing up batteries for its protection. This defeats all the objects of the operations by land in this quarter. I may turn Chippawa, and should General Drummond not retire, may succeed in giving him a good deal of trouble; but if he falls back on Fort George or Burlington Heights, every step I take in pursuit exposes me to be cut off by the large reinforcements it is in the power of the enemy to throw in twenty-four hours upon my flank or rear."

[1] Izard to Monroe, Oct. 16, 1814 ; Izard's Correspondence, p. 100.

[2] Izard to Monroe, Oct. 16, 1814 ; Izard's Correspondence, p. 103.

In this state of mind, notwithstanding a successful skirmish, October 19, between Bissell's brigade and a strong detachment of the enemy, Izard made a decision which ruined his military reputation and destroyed his usefulness to the service. He reported to the Department, October 23,[1] —

" On the 21st, finding that he [Drummond] still continued within his works, which he had been assiduously engaged in strengthening from the moment of our first appearance, the weather beginning to be severe, and a great quantity of our officers and men suffering from their continued fatigues and exposure, at twelve at noon I broke up my encampment, and marched to this ground [opposite Black Rock] in order to prepare winter quarters for the troops."

Nothing remained but to break up the army. Brown was sent at his own request to Sackett's Harbor, where the next fighting was expected. A division of the army went with him. The remainder were placed in winter quarters near Buffalo. Fort Erie was abandoned and blown up, November 5, and the frontier at Niagara relapsed into repose.

Izard felt the mortification of his failure. His feelings were those of a generous character, and his tone toward Brown contrasted to his advantage both in candor and in temper with Brown's language toward

[1] Izard to Monroe, Oct. 23, 1814; Izard's Correspondence, p. 105. Cf. Brown to Armstrong, Nov. 28, 1814 ; Kosciusko Armstrong's " Notice of J. Q. Adams's Eulogy on James Monroe," p. 29.

him; but great energy generally implied great faults, and Brown's faults were better suited than Izard's virtues for the work of an American general at Niagara. Greatly to Izard's credit, he not only saw his own inferiority, but advised the government of it. He wrote to the Secretary of War, November 20,[1] —

"The success of the next campaign on this frontier will in a great measure depend on concert and good understanding among the superior officers. . . . General Brown is certainly a brave, intelligent, and active officer. Where a portion of the forces is composed of irregular troops, I have no hesitation in acknowledging my conviction of his being better qualified than I to make them useful in the public service."

So sensitive was Izard to the public feeling and his loss of standing that he sent his resignation to the secretary, December 18,[2] in terms which betrayed and even asserted his consciousness of shrinking under the weight of responsibility : —

"I am fully aware that attempts have been made to lessen the confidence of government as well as of the public in my ability to execute the important duties intrusted to me, — duties which were imposed unexpectedly and much against my inclination. It is therefore not improbable that my voluntary retirement will relieve the Department of War from some embarrassment, and that my individual satisfaction will accord with the public

[1] Izard to Monroe, Nov. 20, 1814; Izard's Correspondence, p. 119.

[2] Izard to Monroe, Dec. 18, 1814; Izard's Correspondence, p. 130.

advantage, — especially as my view of the connection between military command and responsibility differs materially from that entertained by persons in high authority."

A man who showed so little confidence in himself could not claim the confidence of others, and in contact with stronger characters like Armstrong, Brown, Scott, or Andrew Jackson could play no part but that of a victim. His resignation was not accepted, but his career was at an end. When he relieved the pressure kept by Brown constantly applied to the extremity of the British line, the movement of war necessarily turned back to its true object, which was Sackett's Harbor. Drummond no sooner saw Fort Erie evacuated and his lines re-established, November 5, than he hurried on board ship with a part of his troops, and reached Kingston, November 10,[1] where Sir George Prevost had already prepared for an attack on Sackett's Harbor as soon as supplies could be brought from Quebec to Kingston over the winter roads. Soon afterward Sir George Prevost was recalled to England, and a new commander-in-chief, Sir George Murray, supposed to be a man of higher capacity, was sent to take direction of the next campaign. Reinforcements continued to arrive.[2] About twenty-seven thousand regular troops, including officers, were in Canada;[3] a seventy-four-gun ship and a new frigate were launched at Kingston; and

[1] James, ii. 241.          [2] James, ii. 393.
[3] MSS. Canadian Archives.  Freer Papers, 1814, p. 31.

no one doubted that, with the spring, Sackett's Harbor would be formally besieged. Izard remained at Buffalo, doing nothing, and his only influence on the coming as on the past campaign was to leave the initiative to the enemy.

# CHAPTER V.

ARMSTRONG'S management of the Northern campaign caused severe criticism; but his neglect of the city of Washington exhausted the public patience. For two years Washington stood unprotected; not a battery or a breastwork was to be found on the river bank except the old and untenable Fort Washington, or Warburton.[1] A thousand determined men might reach the town in thirty-six hours, and destroy it before any general alarm could be given.[2] Yet no city was more easily protected than Washington, at that day, from attack on its eastern side; any good engineer could have thrown up works in a week that would have made approach by a small force impossible. Armstrong neglected to fortify. After experience had proved his error, he still argued in writing to a committee of Congress[3] that fortifications would have exhausted the Treasury; " that

[1] Lieutenant Edwards's Report of July 25, 1814; State Papers, Military Affairs, i. 545.

[2] Winder to Armstrong, July 9, 1814; State Papers, Military Affairs, i. 543.

[3] Letter of Secretary Armstrong, Oct. 17, 1814; State Papers, Military Affairs, i. 538.

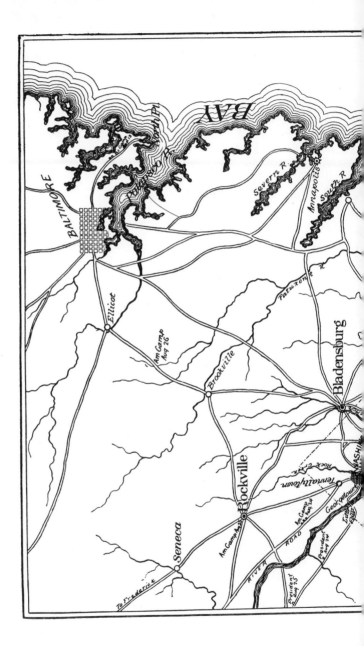

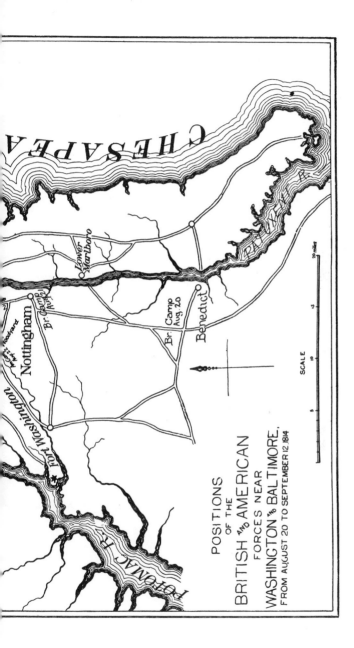

POSITIONS
OF THE
BRITISH AND AMERICAN
FORCES NEAR
WASHINGTON AND BALTIMORE.
FROM AUGUST 20 TO SEPTEMBER 12, 1814

SCALE

CHESAPEA

CHE

Lower Marlboro

Nottingham

Br. Camp
Aug. 20

Br. Camp

Benedict

Fort Washington

POTOMAC R.

PATUXENT R.

bayonets are known to form the most efficient barriers; and that there was no reason in this case to doubt beforehand the willingness of the country to defend itself," — as though he believed that militia were most efficient when most exposed! He did not even provide the bayonets.

In truth, Armstrong looking at the matter as a military critic decided that the British having no strategic object in capturing Washington, would not make the attempt. Being an indolent man, negligent of detail, he never took unnecessary trouble; and having no proper staff at Washington, he was without military advisers whose opinion he respected. The President and Monroe fretted at his indifference, the people of the District were impatient under it, and every one except Armstrong was in constant terror of attack; but according to their account the secretary only replied: "No, no! Baltimore is the place, sir; that is of so much more consequence."[1] Probably he was right, and the British would have gone first to Baltimore had his negligence not invited them to Washington.

In May the President began to press Armstrong for precautionary measures.[2] In June letters arrived from Gallatin and Bayard in London which caused the President to call a Cabinet meeting. June 23

[1] Letter of J. P. Van Ness, Nov. 23, 1814; State Papers, Military Affairs, i. 581.

[2] Madison to Armstrong, May 20, 1814; Madison's Works, iii. 399.

and 24 the Cabinet met and considered the diplomatic situation.[1]  The President proposed then for the first time to abandon impressment as a *sine qua non* of negotiation, and to approve a treaty that should be silent on the subject.  Armstrong and Jones alone supported the idea at that time, but three days afterward, June 27, Monroe and Campbell acceded to it. The Cabinet then took the defences of Washington in hand, and July 1 decided to organize a corps of defence from the militia of the District and the neighboring States.    July 2, the first step toward efficient defence was taken by creating a new military district on the Potomac, with a military head of its own.  Armstrong wished to transfer Brigadier-General Moses Porter from Norfolk, to command the new Potomac District;[2] but the President selected Brigadier-General Winder, because his relationship to the Federalist governor of Maryland was likely to make co-operation more effective.

Political appointments were not necessarily bad; but in appointing Winder to please the governor of Maryland Madison assumed the responsibility, in Armstrong's eyes, for the defence of Washington.  The Secretary of War seemed to think that Madison and Monroe were acting together to take the defence of Washington out of his hands, and to put it in hands in which they felt confidence.  .Armstrong placed Winder instantly in command, and promptly issued

[1] Madison's Works, iii. 408, 409.

[2] Notices, ii. 140.

the orders arranged in Cabinet; but he left further measures to Winder, Monroe, and Madison. His conduct irritated the President; but no one charged that the secretary refused to carry out the orders, or to satisfy the requisitions of the President or of General Winder. He was merely passive.[1]

Winder received his appointment July 5, and went to Washington for instructions. He passed the next month riding between Washington, Baltimore, and points on the lower Potomac and Patuxent,[2] obtaining with great fatigue a personal knowledge of the country. August 1 he established his permanent headquarters at Washington, and the entire result of his labors till that time was the presence of one company of Maryland militia at Bladensburg. No line of defence was selected, no obstructions to the roads were prepared, and not so much as a ditch or a breastwork was marked out or suggested between Annapolis and Washington. Another fortnight passed, and still Winder was not further advanced. He had no more men, arms, fortifications, and no more ideas, on the 18th of August than on the 5th of July. "The call for three thousand militia under the requisition of July 4 had produced only two hundred and fifty men at the moment the enemy landed at Benedict." [3]

[1] Madison's Works, iii. 422, 426.

[2] Winder to Armstrong, July 27, 1814; State Papers, Military Affairs, i. 546.

[3] Winder's letter of Sept. 26, 1814; State Papers, Military Affairs, i. 552.

Winder had then been six weeks in command of the Washington defences.

Meanwhile a British expedition under command of Major General Robert Ross, a distinguished officer of the Peninsula army, sailed from the Gironde, June 27, to Bermuda.   Ross was instructed " to effect a diversion on the coasts of the United States of America in favor of the army employed in the defence of Upper and Lower Canada."   The point of attack was to be decided by Vice-Admiral Cochrane, subject to the general's approval ; but the force was not intended for " any extended operation at a distance from the coast," nor was Ross to hold permanent possession of any captured district.[1]

" When the object of the descent which you may make on the coast is to take possession of any naval or military stores, you will not delay the destruction of them in preference to the taking them away, if there is reasonable ground of apprehension that the enemy is advancing with superior force to effect their recovery.   If in any descent you shall be enabled to take such a position as to threaten the inhabitants with the destruction of their property, you are hereby authorized to levy upon them contributions in return for your forbearance ; but you will not by this understand that the magazines belonging to the government, or their harbors, or their shipping, are to be included in such an arrangement.   These, together with their contents, are in all cases to be taken away or destroyed."

[1] Bathurst to Ross, 1814 ; War Office Despatches, MSS. British Archives.

Negroes were not to be encouraged to rise upon their masters, and no slaves were to be taken away as slaves; but any negro who should expose himself to vengeance by joining the expedition or lending it assistance, might be enlisted in the black corps, or carried away by the fleet.

Nothing in these orders warranted the destruction of private or public property, except such as might be capable of military uses. Ross was not authorized, and did not intend, to enter on a mere marauding expedition; but Cochrane was independent of Ross, and at about the time when Ross reached Bermuda Cochrane received a letter from Sir George Prevost which gave an unexpected character to the Chesapeake expedition. A small body of American troops had crossed Lake Erie to Long Point, May 15, and destroyed the flour-mills, distilleries, and some private houses there. The raid was not authorized by the United States government, and the officer commanding it was afterward court-martialed and censured; but Sir George Prevost, without waiting for explanations, wrote to Vice-Admiral Cochrane, June 2, suggesting that he should " assist in inflicting that measure of retaliation which shall deter the enemy from a repetition of similar outrages." [1]

When Cochrane received this letter, he issued at Bermuda, July 18, orders to the ships under his command, from the St. Croix River to the St. Mary's,

[1] Cochrane to Prevost, July 22, 1814; MSS. Canadian Archives. C. 684, p. 221.

directing general retaliation.[1]   The orders were interesting as an illustration of the temper the war had taken.

" You are hereby required and directed," wrote the Vice-Admiral to the British blockading squadrons, " to destroy and lay waste such towns and districts upon the coast as you may find assailable.   You will hold strictly in view the conduct of the American army toward his Majesty's unoffending Canadian subjects, and you will spare merely the lives of the unarmed inhabitants of the United States.   For only by carrying this retributory justice into the country of our enemy can we hope to make him sensible of the impropriety as well as of the inhumanity of the system he has adopted.   You will take every opportunity of explaining to the people how much I lament the necessity of following the rigorous example of the commander of the American forces. And as these commanders must obviously have acted under instructions from the Executive government of the United States, whose intimate and unnatural connection with the late government of France has led them to adopt the same system of plunder and devastation, it is therefore to their own government the unfortunate sufferers must look for indemnification for their loss of property."

This ill-advised order was to remain in force until Sir George Prevost should send information " that the United States government have come under an obligation to make full remuneration to the injured and

[1] Orders of Vice-Admiral Cochrane, July 18, 1814 ; MSS. Canadian Archives, C. 684, p. 204.

unoffending inhabitants of the Canadas for all the outrages their troops have committed." Cochrane further wrote to Prevost that " as soon as these orders have been acted upon," a copy would be sent to Washington for the information of the Executive government.

Cochrane's retaliatory order was dated July 18, and Ross's transports arrived at Bermuda July 24. As soon as the troops were collected and stores put on board, Cochrane and Ross sailed, August 3, for Chesapeake Bay. They arrived a few days in advance of the transports, and passing up the bay to the mouth of the Potomac, landed, August 15, with Rear Admiral Cockburn, to decide on a plan for using to best effect the forces under their command.

Three objects were within reach. The first and immediate aim was a flotilla of gunboats, commanded by Captain Joshua Barney, which had taken refuge in the Patuxent River, and was there blockaded. The next natural object of desire was Baltimore, on account of its shipping and prize-money. The third was Washington and Alexandria, on account of the navy-yard and the vessels in the Potomac. Baltimore was the natural point of attack after destroying Barney's flotilla; but Cockburn, with a sailor's recklessness, urged a dash at Washington.[1] Ross hesitated, and postponed a decision till Barney's flotilla should be disposed of.

[1] James, ii. 275, 276; Cockburn to Cochrane, Aug. 27, 1814; Ross to Bathurst, Aug. 30, 1814; James, ii. 492–499.

Two days afterward, August 17, the troops arrived, and the squadron, commanded by Vice-Admiral Cochrane, moved twenty miles up the bay to the mouth of the Patuxent, — a point about fifty miles distant from Annapolis on the north, and from Washington on the northwest. Having arrived there August 18, Cochrane wrote, or afterward ante-dated, an official letter to Secretary Monroe: [1] —

"Having been called on by the Governor-General of the Canadas to aid him in carrying into effect measures of retaliation against the inhabitants of the United States for the wanton destruction committed by their army in Upper Canada, it has become imperiously my duty, conformably with the nature of the Governor-General's application, to issue to the naval force under my command an order to destroy and lay waste such towns and districts upon the coast as may be found assailable."

The notice was the more remarkable because Cochrane's order was issued only to the naval force. The army paid no attention to it. Ross's troops were landed at Benedict the next day, August 19; but neither there nor elsewhere did they destroy or lay waste towns or districts. They rather showed unusual respect for private property.

At Benedict, August 19, the British forces were organized in three brigades, numbering, according to different British accounts, four thousand five hun-

[1] Cochrane to Monroe, Aug. 18, 1814; State Papers, Foreign Affairs, iii. 693.

dred, or four thousand rank-and-file.[1]  Cockburn
with the boats of the fleet the next day, August 20,
started up the river in search of Barney's flotilla;
while the land force began its march at four o'clock
in the afternoon abreast of the boats, and camped
four miles above Benedict without seeing an enemy,
or suffering from a worse annoyance than one of the
evening thunder-storms common in hot weather.

The next day at dawn the British army started
again, and marched that day, Sunday, August 21,
twelve miles to the village of Nottingham, where it
camped.[2]  The weather was hot, and the march resembled a midsummer picnic.  Through a thickly
wooded region, where a hundred militia-men with
axes and spades could have delayed their progress
for days, the British army moved in a solitude apparently untenanted by human beings, till they
reached Nottingham on the Patuxent, — a deserted
town, rich in growing crops and full barns.

At Nottingham the army passed a quiet night, and
the next morning, Monday, August 22, lingered till
eight o'clock, when it again advanced.  Among the
officers in the Eighty-fifth regiment was a lieutenant
named Gleig, who wrote afterward a charming narrative of the campaign under the title, " A Subaltern
in America."  He described the road as remarkably
good, running for the most part through the heart of
thick forests, which sheltered it from the rays of the

---

[1] Gleig's Washington and New Orleans, p. 51.  James, ii. 283.
[2] Map of General Ross's Route ; Wilkinson's Memoirs.

sun. During the march the army was startled by the distant sound of several heavy explosions. Barney had blown up his gunboats to prevent their capture. The British naval force had thus performed its part in the enterprise, and the army was next to take the lead. Ross halted at Marlboro after a march of only seven miles, and there too he camped, undisturbed by sight or sound of an armed enemy, although the city of Washington was but sixteen miles on his left, and Baltimore thirty miles in his front. Ross had then marched twenty or twenty-one miles into Maryland without seeing an enemy, although an American army had been close on his left flank, watching him all day.

At Marlboro Ross was obliged to decide what he should next do. He was slow in forming a conclusion. Instead of marching at daybreak of August 23, and moving rapidly on Baltimore or Washington, the army passed nearly the whole day at Marlboro in idleness, as though it were willing to let the Americans do their utmost for defence. "Having advanced within sixteen miles of Washington," Ross officially reported,[1] "and ascertained the force of the enemy to be such as might authorize an attempt to carry his capital, I determined to make it, and accordingly put the troops in movement on the evening of the 23d." More exactly, the troops moved at two o'clock in the afternoon, and marched about six miles on the road to Washington, when they struck Ameri-

[1] Ross's Report of Aug. 30, 1814 ; Niles, vii. 277.

can outposts at about five o'clock, and saw a force
posted on high ground about a mile in their front.
As the British formed to attack, the American force
disappeared, and the British army camped about nine
miles from Washington by way of the navy-yard
bridge over the Eastern Branch.

Thus for five days, from August 18 to August 23,
a British army, which though small was larger than
any single body of American regulars then in the
field, marched in a leisurely manner through a long-
settled country, and met no show of resistance before
coming within sight of the Capitol. Such an adventure resembled the stories of Cortez and De Soto; and
the conduct of the United States government offered
no contradiction to the resemblance.

News of the great fleet that appeared in the Patuxent August 17 reached Washington on the morning
of Thursday, August 18, and set the town in commo-
tion. In haste the President sent fresh militia requisitions to the neighboring States, and ordered out
the militia and all the regular troops in Washington
and its neighborhood. Monroe started again as a
scout, arriving in the neighborhood of Benedict at
ten o'clock on the morning of August 20, and remaining there all day and night without learning
more than he knew before starting.[1] Winder was
excessively busy, but did, according to his own account, nothing. " The innumerably multiplied or-

---

[1] Monroe to Madison, Aug. 20 and 21, 1814; State Papers,
Military Affairs, i. 537. Winder's Narrative, Ibid. 554.

ders, letters, consultations, and demands which crowded upon me at the moment of such an alarm can more easily be conceived than described, and occupied me nearly day and night, from Thursday the 18th of August till Sunday the 21st, and had nearly broken down myself and assistants in preparing, dispensing, and attending to them." Armstrong, at last alive to the situation, made excellent suggestions,[1] but could furnish neither troops, means, nor military intelligence to carry them out; and the President could only call for help. The single step taken for defence was taken by the citizens, who held a meeting Saturday evening, and offered at their own expense to erect works at Bladensburg. Winder accepted their offer. Armstrong detailed Colonel Wadsworth, the only engineer officer near the Department, to lay out the lines, and the citizens did such work as was possible in the time that remained.

After three days of confusion, a force was at last evolved. Probably by Winder's order, although no such order was preserved, a corps of observation was marched across the navy-yard bridge toward the Patuxent, or drawn from Bladensburg, to a place called the Woodyard, twelve miles beyond the Eastern Branch. The force was not to be despised. Three hundred infantry regulars of different regiments, with one hundred and twenty light dragoons, formed the nucleus; two hundred and fifty Maryland

[1] State Papers, Military Affairs, i. 547, 549.

militia, and about twelve hundred District volunteers
or militia, with twelve six-pound field-pieces, composed a body of near two thousand men,[1] from whom
General Brown or Andrew Jackson would have got
good service. Winder came out and took command
Sunday evening, and Monroe, much exhausted, joined
them that night.

There the men stood Monday, August 22, while
the British army marched by them, within sight
of their outposts, from Nottingham to Marlboro.
Winder rode forward with his cavalry and watched
all day the enemy's leisurely movements close in
his front,[2] but the idea of attack did not appear to
enter his mind. " A doubt at that time," he said,[3]
" was not entertained by anybody of the intention
of the enemy to proceed direct to Washington." At
nine o'clock that evening Monroe sent a note to the
President, saying that the enemy was in full march
for Washington ; that Winder proposed to retire till
he could collect his troops ; that preparations should
be made to destroy the bridges, and that the papers
in the government offices should be removed.[4] At
the same time Monroe notified Serurier, the only
foreign minister then in Washington, that the sin-

[1] Winder's Narrative ; State Papers, Military Affairs, i. 554.
General W. Smith's Statement ; State Papers, Military Affairs,
i. 563.

[2] Winder's Narrative ; State Papers, Military Affairs, i. 554.
General W. Smith's Statement, i. 563.

[3] Winder's Narrative ; State Papers, Military Affairs, i. 555.

[4] State Papers, Military Affairs, i. 538.

gle hope of saving the capital depended on the very
doubtful result of an engagement, which would probably take place the next day or the day after, at
Bladensburg.[1]

At Bladensburg, of necessity, the engagement
must take place, unless Winder made an attack or
waited for attack on the road. One of two courses
was to be taken, — Washington must be either defended or evacuated. Perhaps Winder would have
done better to evacuate it, and let the British take
the undefended village ; but no suggestion of the
sort was made, nor did Winder retreat to Bladensburg as was necessary if he meant to unite his troops
and make preparations for a battle. Instead of retreating to Bladensburg as soon as he was satisfied —
at noon of Monday, August 22 — that the British were
going there, he ordered his troops to fall back, and
took position at the Old Fields, about five miles in
the rear of the Woodyard, and about seven miles by
road from the navy-yard. Another road led from
the Old Fields to Bladensburg about eight miles
away. The American force might have been united
at Bladensburg Monday evening, but Winder camped
at the Old Fields and passed the night.

That evening the President and the members of
the Cabinet rode out to the camp, and the next
morning the President reviewed the army, which
had been reinforced by Commodore Barney with four

[1] Serurier to Talleyrand, Aug. 22, 1814; Archives des Aff.
Étr. MSS.

hundred sailors, the crews of the burned gunboats. Winder then had twenty-five hundred men, of whom near a thousand were regulars, or sailors even better fighting troops than ordinary regulars. Such a force vigorously led was sufficient to give Ross's army a sharp check, and at that moment Ross was still hesitating whether to attack Washington. The loss of a few hundred men might have turned the scale at any moment during Tuesday, August 23 ; but Winder neither fought nor retreated, but once more passed the day on scout. At noon he rode with a troop of cavalry toward Marlboro. Satisfied that the enemy was not in motion and would not move that day, he started at one o'clock for Bladensburg, leaving his army to itself. He wished to bring up a brigade of militia from Bladensburg.[1]

Winder had ridden about five miles, when the British at two o'clock suddenly broke up their camp and marched directly on the Old Fields. The American army hastily formed in line, and sent off its baggage to Washington. Winder was summoned back in haste, and arrived on the field at five o'clock as the British appeared. He ordered a retreat. Every military reason required a retreat to Bladensburg. Winder directed a retreat on Washington by the navy-yard bridge.

The reasons which actuated him to prefer the navy-yard to Bladensburg, as explained by him, consisted

[1] Winder's Narrative; State Papers, Military Affairs, pp. 555, 556.

in anxiety for the safety of that " direct and important pass," which could not without hazard be left
unguarded.[1]  In order to guard a bridge a quarter
of a mile long over an impassable river covered by
the guns of war-vessels and the navy-yard, he left
unguarded the open high-road which led through
Bladensburg directly to the Capitol and the White
House.    After a very rapid retreat that " literally
became a run of eight miles," [2] Winder encamped in
Washington near the bridge-head at the navy-yard
at eight o'clock that night, and then rode three miles
to the White House to report to the President.    On
returning to camp, he passed the night until three
or four o'clock in the morning making in person
arrangements to destroy the bridge " when necessary," assuring his officers that he expected the
enemy to attempt a passage there that night.[3]  Toward dawn he lay down, exhausted by performing a
subaltern's duty all day, and snatched an hour or
two of sleep.

The British in their camp that evening were about
eight miles from Bladensburg battle-field.    Winder
was about five miles distant from the same point.
By a quick march at dawn he might still have arrived there, with six hours to spare for arranging

[1] Winder's Narrative ; State Papers, Military Affairs, pp.
556, 557.

[2] Statement of John Law ; State Papers, Military Affairs,
i. 585.

[3] Winder's Narrative ; State Papers, Military Affairs, i. 557.

his defence. He preferred to wait till he should know with certainty that the British were on their way there. On the morning of Wednesday, August 24, he wrote to Armstrong : [1] —

" I have found it necessary to establish my headquarters here, the most advanced position convenient to the troops, and nearest information. I shall remain stationary as much as possible, that I may be the more readily found, to issue orders, and collect together the various detachments of militia, and give them as rapid a consolidation and organization as possible. . . . The news up the river is very threatening. Barney's or some other force should occupy the batteries at Greenleaf's Point and the navy-yard. I should be glad of the assistance of counsel from yourself and the Government. If more convenient, I should make an exertion to go to you the first opportunity."

This singular note was carried first to the President, who, having opened and read it, immediately rode to headquarters. Monroe, Jones, and Rush followed. Armstrong and Campbell arrived last. Before Armstrong appeared, a scout arrived at ten o'clock with information that the British army had broken up its camp at daylight, and was probably more than half way to Bladensburg.[2]

Winder's persistence in remaining at the navy-yard was explained as due to the idea that the enemy might move toward the Potomac, seize Fort

[1] State Papers, Military Affairs, i. 548.

[2] Captain Burch's Statement, Oct. 12, 1814 ; State Papers, Military Affairs, i. 574.

Washington or Warburton, secure the passage of his ships, and approach the city by the river.[1] The general never explained how his presence at the navy-yard was to prevent such a movement if it was made.

The whole eastern side of Washington was covered by a broad estuary called the Eastern Branch of the Potomac, bridged only at two points, and impassable, even by pontoons, without ample warning. From the Potomac River to Bladensburg, a distance of about seven miles, the city was effectually protected. Bladensburg made the point of a right angle. There the Baltimore road entered the city as by a pass ; for beyond, to the west, no general would venture to enter, leaving an enemy at Bladensburg in his rear. Roads were wanting, and the country was difficult. Through Bladensburg the attacking army must come; to Bladensburg Winder must go, unless he meant to retreat to Georgetown, or to re-cross the Eastern Branch in the enemy's rear. Monroe notified Serurier Monday evening that the battle would be fought at Bladensburg. Secretary Jones wrote to Commodore Rodgers, Tuesday morning, that the British would probably "advance to-day toward Bladensburg."[2] Every one looked instinctively to that spot[3],

---

[1] Rush's Narrative; State Papers, Military Affairs, i. 542. Winder's Narrative ; State Papers, Military Affairs, i. 557.

[2] Review of J. Q. Adams by Kosciusko Armstrong, p. 7.

[3] William Pinkney's Statement; State Papers, Military Affairs, i. 572.

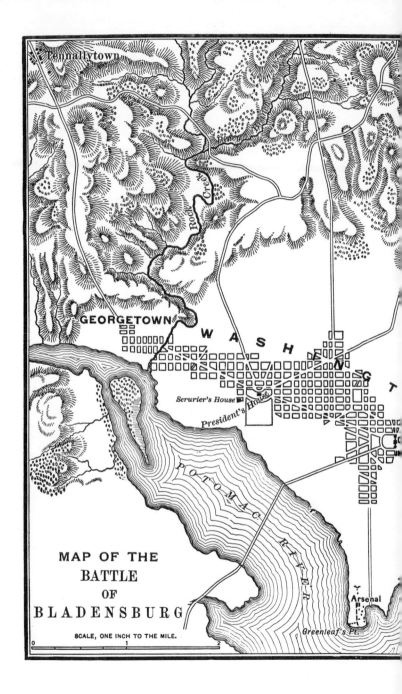

MAP OF THE
BATTLE
OF
BLADENSBURG

SCALE, ONE INCH TO THE MILE.

Tennallytown

Rock Creek

GEORGETOWN

W A S H I N G T

Serurier's House

President's House

P O T O M A C   R I V E R

Arsenal

Greenleaf's Pt.

0        1        2

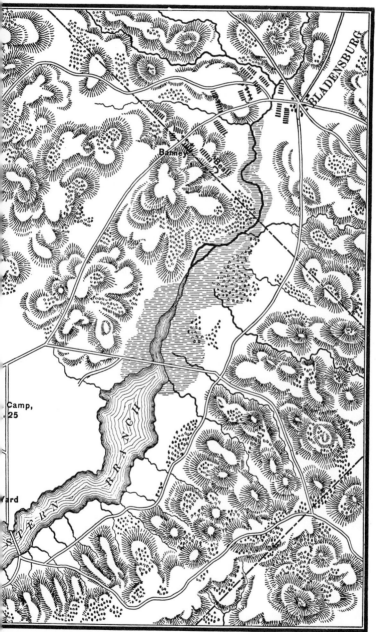

BLADENSBURG

Barney

Beal

Camp,
25

ard

SHERY BRANCH

yet Winder to the last instant persisted in watching the navy-yard bridge, using the hours of Wednesday morning to post Barney's sailors with twenty-four-pound guns to cover an approach [1] where no enemy could cross.

No sooner did Winder receive intelligence at ten o'clock Wednesday morning that the British were in march to Bladensburg, than in the utmost haste he started for the same point, preceded by Monroe and followed by the President and the rest of the Cabinet and the troops. Barney's sailors and their guns would have been left behind to guard the navy-yard bridge had Secretary Jones not yielded to Barney's vigorous though disrespectful remonstrances, and allowed him to follow.[2]

In a long line the various corps, with their military and civil commanders, streamed toward Bladensburg, racing with the British, ten miles away, to arrive first on the field of battle. Monroe was earliest on the ground. Between eleven and twelve o'clock he reached the spot where hills slope gently toward the Eastern Branch a mile or more in broad incline, the little straggling town of Bladensburg opposite, beyond a shallow stream, and hills and woods in the distance. Several militia corps were already camped on the ground, which had been from the first desig-

[1] Secretary Jones's Report, Oct. 3, 1814; State Papers, Military Affairs, i. 576.

[2] Armstrong's Letter; State Papers, Military Affairs, i. 540. Ingersoll's History, ii. 173.

nated as the point of concentration. A Baltimore
brigade, more than two thousand strong, had arrived
there thirty-six hours before. Some Maryland regiments arrived at the same time with Monroe. About
three thousand men were then on the field, and their
officers were endeavoring to form them in line of
battle. General Stansbury of the Baltimore brigade
made such an arrangement as he thought best. Monroe, who had no military rank, altered it without
Stansbury's knowledge.[1] General Winder arrived at
noon, and rode about the field. At the same time
the British light brigade made its appearance, and
wound down the opposite road, a mile away, a long
column of redcoats, six abreast, moving with the
quick regularity of old soldiers,[2] and striking directly
at the American centre. They reached the village on
one side of the stream as Winder's troops poured
down the hill on the other; and the President with
two or three of his Cabinet officers, considerably in
advance of all their own troops, nearly rode across
the bridge into the British line, when a volunteer
scout warned them of their danger.[3]

Much the larger portion of the American force
arrived on the ground when the enemy was in sight,
and were hastily drawn up in line wherever they

[1] Stansbury's Report; Monroe's Letter; State Papers, Military
Affairs, i. 561, 536.

[2] Gleig's Subaltern, p. 68.

[3] Letter of William Simmons; State Papers, Military Affairs,
i. 596.

could be placed.[1] They had no cover. Colonel Wadsworth's intrenchments were not used,[2] except in the case of one field-work which enfiladed the bridge at close range, where field-pieces were placed. Although some seven thousand men were present, nothing deserving the name of an army existed. " A few companies only," said the Subaltern, " perhaps two or at the most three battalions, wearing the blue jacket which the Americans have borrowed from the French, presented some appearance of regular troops. The rest seemed country-people, who would have been much more appropriately employed in attending to their agricultural occupations than in standing with muskets in their hands on the brow of a bare, green hill." Heterogeneous as the force was, it would have been sufficient had it enjoyed the advantage of a commander.

The British light brigade, some twelve or fifteen hundred men, under Colonel Thornton of the Eighty-fifth regiment, without waiting for the rear division, dashed across the bridge, and were met by a discharge of artillery and musketry directly in their face. Checked for an instant, they pressed on, crossed the bridge or waded the stream, and spread to the right and left, while their rockets flew into the American lines. Almost instantly a portion of the American line gave way; but the rest stood firm, and

[1] Winder's Narrative; State Papers, Military Affairs, i. 557. Stansbury's Report; State Papers, Military Affairs, i. 562.

[2] Van Ness's Letter; State Papers, Military Affairs, i. 580.

drove the British skirmishers back under a heavy fire
to the cover of the bank with its trees and shrubs.
Not until a fresh British regiment, moving well to the
right, forded the stream and threatened to turn the
American left, did the rout begin. Even then several
strong corps stood steady, and in good order retired
by the road that led to the Capitol; but the mass,
struck by panic, streamed westward toward Georgetown and Rockville.

Meanwhile Barney's sailors, though on the run,
could not reach the field in time for the attack, and
halted on the hillside, about a mile from Bladensburg,
at a spot just outside the District line. The rout had
then begun, but Barney put his five pieces in position
and waited for the enemy. The American infantry
and cavalry that had not fled westward moved con-
fusedly past the field where the sailors stood at their
guns. Winder sent Barney no orders, and Barney,
who was not acting under Winder, but was commander-in-chief of his own forces under authority of
the Navy Department, had no idea of running away.
Four hundred men against four thousand were odds
too great even for sailors, but a battle was not wholly
disgraceful that produced such a commander and
such men. Barney's account of the combat was as
excellent as his courage : [1] —

" At length the enemy made his appearance on the
main road in force and in front of my battery, and on

[1] Barney's Report of Aug. 29, 1814; State Papers, Military
Affairs, i. 579.

seeing us made a halt. I reserved our fire. In a few
minutes the enemy again advanced, when I ordered an
eighteen-pounder to be fired, which completely cleared
the road; shortly after, a second and a third attempt
was made by the enemy to come forward, but all were
destroyed. They then crossed over into an open field,
and attempted to flank our right. He was met there by
three twelve-pounders, the marines under Captain Miller,
and my men acting as infantry, and again was totally
cut up. By this time not a vestige of the American
army remained, except a body of five or six hundred
posted on a height on my right, from which I expected
much support from their fine situation."

Such a battle could not long continue. The British
turned Barney's right; the corps on the height broke
and fled,[1] and the British, getting into the rear, fired
down upon the sailors. The British themselves were
most outspoken in praise of Barney's men. "Not
only did they serve their guns with a quickness and
precision that astonished their assailants," said the
Subaltern, "but they stood till some of them were actually bayoneted with fuses in their hands; nor was
it till their leader was wounded and taken, and they
saw themselves deserted on all sides by the soldiers,
that they left the field." Barney held his position
nearly half an hour, and then, being severely wounded,
ordered his officers to leave him where he lay. There
he was taken by the British advance, and carried to
their hospital at Bladensburg. The British officers,
admiring his gallantry, treated him, he said, " with

[1] Colonel Beall's Statement; State Papers, Military Affairs,
i. 571.

the most marked attention, respect, and politeness
as if I was a brother," — as though to show their opinion that Barney instead of Winder should have led
the American army.

After the sailors retired, at about four o'clock, the
British stopped two hours to rest. Their victory,
easy as it seemed, was not cheaply bought. General
Ross officially reported sixty-four killed and one
hundred and eighty-five wounded.[1] A loss of two
hundred and fifty men among fifteen hundred said
to be engaged[2] was not small ; but Gleig, an officer
of the light brigade, himself wounded, made twice,
at long intervals, an assertion which he must have
intended as a contradiction of the official report.
" The loss on the part of the English was severe," he
said,[3] " since out of two thirds of the army which
were engaged upward of five hundred men were killed
and wounded." According to this assertion, Ross
lost five hundred men among three thousand engaged,
or one in six. Had Winder inflicted that loss while
the British were still on the Patuxent, Ross would
have thought long before risking more, especially as
Colonel Thornton was among the severely injured.
The Americans reported only twenty-six killed and
fifty-one wounded.

At six o'clock, after a rest of two hours, the British
troops resumed their march ; but night fell before

[1] James, ii. 499.

[2] Cockburn to Cochrane, Aug. 27, 1814; James, ii. 493.

[3] Campaigns, p. 67; Cf. Barney to the National Intelligencer.
Niles, vii. Supplement, p. 159.

they reached the first houses of the town. **As Ross** and Cockburn, with a few officers, advanced before the troops, some men, supposed to have been Barney's sailors, fired on the party from the house formerly occupied by Gallatin, at the northeast corner of Capitol Square. Ross's horse was killed, and the general ordered the house to be burned, which was done. The army did not enter the town, but camped at eight o'clock a quarter of a mile east of the Capitol. Troops were then detailed to burn the Capitol, and as the great building burst into flames, Ross and Cockburn, with about two hundred men, marched silently in the darkness to the White House, and set fire to it. At the same time Commodore Tingey, by order of Secretary Jones, set fire to the navy-yard and the vessels in the Eastern Branch. Before midnight the flames of three great conflagrations made the whole country light, and from the distant hills of Maryland and Virginia the flying President and Cabinet caught glimpses of the ruin their incompetence had caused.

Serurier lived then in the house built by John Tayloe in 1800, called the Octagon, a few hundred yards from the War and Navy Departments and the White House.[1] He was almost the only civil official left in Washington, and hastened to report the event to Talleyrand:[2] —

[1] Benjamin Ogle Tayloe. In Memoriam, p. 154.
[2] Serurier to Talleyrand, Aug. 22 and 27, 1814. Archives des Aff. Étr. MSS.

"I never saw a scene at once more terrible and more magnificent. Your Highness, knowing the picturesque nature and the grandeur of the surroundings, can form an idea of it. A profound darkness reigned in the part of the city that I occupy, and we were left to conjectures and to the lying reports of negroes as to what was passing in the quarter illuminated by these frightful flames. At eleven o'clock a colonel, preceded by torches, was seen to take the direction of the White House, which is situated quite near mine; the negroes reported that it was to be burned, as well as all those pertaining to government offices. I thought best, on the moment, to send one of my people to the general with a letter, in which I begged him to send a guard to the house of the Ambassador of France to protect it. . . . My messenger found General Ross in the White House, where he was collecting in the drawing-room all the furniture to be found, and was preparing to set fire to it. The general made answer that the King's Hotel should be respected as much as though his Majesty were there in person; that he would give orders to that effect; and that if he was still in Washington the next day, he would have the pleasure to call on me."

Ross and Cockburn alone among military officers, during more than twenty years of war, considered their duty to involve personal incendiarism. At the time and subsequently various motives were attributed to them, — such as the duty of retaliation, — none of which was alleged by either of them as their warranty.[1] They burned the Capitol, the White House, and the Department buildings because they

[1] Reports of Ross and Cockburn; James, ii. 499.

thought it proper, as they would have burned a negro kraal or a den of pirates. Apparently they assumed as a matter of course that the American government stood beyond the pale of civilization; and in truth a government which showed so little capacity to defend its capital, could hardly wonder at whatever treatment it received.

A violent thunder-storm checked the flames; but the next morning, Thursday, August 25, fresh detachments of troops were sent to complete the destruction of public property. Without orders from his Government, Ross converted his campaign, which till then had been creditable to himself and flattering to British pride, into a marauding raid of which no sensible Englishman spoke without mortification. Cockburn amused himself by revenging his personal grievances on the press which had abused him. Mounted on a brood mare, white, uncurried, with a black foal trotting by her side, the Admiral attacked the office of the " National Intelligencer," and superintended the destruction of the types. " Be sure that all the C's are destroyed," he ordered, " so that the rascals cannot any longer abuse my name." [1] Ross was anxious to complete the destruction of the public buildings with the least possible delay, that the army might retire without loss of time; [2] and the work was pressed with extreme haste. A few private buildings were burned, but as a rule private property was

[1] Ingersoll's History, ii. 189.
[2] Ross's Report of Aug. 30, 1814; James, ii. 496.

respected, and no troops except small detachments were allowed to leave the camp.

Soon after noon, while the work was still incomplete, a tornado burst on the city and put an end to the effort. An accidental explosion at the navyyard helped to check destruction. Ross could do no more, and was in haste to get away. No sooner had the hurricane, which lasted nearly two hours and seemed especially violent at the camp, passed over, than Ross began preparations to retire. With precautions wholly unnecessary, leaving its camp-fires burning, the British column in extreme silence, after nine o'clock at night, began its march. Passing Bladensburg, where the dead were still unburied, Ross left his wounded in the hospital to American care, and marched all night till seven o'clock Friday morning, when the troops, exhausted with fatigue, were allowed a rest. At noon they were again in motion, and at night-fall, after marching twenty-five miles within twenty-four hours, they arrived at Marlboro. Had the advance from Benedict been equally rapid, Ross would have entered Washington without a skirmish.

## CHAPTER VI.

WHILE Ross and Cockburn were hastily burning the White House and the Department buildings, anxious only to escape, and never sending more than two hundred soldiers beyond Capitol Square, the President, his Cabinet, his generals, and his army were performing movements at which even the American people, though outraged and exasperated beyond endurance, could not but laugh.

The President, after riding over the battle-field until the action began, remarked to Monroe and Armstrong that " it would be now proper for us to retire in the rear, leaving the military movement to military men," which they did.[1] A moment afterward the left of the line gave way, and the panic-stricken militia poured along the road leading westward toward the point which in later times became known as the Soldier's Home. The President retired with them, " continuing to move slowly toward the city," according to Monroe, in company with Attorney-General Rush. The slowness of movement, on which Monroe seemed to lay stress, was compen-

[1] Monroe's Letter, Nov. 13, 1814; State Papers, Military Affairs, i. 537.

sated by steadiness.  The President left Bladensburg
battle-field  toward  two  o'clock.    He  had  already
ridden in the early morning from the White House
to the navy-yard, and thence to Bladensburg, — a
distance of eight miles at the least.  He had six
miles to ride, on a very hot August day, over a road
encumbered by fugitives.  He was sixty-three years
old, and had that day already been in the saddle
since eight o'clock in the morning, probably without
food.  Soon after three o'clock he reached the White
House, where all was confusion and flight.[1]  He had
agreed with his Cabinet, in case of disaster, to meet
them at Frederick in Maryland, fifty miles away, but
he did not go toward Frederick.  Before six o'clock
he crossed the Potomac in a boat from the White
House grounds, and started by carriage westward,
apparently intending to join his wife and accompany her to his residence at Montpelier in Loudoun
County, adjoining Frederick County, on the south side
of the Potomac.  Secretary Jones, Attorney-General
Rush, and one or two other gentlemen accompanied
him.  In the midst of a troop of fugitives they trav-
elled till dark, and went about ten miles, passing
the night at a house " a few miles above the lower
falls." [2]

The next morning, August 25, the President trav-

[1] Mrs. Madison to her sister, Aug. 24, 1814; Memoirs and
Letters of Dolly Madison, p. 108.

[2] Memorandum of Colonel Monroe ; MSS. State Department
Archives.

elled about six miles and joined his wife at an inn
on the same road, where he remained during the tornado, subjected to no little discomfort and some insult from fugitives who thought themselves betrayed.
Although far beyond reach of the British troops and
some twenty miles from their camp, the panic was
still so great as to cause an alarm on the following
night, which drove Madison from his bed for refuge
in the Virginia woods,[1] at the time when Ross's army,
more than twenty miles distant, was marching at the
utmost speed in the opposite direction.

Of all the rulers, monarchical or republican, whose
capitals were occupied by hostile armies in the Napo-
leonic wars, Madison was personally the most roughly
treated.      Monroe's adventures were not less mortifying.     As a scout the Secretary of State's services were hardly so valuable as those of a common
trooper, for he was obliged to be more cautious ; as
a general, his interference with the order of battle
at Bladensburg led to sharp criticisms from General
Stansbury, whose arrangements he altered,[2] and to
the epithet of " busy and blundering tactician " from
Armstrong.[3]   After the battle he was not less busy,
and opinions greatly differed whether he was less
blundering.   He did not return to the White House

[1] Ingersoll's History, ii. 208 ; Memoirs and Letters of Dolly
Madison, p. 116.

[2] Report of General Stansbury, Nov. 15. 1814 ; State Papers,
Military Affairs, i. 560.

[3] Notices, ii. 148.

with Madison, but joined Winder and rode with him
to the Capitol, where he assented to an evacuation,
and retired after the flying troops through Georgetown, passing the night on the Maryland side of the
Potomac. The next morning, August 25, he crossed
the river and overtook the President. After an
interview with him, Monroe recrossed the river to
Winder's headquarters at Montgomery Court House,
where he resumed military functions.

The Secretary of the Treasury, G. W. Campbell,
on the morning of the battle went to the Cabinet
meeting at the navy-yard, but his health, which had
become much affected, obliged him to return to his
lodgings instead of riding to Bladensburg. In part-
ing from Madison, Campbell lent him a pair of pistols, which the President put in his holsters. Federalists were curious to know whether the pistols were
the same with which he shot Barent Gardenier, but
learned only that they were fine duelling pistols, and
that they were stolen from the President's holsters
during his short stay at the White House after the
battle. The secretary's duelling pistols became the
best known of all the weapons unused that day ; but
the secretary himself made no further appearance on
the scene. He went to Frederick. The Secretary
of the Navy and the Attorney-General accompanied
the President, and shared his fortunes.

Although ridicule without end was showered on
the President and the other civilians, their conduct
was on the whole creditable to their courage and

character; but of the commanding general no kind word could be said. Neither William Hull, Alexander Smyth, Dearborn, Wilkinson, nor Winchester showed such incapacity as Winder either to organize, fortify, fight, or escape. When he might have prepared defences, he acted as scout; when he might have fought, he still scouted; when he retreated, he retreated in the wrong direction; when he fought, he thought only of retreat; and whether scouting, retreating, or fighting, he never betrayed an idea. In the brief moment of his preparations on the field at Bladensburg he found time to give the characteristic order to his artillery: " When you retreat, take notice that you must retreat by the Georgetown road." [1] When he left the field of Bladensburg he rode past Barney's sailors, at their guns, and sent his aid to Colonel Beall, on the hill covering Barney's right, with an order to retreat.[2] " After accompanying the retreating army within two miles of the Capitol, I rode forward for the purpose of selecting a position." [3] He reached the Capitol first, and was presently joined there by Monroe and Armstrong. Having decided not to fight at the Capitol, or at any point between the Capitol and Georgetown, he rode to Georgetown.[4] Behind Rock Creek his army would

[1] Statement of John Law, Nov. 10, 1814; State Papers, Military Affairs, p. 585.

[2] Wilkinson's Memoirs, i. 786.

[3] Winder's Narrative; State Papers, Military Affairs, p. 558.

[4] Armstrong's Notices, ii. 231; Appendix no. 28. Winder's Narrative; State Papers, Military Affairs, p. 559.

have been safe, and he could certainly have rallied
more than a thousand men to stop the panic; but he
thought a farther retreat necessary, and went on to
the heights. On the heights nothing could reach
him without hours of warning, but he rode three
miles farther to Tenallytown. At Tenallytown his
exhausted men stopped a moment from inability to
run farther, yet he seemed angry at their fatigue.
Struck by a fresh panic at the glare of the burning
city, he pressed his men on at midnight. "After
waiting in this position [Tenallytown] until I supposed I collected all the force that could be gathered,
I proceeded about five miles farther on the river road,
which leads a little wide to the left of Montgomery
Court House, and in the morning gave orders for the
whole to assemble at Montgomery Court House." The
river road was the road that led farthest from the
enemy westward, when every motive required retreat
toward Baltimore if anywhere. The next morning
Winder returned to the Rockville road, till he reached
Rockville, or Montgomery Court House, sixteen miles
from Washington, where at last he paused.

From the beginning to the end of the campaign
Winder showed no military quality. In other respects his conduct tallied with his behavior in the
field. He lost no opportunity of throwing responsibility on the President and on his troops, and he so
far succeeded as to save himself from public anger
by encouraging the idea that the President and the
Cabinet had directed the campaign. Universal as

that belief was, and continued to be, it was without foundation. While Winder courted advice from every quarter, and threw on the President at every instant the responsibility for every movement, neither the President nor the Cabinet showed a disposition to interfere with his authority in any way except to give the support he asked. Under the strongest temptation they abstained even from criticism.

More than all the rest, Armstrong refrained from interference with the movements of Winder. Of all the unfortunate or incapable generals of the war, Winder was the one whom Armstrong treated with least bitterness,[1] although he was not Armstrong's choice, and was the direct cause of the secretary's ruin. So careful was Armstrong not to interfere, that his non-interference became the chief charge against him. At one moment the President told the secretary that he interfered too much, at another moment that he should interfere more ; but in truth Armstrong was the only man connected with the defence of Washington whom no one charged with being ridiculous. After August 20 his conduct was not open to reproach. He was cool when others were excited ; he tried to check the panic; his suggestions were sensible ; he gave all possible aid both to Winder and to the citizens ; he attended the President in his expeditions, used wisely such power as he had, and indulged in few words.[2]

[1] Notices, vol. ii. chap. v.
[2] Madison's Memorandum, Aug. 24, 1814; Works, iii.. 422.

At the President's request he went to Bladensburg to support and assist Winder; at the President's order he retired after the battle began. He returned, after Winder, to the Capitol, hoping to convert that strong building into a fortress, — a measure not unreasonable, if the regulars and sailors were rallied to make a stand there. When Winder decided to retire to Georgetown, the secretary acquiesced without a word. Then, in pursuance of a Cabinet decision made a few hours before, he set out in company with Secretary Campbell for Frederick, and arrived there in the course of the next day.

Armstrong and Campbell were at Frederick when the British army began its retreat Thursday night; the President was in Virginia, sixteen miles up the river; Winder and Monroe, with the remaining troops, were at Montgomery Court House sixteen miles from Washington. There they learned, Friday morning, that the British had marched toward Bladensburg, probably going to Baltimore; and at about ten o'clock in the morning Winder marched from Montgomery Court House toward Brookville and Baltimore with all his force. Passing through Brookville, they camped, Friday night, " about half way between Montgomery Court House and Ellicott's upper mills," [1] and Winder there left them, starting late that evening alone for Baltimore, and leaving Monroe and Stansbury in command, with directions to follow.

[1] Stansbury's Report; State Papers, Military Affairs, i. 562.

Meanwhile the President had crossed the Potomac that morning, expecting to find Winder and Monroe at Montgomery Court House; but on arriving there at six o'clock in the evening, and learning that the army had marched toward.Baltimore, he followed as far as Brookville, about ten miles, where he passed the night.[1] Attorney-General Rush was with him. Saturday morning, August 27, the President sent notes to all his Cabinet requesting them to unite in Washington.[2] The same afternoon he returned with Monroe and Rush to the city, which they reached at about six o'clock, after three days' absence.

Armstrong and Campbell, ignorant of the change in plan, waited at Frederick for the President's arrival, while the President and Monroe, Sunday, August 28, began the task of restoring the functions of government. The task was difficult, not so much on account of the British ravages, which had been confined to public property, as on account of the general irritation and the continued panic. Hardly had Ross's army disappeared when a squadron of British war-vessels, under Captain Gordon of the frigate "Seahorse," worked its way up the river, approaching Fort Washington or Warburton August 27. The commander of that post, misunderstanding his orders, abandoned it and crossed the river with his men. Gordon's squadron reached Alexandria the

[1] Madison to Monroe, Aug. 26, ten o'clock P.M.; Ingraham's "Sketch of the Events," p. 61.

[2] Note of Aug. 27, 1814; MSS. War Department Archives.

next day, and the town capitulated, since it could not resist. Until August 31 the frigates remained at Alexandria, loading such vessels as were there with the tobacco and other produce which the warehouses contained.[1]

The citizens of Washington and Georgetown, expecting to be visited in their turn, and conscious of their inability to resist, talked of a capitulation. Public feeling ran strong against the President. Armstrong was absent. Winder was at Baltimore. Monroe alone was in a position to act, and upon Monroe the President was obliged to depend.

" Under these circumstances," said Monroe in the only authentic account of the event which remains,[2] " the President requested Mr. Monroe to take charge of the Department of War and command of the District *ad interim*, with which he immediately complied. On the 28th, in the morning, the President with Mr. Monroe and the Attorney-General visited the navy-yard, the arsenal at Greenleaf's Point, and passing along the shore of the Potomac up toward Georgetown. Mr. Monroe, as Secretary of War and military commander, adopted measures under sanction of the President for the defence of the city and of Georgetown."

Colonel W [adsworth ?] who was placing some guns on the opposite shore refused to obey an order of Monroe to change their position. Monroe rode across the bridge and gave the order in person. The

[1] Report of Captain Gordon, Sept. 9, 1814; James, Appendix no. 84.

[2] Monroe's Memorandum; Gilman's Monroe, p. 119.

colonel replied that he did not know Mr. Monroe as
Secretary of War or commanding general. Monroe ordered him to obey or leave the field, and the
colonel left the field.

Monroe's act, whether such was his intention or
not, was a *coup d'état*. The citizens, unable to pun-
ish the President, were rabid against Armstrong.
No one could deny that they had reason for their
anger, although the blame for their misfortunes was
so evenly distributed between every officer and every
branch of government that a single victim could not
justly be selected for punishment. Monroe, instead
of giving to Armstrong in his absence such support
as might have sustained him, took a position and exercised an authority that led necessarily to his overthrow. The influence of such acts on the citizens was
obvious. That evening the first brigade of militia
held a meeting, and passed a formal and unanimous
resolution that they would no longer serve under the
orders or military administration of General Armstrong, whom they denounced as the willing cause of
the fate of Washington.[1] This mutinous resolution,
adopted in the immediate presence of the enemy,
was taken to the President by two officers of the
brigade, one of whom at least was a strong friend
of Monroe.[2]

The resolution of the first brigade was communi-
cated to the President the next morning, Monday,

---

[1] Williams; Capture of Washington, p. 105.

[2] McKenney's Memoirs, p. 47.

August 29. All the President's recorded acts and
conversation for months after the capture of Washington implied that he was greatly shaken by that
disaster. He showed his prostration by helplessness.
He allowed Monroe for the first time to control him;
but he did not dismiss Armstrong. At one o'clock
on the afternoon of the same day the Secretary of
War arrived in Washington.[1] The President that
evening rode to his lodgings. Madison preserved a
memorandum of their conversation, and Armstrong
also immediately afterward recorded what passed.[2]
The President described to the secretary the violent
prejudices which existed in the city against the Administration, and especially against himself and the
Secretary of War. " Before his arrival there was
less difficulty, as Mr. Monroe, who was very acceptable to them, had, as on preceding occasions of his
absence, though very reluctantly on this, been the
medium for the functions of Secretary of War;"
but since Armstrong had returned, something must
be done.

Armstrong replied that he was aware of the excitement, and knew its sources; that evidently he could
not remain if his functions were exercised by any one
else; that he would resign, or retire from Washington
at once, as the President preferred.

Madison deprecated resignation, and recommended

[1] Madison's Memorandum; Works, iii. 424. Letter of Jacob
Barker, Feb. 8, 1843; Life of Barker, pp. 114, 115.

[2] Armstrong's Letter of Sept. 13, 1814; Niles, vii. 6.

" a temporary retirement, as he suggested;" and after some further conversation, in which the President complained of the secretary's mistakes, they parted with the understanding that Armstrong should leave Washington the next morning. Armstrong behaved with dignity and with his usual pride ; but he understood, if Madison did not, the necessary consequences of his retirement, and on reaching Baltimore sent his resignation to the President. At the same time he announced it to the public in a letter, dated September 3, containing comments on the weakness of Madison's conduct calculated to close their relations.

Between conscious intrigue and unconscious instinct no clear line of division was ever drawn. Monroe, by the one method or the other, gained his point and drove Armstrong from the Cabinet; but the suspicion that he had intrigued for that object troubled his mind to the day of his death.[1] Even after Armstrong's departure, the dangers and disadvantages of appointing Monroe his successor were so great that for three weeks the post remained unfilled, until, after many doubts and hesitations, Monroe wrote to Madison a letter claiming the appointment of Secretary of War.

" I have thought much of the state of the Departments at this time," he informed the President, September 25,[2]

[1] McKenney's Memoirs, p. 44.

[2] Monroe to Madison, Sept. 25, 1814; Madison MSS. State Department Archives.

" and of the persons whom it may be proper to place in
them, and have concluded that whatever may be the arrangement with respect to other Departments, the Department of War ought to be immediately filled.    I think also
that I ought to take charge of it. . . .  By taking charge
of the Department twice, and withdrawing from it a second time, it may be inferred that I shrink from the responsibility from a fear of injuring my reputation ; and
this may countenance the idea that the removal of the
others was an affair of intrigue in which I partook, especially in the latter instance, from selfish and improper
motives, and did not proceed from his incompetency or
misconduct.    It seems due, therefore, to my own reputation to go through with the undertaking by accepting
permanently a trust which I have not sought, never
wished, and is attended with great responsibility and
hazard.    By taking the place, all clamor will be silenced.
It is known, here at least, that I was put into it when the
other could no longer hold it.    Those who wished it in
the first instance will be satisfied, and I shall go on with
your support and a favorable expectation of the public
that I shall discharge to advantage its duties."

While Monroe in private communications with Madison thus treated Armstrong's retirement as a " removal," due to his " incompetency or misconduct,"
and Madison apparently acquiesced in that view, in
public Madison seemed inclined to convey the idea
that Armstrong was not removed or meant to be removed from office, but rather deserted it.    Which-
ever view was correct, Madison certainly dreaded the
political effect of appearing to remove Armstrong;

and while he gave to Monroe the appointment of Secretary of War, he wrote, September 29, to Governor Tompkins of New York, offering him the State Department.

Governor Tompkins declined the offer. Apart from the great need of his services as governor, the experience of Northern men in Virginia Cabinets was not calculated to encourage any aspirant to the Presidency in seeking the position. Monroe remained Secretary of State as well as Secretary of War. As Secretary of State he had little or nothing to do, which was partly the cause of his activity in military matters; but as Secretary of War he was obliged to undertake a task beyond the powers of any man.

During an entire month after the appearance of the British in the Patuxent, the United States government performed few or none of its functions. The war on the frontiers was conducted without orders from Washington. Every energy of the government was concentrated on its own immediate dangers, as though Washington were a beleaguered fortress. Slowly the tide of war ebbed from the Potomac and Chesapeake, and not until it had wholly subsided could men cease to dread its possible return.

Captain Gordon's squadron began its descent of the river September 1, greatly annoyed [1] by batteries

[1] Report of Captain Gordon, Sept. 9, 1814; James, ii. Appendix no. 84.

erected on the banks by Commodore Rodgers, Perry, and Porter, who were sent from Baltimore, by order of Secretary Jones, for the purpose. Not until September 6 did Captain Gordon escape from his perilous position and rejoin the fleet. Meanwhile the shores of Chesapeake Bay continued to be ravaged with all the severity threatened by Cochrane. Frederick Chamier, afterward the author of several popular sea-stories, was then a lieutenant on the "Menelaus" in Cochrane's squadron, and his recollections in "The Life of a Sailor" gave a lively picture of the marauding in which he took part.[1] Like Napier, Chamier was too tender-hearted for his work. "I am willing to make oath," he wrote, in reply to Captain Scott's contradictions, "that on the day that the 'Menelaus' entered the Potomac, three houses were burning at the same time on the left-hand bank of the river. We burnt more than five ourselves." War was commonly accompanied by destruction, but the war in the Chesapeake was remarkable for the personal share taken by the highest officers, especially by Cockburn and Ross, in directing the actual operation of setting fire to private and public property.[2]

At last the practice caused a disaster that cost the British navy a life more valuable than all the property it could destroy or carry away. The "Menelaus," commanded by Sir Peter Parker, was sent up

[1] Chamier's "Life of a Sailor." Preface to Second Edition, chap. xviii.

[2] Life of a Sailor, Bentley, 1850, p. 180.

Chesapeake Bay to divert attention from the general movement of troops and ships on the Potomac.[1] The " Menelaus " took position off the Sassafras River, which Cockburn had cleared of vessels the year before. Nothing in the river could injure the navy, but the " Menelaus " was ordered to make a diversion; and Sir Peter Parker learned from negroes that two hundred militia, encamped behind a wood half a mile from the beach, intended to cross the bay for the protection of Baltimore.[2] One hundred and twenty-four men were landed at eleven o'clock on the night of August 30, and went in search of the militia. Instead of half a mile, they were led by their guides three or four miles, and at last found the militia drawn up, ready to receive them. Sir Peter Parker ordered an attack, and while cheering it on in the moonlight was struck by a buckshot, which severed the femoral artery. The sailors carried him back to the ship, but he died long before reaching it.[3] His party escaped with a loss of thirteen killed and twenty-seven wounded besides their captain.

The Americans regretted only that the punishment had fallen on the wrong person, for Cochrane and Cockburn rather than Parker were the true marauders; but the lesson was effectual, and the British

[1] James, ii. 276.

[2] Report of Acting-Commodore Crease, Sept. 1, 1814; Niles, vii., Supplement, p. 150.

[3] Chamier's " Life of a Sailor," pp. 183–191.

became more cautious after Parker's death. Indeed, their activity in the Chesapeake centred thenceforward in an effort to capture Baltimore, which required all their strength.

Baltimore should have been first attacked, but Cockburn's influence by diverting Ross to Washington gave the larger city time to prepare its defence. The citizens themselves, headed by the mayor, took charge of the preparations; and their first act, contrary to the course pursued by Armstrong and Winder at Washington, was to construct intrenchments round the city, and to erect semi-circular batteries at a number of points, mounted with cannon and connected by a line of works. After the capture of Washington the citizens toiled still more earnestly at their task, until a formidable line of redoubts protected the town, and, though not wholly finished, gave cover to the militia. The batteries were manned by sailors, commanded by officers of the navy. The harbor was protected by Fort McHenry, small but capable of defence, and occupied by a strong force of regular troops, sailors, and volunteer artillerists numbering about one thousand, under the command of Lieutenant-Colonel Armistead of the Artillery.[1]

These precautions made the capture of Baltimore impossible by such a force as had taken Washington, even though aided by the fleet. The precise number of troops present in the city, according to the official

[1] Report of Lieutenant-Colonel Armistead, Sept. 24, 1814; Niles, vii. 40.

return for September 10, was twelve thousand nine
hundred and ninety-one men present for duty, with
eight hundred and ninety-seven officers. The aggregate of present and absent was sixteen thousand
eight hundred and five men.[1] The force was ample
to man the works, but the fortifications chiefly decided the result. No army on either side during the
war succeeded in storming works in face, except by
surprise; and to turn the works of Baltimore a
larger army was required than Ross had at his
command.

The militia major-general commanding at Baltimore
was no other than Samuel Smith, senator of the
United States. He had lately passed his sixty-second
year. The brigadier-general in the United States
service who commanded the military district was
W. H. Winder, whose defence of Washington ended
abruptly August 24, and who left that neighborhood
on the evening of August 26 to take command of
the defences of Baltimore. Winder was a Baltimore
lawyer, only three years Smith's junior, when Eustis
and Madison gave him a regiment in March, 1812.
Smith was not disposed to accept the idea of sub-
ordination to a man of inferior rank, military and
civil, who knew no more of war than Smith knew,
and whose career had been twice marked by unusual
ridicule. Winder on arriving in Baltimore notified
Smith that he should take command, and was as-

[1] Army Returns; MSS. Adjutant-General's office, War
Department.

tonished when the senator declined to surrender his authority. Winder appealed to the President and to the governor of Maryland, his cousin Levin Winder; but nothing could be done to assist him, and in the end he submitted. Samuel Smith remained in command.

The British leaders having succeeded in turning their demonstration up the Patuxent into an attack on Washington, next decided to make " a demonstration upon the city of Baltimore, which might be converted into a real attack should circumstances appear to justify it,"[1] and sailed from the Potomac September 6 for the Patapsco River. They anchored September 11 off its mouth. From that point Ross's army when landed had only fourteen miles to march, and no water in their way, while Cochrane's fleet had but twelve miles to sail. Compared with the approaches to Washington, the approach to Baltimore was easy.

Ross's troops were all landed at daylight on the northern point, and were in motion by eight o'clock September 12, without firing a shot. Their numbers were differently given by British authorities, — one reporting them at three thousand two hundred and seventy rank-and-file;[2] the other reckoning them at upward of five thousand.[3] Ross made on the Patap-

---

[1] Cochrane's Report of Sept. 17, 1814; James, ii. Appendix no. 73.

[2] James, ii. 313, 314.

[3] Gleig's Campaigns, p. 116.

sco no such leisurely movements as on the Patuxent, but began his march at once, and proceeded about five miles without meeting resistance. The light brigade with the Eighty-fifth regiment was in advance; the second brigade, under Colonel Brooke of the Forty-fourth, followed; and the third brigade, under Colonel Patterson of the Twenty-first, formed the rear. At the same time the fleet moved up the channel toward Fort Henry.

The city was naturally excited at the news that the British had arrived. General Smith, on receiving the intelligence September 11, detached a brigade of Baltimore militia, under General Stricker, to check the enemy if possible, and Stricker advanced that evening about seven miles toward North Point. His force numbered about three thousand two hundred men;[1] and with that body of raw militia, a part of whom had been routed at Bladensburg only a fortnight before, General Stricker attempted to fight a battle with five thousand old soldiers. On the morning of September 12 he formed his troops in three lines three hundred yards apart, apparently in close order, without cover or protection of any kind, standing in fields more or less open, and with an exposed flank.[2] Of all his arrangements, the only one which showed ordinary caution was to send a detachment of cavalry and riflemen a mile or two in his front. As the Brit-

---

[1] Report of General Stricker, Sept. 15, 1814; Niles, vii. 26.

[2] Drawing of line of battle; Lossing, p. 953. Report of Colonel Brooke, Sept. 17, 1814; James, ii. Appendix no. 71.

ish advance approached, the American outposts fell
back, and General Stricker sent forward some four
hundred men, partly rifles, as skirmishers. The British advanced guard coming up, the skirmishing party
fired, but was soon driven back. Ross and Cockburn
were walking together with the advance, and after the
firing ceased, Ross turned back alone to order up the
light companies in anticipation of more serious resistance. On his way he was shot through the breast
from the wood, and fell in the road, where he lay till
he was found by the light companies hurrying forward to the scene of the firing. He barely spoke
afterward.[1]

The loss of their commanding general was the
second heavy penalty paid by the British for their contempt of militia. Colonel Brooke immediately took
command, and the advance was not checked; but the
loss was not the less serious. When Brooke saw
Stricker's line stretching across the field, he did not
dash at them at once with the light brigade as Thornton had attacked the larger force and stronger position at Bladensburg, but deployed the whole army and
formed a regular order of battle. Although his force
easily overlapped and outflanked the American, the
engagement that followed was sharp, and the Americans were not routed without considerable loss to the
British, who reported forty-six killed and two hundred
and seventy-three wounded, — or more than they reported at Bladensburg. The Americans, though routed,

[1] James, ii. 315.

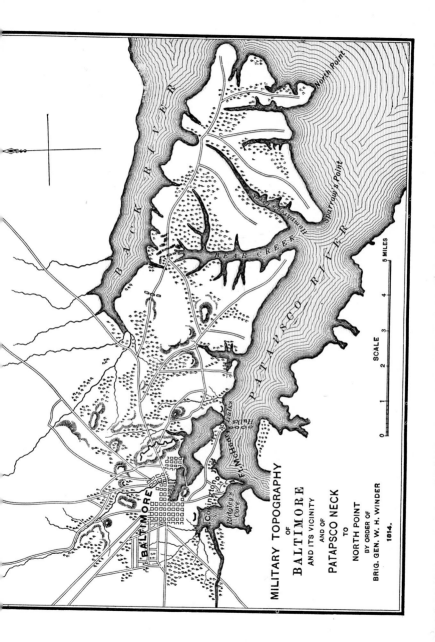

MILITARY TOPOGRAPHY
OF
BALTIMORE
AND ITS VICINITY
AND OF
PATAPSCO NECK
TO
NORTH POINT
BY ORDER OF
BRIG. GEN. W. H. WINDER
1814.

SCALE

0   1   2   3   4   5 MILES

suffered less, losing only twenty-four killed, one hundred and thirty-nine wounded, and fifty prisoners, with two field-pieces.

This spirited little battle detained the British so long that they bivouacked on the field, and passed the night in a drenching rain, resuming their march the next morning, September 13, when they found the roads obstructed, and were obliged to move so slowly that evening arrived before they came in sight of Baltimore.[1] When at last they saw on the distant heights the long line of intrenchments that surrounded Baltimore on the side of their approach, they stopped short. Colonel Brooke had gone forward with the advance, and was engaged all day, at about a mile and a half distance, in studying the American lines. He made arrangements for a night attack, hoping to avoid the effects of the American artillery,[2] and then waited for the fleet to support him.

The fleet all day bombarded the forts and batteries that covered the entrance to the harbor, and continued the bombardment till past midnight. Unlike most naval engagements during the war, this battle was harmless to either party. The heavier British ships feared to approach within range, owing to a barrier of sunken vessels, covered by the guns on shore and by gunboats. Without the heavy ships, the

[1] Gleig's Campaigns, p. 102.

[2] Brooke's Report of Sept. 17, 1814 ; James, ii. Appendix no. 71, p. 508.

lighter vessels could not maintain a position. The fort sustained no great injury, and only four men were killed and twenty-four wounded.[1] The fleet as far as was reported sustained no injury whatever. The firing ceased toward midnight, and Admiral Cochrane sent word to Colonel Brooke that he could do no more.[2]

" Under these circumstances," reported Colonel Brooke, " and keeping in view your Lordship's instructions, it was agreed between the Vice-admiral and myself that the capture of the town would not have been a sufficient equivalent to the loss which might probably be sustained in storming the heights."

Sir George Prevost at Plattsburg only two days before, with three times the number of troops and a much smaller number of opponents, came to the same conclusion. That both officers were probably wise was shown by the experience of Lieutenant-General Drummond, a month earlier, in attempting to storm the lines of Fort Erie. Brooke and Prevost followed the same course in another respect, for Brooke withdrew his army so rapidly that at noon of September 14 it had already passed the battle-field of two days before, and in another day the whole force was re-embarked.[3]

As soon as the wind allowed, the fleet returned to the lower Chesapeake; and September 19 Admiral

---

[1] Armistead's Report, Sept. 24, 1814; Niles, vii. 40.

[2] Cochrane's Report of Sept. 17, 1814; James, ii. 514.

[3] Subaltern, chap. xiii.

Cochrane sailed for Halifax to prepare for a new expedition. The troops remained till October 14 in their transports in the bay, and then set sail for Jamaica, leaving Virginia and Maryland to a long repose, which the vexed shores sorely needed.

## CHAPTER VII.

AFTER balancing gains and losses, the result of the campaign favored Great Britain by the amount of plunder which the navy obtained in Alexandria, and by the posts which Governor Sherbrooke occupied between the Penobscot and the Passamaquoddy in Maine. Considering the effort made and the waste of money, the result was a total disappointment to the British people; but even these advantages on land could not be regarded as secure until the British navy and mercantile marine had summed up their profits and losses on the ocean.

At the beginning of the year 1814 the American navy had almost disappeared. Porter in the "Essex" still annoyed British interests in the Pacific; but of the five large frigates only the "President" was at sea. January 1 the "Constitution," Captain Charles Stewart, left Boston and cruised southward, making a few prizes and destroying a British fourteen-gun schooner, but fighting no battle and effecting no object equivalent to her cost. In returning to Boston, April 3, she narrowly escaped capture by the two British frigates blockading the port, and with difficulty got into Marblehead harbor. The "Constitution" did not again go to sea until December 17. During her cruise of three months, from January 1 to April 3, she made four prizes.

The " President " regained New York February 18, and was blockaded during the rest of the year. The " United States " and " Macedonian " remained blockaded at New London. The " Constellation " remained blockaded at Norfolk. The corvette " Adams," twenty-eight guns, ran the blockade of Chesapeake Bay January 18, and cruised until August 17, making nine prizes and several narrow escapes before striking on the Isle of Haut and taking refuge in the Penobscot as the British forces occupied Castine. The story of her destruction has been told. Her fate was the same she would have met had she remained in Washington, where a week earlier the new forty-four-gun frigate " Columbia " and the new twenty-two-gun sloop-of-war " Argus " were burned to prevent them from falling prize to the British army.

This short abstract accounted for all the frigates except the " Essex," whose fortune was no happier than that of the larger ships. October 27, 1812, the " Essex," Captain David Porter, left the Delaware, intending to meet Bainbridge and form part of a squadron under his command. Failing to meet Bainbridge, though constantly near him, Porter at last decided to sail southward ; and when Bainbridge in the " Constitution " reached Boston February 27, 1813, the " Essex " had already passed Cape Horn,

and was running up the western coast of South
America to Valparaiso.

At Valparaiso Porter arrived March 14, 1813, to
the consternation of commerce. Chili had recently
asserted independence of Spain, and as yet no English war-vessels were stationed in the Pacific. The
chief British interest was the whale fishery which
centred in the Galapagos Islands, — a group lying under the equator, about a thousand miles from Panama.
Although the influence of England was supreme, on
account of her naval power, her commerce, and her
political alliance with the Spanish people, and although Porter had neither a harbor of his own, nor
the support of a diplomatic officer on the Pacific, he
had nothing to fear. He was well received at Valparaiso, where since 1811 J. R. Poinsett had held the
post of United States Consul-General for Buenos
Ayres, Chili, and Peru; but the "Essex" tarried
only for supplies, and soon sailed for the Galapagos
Islands. There she arrived in April, 1813, and in
the course of the summer captured all the British
whalers known to be in those seas. These were
twelve in number, and after sending some of them
away, Porter still had a fleet of five armed ships
besides his own, and nothing more to do.

The "Essex" had then been a year at sea, and
needed repairs. Porter determined to take his entire
fleet of six vessels about three thousand miles to
the Marquesas Islands, — as though to make a voyage
of discovery, or to emulate the mutineers of the

" Bounty." The squadron sailed three weeks over
the southern seas, until, October 23, the Marquesas
Islands were sighted. There Porter remained seven
weeks, amusing himself and his crew by interven-
tion in native Marquesan politics, ending in his conquest of the principal tribes, and taking possession
of the chief island in the name of his Government.
That he should have brought away his whole crew
after such relaxation, without desertion, was surprising. The men were for a time in a state of mutiny
on being ordered to sea ; but they did not desert, and
the squadron sailed, Dec. 12, 1813, for Valparaiso.

Porter would have done better to sail for the China
seas or the Indian Ocean. He knew that British
war-vessels were searching for him, and that Valparaiso was the spot where he would be directly in their
way. He arrived February 3, and five days afterward two British vessels of war sailed into the
harbor, making directly for the " Essex " with the
appearance of intending to attack and board her.
The crew of the " Essex " stood at quarters ready to
fire as the larger ship ran close alongside, until her
yards crossed those of the " Essex," and Porter
probably regretted to the end of his life that he did
not seize the opportunity his enemy gave him ; but
the British captain, from his quarter-deck only a few
feet away, protested that the closeness of his approach
was an accident, and that he intended no attack.
The moment quickly passed, and then Porter found
himself overmatched.

The British frigate " Phœbe," thirty-six guns, had
sailed from England in March, 1813, under secret
orders to break up the United States fur-establish-
ment on the Columbia River.[1]  At Rio Janeiro the
" Phœbe " was joined by the "Cherub," a sloop-of-war
rated at eighteen guns, and both sailed in search
of the " Essex."    The " Phœbe " was one hundred
and forty-three and three quarters feet in length, by
thirty-eight and a quarter in breadth; the " Essex "
was one hundred and thirty-eight and a half feet
in length, and thirty-seven and a quarter in breadth.
The " Phœbe " carried a crew of three hundred men
and boys ; the " Essex " carried two hundred and
fifty-five.    The " Essex " was the better sailer, and
the result of an action depended on her ability to use
this advantage.    The broadside of the " Essex " consisted of seventeen thirty-two-pound carronades and
six long twelve-pounders; the " Phœbe " showed only
eight carronades, but had thirteen long eighteen-
pounders, one long twelve-pounder, and one long
nine-pounder.    At close range, Porter's battery
would overpower the " Phœbe's " long guns, but the
" Phœbe's " thirteen long-range eighteen-pounders
could destroy her enemy without receiving a shot
in return.    Porter knew all this, and knew also
that he could not depend on Chilian protection.
No British captain in such a situation could afford
to be delicate in regard to the neutrality of Chili,
which was not even a recognized nation.    At most

[1] James, p. 305.

Porter could hope for immunity only in the port of Valparaiso.

Captain Hillyar of the " Phœbe " made no mistakes. During an entire month he blockaded the " Essex " with his two vessels, acting with extreme caution. At last Porter determined to run out, trusting to a chase to separate the blockading cruisers ; and March 28, 1814, with a strong southerly wind, he got under way. As he rounded the outermost point a violent squall carried away his maintopmast. The loss threw on Porter a sudden emergency and a diffi- cult, instantaneous decision. He decided to return to harbor. A young midshipman, David Farragut, who made his first cruise in the " Essex," gave his high authority in after years to the opinion that Por- ter's decision was wrong. " Being greatly superior in sailing powers," said Farragut, " we should have borne up, and run before the wind." The chance of outsailing the " Phœbe," or separating her from her consort, was better than that of regaining the anchorage.

The wind did not allow of a return to port, and the " Essex " was run into a small bay three miles from Valparaiso, and anchored within pistol-shot of the shore. There Hillyar had her wholly at his mercy. At first he attacked somewhat timidly. Al- though Porter could bring only three long twelve- pounders to bear, he damaged the " Phœbe's " rigging until Hillyar, in half an hour, hauled off to repair the injury, — or, according to Hillyar's account, the

" Phœbe " was prevented by the freshness of the
wind from holding a position.[1]    Finally the " Phœbe "
anchored, and began firing her broadsides of long
eighteen-pounders into the " Essex's " quarter.    The
" Cherub " kept under way, using only her bow guns.
Reply was impossible.    The crew of the " Essex "
fired what guns would bear, and got the ship under
way ; but the " Phœbe " kept her distance, throwing
thirteen eighteen pound shot into the " Essex " every
five or ten minutes, until the " Essex " was cut to
pieces and her decks were shambles.

The last attack continued, according to Captain
Hillyar, from 5.35 till 6.20 P. M., when the " Essex "
struck.    The entire battle lasted from four o'clock
until the surrender.    The carnage was frightful and
useless.    Porter declared that fifty-eight of his crew
were killed.    Hillyar claimed one hundred and nineteen unwounded prisoners, while Porter declared the
number of unwounded prisoners to be seventy-five.
The British ships, with five hundred men, lost only
fifteen killed and wounded.

The loss of the " Essex," like the loss of the " Chesapeake" and "Argus," was unnecessary.    Porter need
not have gone to Valparaiso, or might have tried to
run out at night, or might have fought, even after
the loss of his maintopmast, under less disadvantage.    The disaster completed the unfortunate record
of the frigates for the year.    They made some six-

[1] Report of Captain Hillyar; James, ii. Appendix no. 71.
Naval History, vi. 153.

teen prizes and busied many British cruisers, but won
no victories and suffered one bloody defeat.

The sloops told a different story. Early in 1814
three of the new sloops-of-war were ready for sea, —
the " Frolic," the " Peacock," and the " Wasp."
They were heavy vessels of their class, about one
hundred and twenty feet long on the main-deck, and
thirty-two feet in extreme breadth ; carrying crews
of about one hundred and sixty men, with an armament of twenty thirty-two-pound carronades and two
long eighteen-pounders. Although only one third the
tonnage of the forty-four-gun frigates, and carrying
only one third the crew, the new sloops-of-war threw
nearly half the weight of metal, — for the broadside
of the " Constitution " commonly exceeded but little
the weight of seven hundred pounds, while the sloops
threw three hundred and thirty-eight. The difference was due not to the weight, but to the range.
The frigates carried thirty long twenty-four-pounders ;
the sloops carried only two long eighteen-pounders.
The sloops were rigged as ships, and built with the
usual solidity of war-vessels, costing about seventy-
five thousand dollars each.

The first to sail was the " Frolic," from Boston.
in February. She captured only two prizes before
she was herself taken, April 20, off Matanzas, after a
chase by the thirty-six-gun British frigate "Orpheus,"
assisted by a twelve-gun schooner.

The second sloop-of-war, the " Peacock," commanded by Lewis Warrington, sailed from New York

in March. Warrington was a Virginian, thirty-two
years old and fourteen years in the service, with
the rank of master-commandant in 1813. Cruising
down the coast, the " Peacock " first ran in to St.
Mary's on the Florida frontier; and then continuing southward, on the morning of April 29, off the
Indian River Inlet, she discovered a small convoy
on its way from Havana to Bermuda, under charge
of the British eighteen-gun brig " Epervier." The
British brig was no match for the American ship.
She was smaller, and carried only sixteen thirty-two
and two eighteen-pound carronades, with a crew of
one hundred and three men and fifteen boys.[1] The
inferiority was something like four to three; but
Captain Wales of the " Epervier " gallantly brought
his vessel into action at the usual close-range of these
murderous combats.

Captain Wales told the result in an official report,
dated May 8, to Vice-Admiral Cochrane.[2] The report
was not published, the British Admiralty having become sensitive to the popular outcry against their
naval management.

" At eight A. M.," reported Captain Wales, " the wind
being about east-south-east, I saw a strange sail in the
southwest apparently in chase of us; at nine, perceiving
her to near very fast and to be a square-rigged vessel-of-
war, I shortened sail and hauled to the wind on the lar-

[1] Commander R. W. Wales to Sir Alexander Cochrane, May 8,
1814; MSS. British Archives.

[2] Commander R. W. Wales to Sir Alexander Cochrane, May 8,
1814; MSS. British Archives.

board tack to be between her and the convoy, being rather
ahead of them.   The wind at this time veering round to
the southward enabled the stranger to lay up for us. . . .
At 9.50 A. M. we weathered her and exchanged broadsides; having passed her beam, we tacked, shortened
sail, and continued in close action until eleven A. M.,
when — five of our larboard guns being disabled by the
breeching-bolts giving way, and three others by shot,
and unable to manœuvre so as to get the starboard guns
to bear in consequence of the rigging and sails being cut
to pieces in the early part of the action by star-shot, the
main boom shot away, the foremast wounded in several
places, and several shot between wind and water, with
four-and-a-half feet of water in the hold, and the enemy
seemingly in a state to continue the action — I deemed it
prudent to surrender."

The giving way of the breeching-bolts did not
wholly disable the guns, for Captain Wales specially
commended " Mr. Lawrence Kennedy the Purser,
who rendered much service in his exertions at the
after-guns by getting them in a fighting state again
when unshipped by the fighting-bolts coming out of
their places."

At the close of the battle the " Peacock's " hull
had not been touched; aloft, her foreyard was disabled and a few upper stays were cut away; of her
crew, two men were slightly wounded, — but this
was all the injury sustained in running for three
quarters of an hour under the close fire of nine
heavy guns.[1]   The " Epervier " was reported by Cap-

[1] James's Naval History, vi. 160.

tain Warrington as showing forty-five shot-holes in her hull; masts and rigging much cut up, and twenty-three men killed or wounded in a crew of one hundred and twenty-eight. The difference between the force of the two vessels amply accounted for the capture; but the Admiralty might well show unwillingness to admit the bad condition of the vessels-of-war to which it intrusted the duty of convoying British mercantile shipping.[1] So complete was the " Epervier's " disaster that no excuse was offered for it, except the plea that she was in almost every respect inferior to the standard that British vessels of her class were supposed to maintain.

Captain Warrington saved the " Epervier" and brought her into Savannah in spite of two British frigates encountered on the way. He sailed again early in June, and passed the months of July and August in British waters or in the track of British commerce from the Faroe Islands to the Canaries. He burned or sunk twelve prizes, besides making cartels of two more, and brought his ship through the blockade into New York harbor, October 30, without injury, with only one man lost and the crew in fine health.[2]

The third new sloop was named the " Wasp " after the famous victor over the " Hornet." The new " Wasp " sailed from Portsmouth, New Hampshire, May 1, under command of Johnston Blakeley. Born

[1] James, pp. 342–347.

[2] Report of Captain Warrington, Oct. 30, 1814; Niles, vii. 155.

in Ireland in 1781, Blakeley was from infancy a
North Carolinian. He became in 1800 an officer in
the navy. Blakeley and the "Wasp" of 1814, like
Jones and the "Wasp" of 1813, ran a career in
which tragedy gave a deeper tinge than usual to the
bloody colors they won; but their success was on
the whole greater than that of any other national
cruiser from the beginning to the end of the war.
Merely as a story of adventure Blakeley's career
was exciting, but romance was its smallest interest.
For several reasons the sloop battles and cruises afforded one of the best relative tests of American
character and skill among all that were furnished
in the early period of the national history ; and
among the sloops, Blakeley's "Wasp" was the most
distinguished.

Blakeley ran directly across the ocean into sound-
ings at the mouth of the British Channel. There he
remained during the month of June, searching every
vessel that passed. The number of neutrals constantly diverting his attention kept him actively employed, and led him farther into the Channel than
was intended ; but although three British frigates
and fourteen sloops were at sea for the protection of
British waters, the "Wasp" continued to burn and
sink such British merchantmen as she met, — the first,
June 2, and subsequently June 13, 18, 23, and 26, —
until on the morning of June 28 a man-of-war brig
appeared to windward, and bore down on the American ship.

The day was warm and overcast. During the whole morning the two vessels approached each other so slowly that each had more than time to study his opponent. Once more the foresight of the American ship-builders secured a decisive advantage. The British brig, the " Reindeer," was altogether unequal to the contest. In tonnage she resembled the " Epervier," and her armament was even lighter. Captain Manners, her commander, had substituted twenty-four-pound carronades for the usual thirty-two-pounders, and his broadside of ten guns threw only two hundred and ten pounds of metal,[1] while the " Wasp's " eleven guns threw three hundred and thirty-eight pounds. The American crew numbered one hundred and seventy-three men ; the British numbered one hundred and eighteen. Contest under such conditions was a forlorn hope, but the " Reindeer's " crew were the pride of Portsmouth, and Manners was the idol of his men. They might cripple the " Wasp " if they could not capture her ; and probably the fate of the " Argus," a year before, encouraged the hope that the " Reindeer " could do at least as well as the " Pelican."

Each captain manœuvred for the weather-gauge, but the Englishman gained it, and coming up on the " Wasp's " weather-quarter, repeatedly fired his light twelve-pound bow-carronade, filled with round and grape shot, into the American ship. Blakeley, " finding the enemy did not get sufficiently on the

[1] Blakeley's Report of July 8, 1814 ; Niles, vii. 114.

beam to enable us to bring our guns to bear, put the
helm a-lee," and fired as his guns bore. The firing
began at 3.26 P. M. and lasted until 3.40, fourteen
minutes, at close range. In that space of time each
gun in the broadside could be fired at the utmost
three times. Apparently Manners felt that he had
no chance with his guns, for he brought his vessel's
bow against the " Wasp's " quarter and repeatedly
attempted boarding. Early in the action the calves
of his legs were shot away; then a shot passed
through both his thighs; yet he still climbed into
the rigging to lead his boarders, when two balls
at the same moment struck him in the head. His
fall ended the battle; and such had been the losses
of his company that the highest officer remaining
unhurt on the British brig to surrender the vessel
was said to be the captain's clerk. At 3.45 the
" Reindeer's " flag was struck, — the whole action,
from the " Wasp's " first gun, having lasted nineteen
minutes.

Had every British vessel fought like the " Reindeer," Englishmen would have been less sensitive to
defeat. In this desperate action the " Wasp " suffered severely. Her foremast was shot through; her
rigging and spars were much injured; her hull was
struck by six round shot and much grape; eleven
men were killed and fifteen wounded, or nearly
one man in six, " chiefly in repelling boarders," reported Blakeley. The " Reindeer " was a wreck, and
was blown up as soon as the wounded could be

removed. Of her crew, numbering one hundred and eighteen, thirty-three lost their lives; thirty-four were wounded,— in all, sixty-seven, or more than half the brig's complement.

Ten days afterward Blakeley ran into Lorient, where his ship was well received by the French, whose British antipathies were increased rather than lessened by their enforced submission. After refitting, the "Wasp" sailed again August 27, and four days later cut out a valuable ship from a convoy under the eyes of a seventy-four. The same evening, September 1, at half-past six, Blakeley sighted four vessels, two on either bow, and hauled up for the one most to windward. At 9.26 at night the chase, a brig, was directly under the "Wasp's" lee-bow, and Blakeley began firing a twelve-pound bow-carronade, which he must have taken from the "Reindeer," for no such gun made part of his regular armament.

The battle in the dark which followed has been always deeply interesting to students of naval history, the more because the British Admiralty suppressed the official reports, and left an air of mystery over the defeat which rather magnified than diminished its proportions. The British brig was the sloop-of-war "Avon," commanded by Captain James Arbuthnot, and carrying the usual armament of sixteen thirty-two-pound carronades with two long six-pounders. Her crew was reported as numbering one hundred and four men and thirteen boys. Captain Arbuth-

not's official report[1] said that the " Avon " had been
cruising in company with the sloop-of-war " Castilian," when at daylight, September 1, he " discovered
an enemy's schooner in the rear of the Kangaroo
convoy," and gave chase. The " Castilian " also
gave chase, and at seven o'clock the twenty-gun ship
" Tartarus " was signalled, also in chase.[2] All day
the three British sloops-of-war chased the privateer
schooner, until at half-past six o'clock in the evening
the " Castilian's " superiority in sailing free left the
" Avon " out of sight, nine miles astern. The position of the " Tartarus " was not mentioned in the
reports, but she could hardly have been ahead of the
" Castilian." The three British sloops were then
within ten miles of each other, under full sail, with
a ten-knot wind. The weather was hazy, and neither
the " Castilian " nor the " Tartarus " could see that
the " Avon " was signalling the " Castilian " a recall.
The " Avon " saw at four o'clock a large sail on her
weather-beam standing directly for her, and knowing that the " Wasp " was cruising in these waters,
Captain Arbuthnot felt natural anxiety to rejoin his
consort.

Captain Arbuthnot's report continued : —

" The stranger closing with us fast, I kept away and
set the weather studding-sails in hopes of nearing the·

[1] Report of Captain James Arbuthnot, Sept. 1, 1814; MSS.
British Archives.

[2] Report of Lieutenant George Lloyd of the "Castilian," Sept.
2, 1814 ; MSS. British Archives.

'Castilian' or 'Tartarus,' the latter of which I had only lost sight of at 3 p. m.    At 7.30 p. m. the stranger had approached within hail, and being unable to get a satisfactory answer I had not a doubt of her being an enemy's corvette.    At 8.30 he fired a shot over us which was instantly returned with a broadside.    He then bore up and endeavored to rake us, but was prevented.    The action then became general within half pistol-shot, and continued without intermission until 10.30 p. m., when — having seven feet of water in the hold, the magazine drowned; tiller, foreyard, main-boom, and every shroud shot away, and the other standing and the running rigging cut to pieces; the brig quite unmanageable, and the leak gaining fast on the pumps; with forty killed and wounded, and five of the starboard guns dismounted; and conceiving further resistance only would cause a useless sacrifice of lives — I was under the painful necessity of ordering the colors to be struck to the American corvette 'Wasp,' the mainmast, almost immediately after, going over the side."

Lieutenant George Lloyd, commanding the " Castilian," reported September 2 the circumstances attending the loss of the " Avon," as far as they concerned his share in the matter.[1]    At nine o'clock the " Castilian " heard a very heavy firing in the northnortheast, and immediately wore and made all possible sail in that direction, burning blue lights.    At quarter past ten the firing ceased, " and on coming up I had the mortification to observe the ' Avon ' a

[1] Lieutenant Lloyd to Vice-Admiral Sawyer, Sept 2, 1814; MSS. British Archives.

totally dismantled and ungovernable wreck, with her mainmast gone, — the enemy, apparently a large ship corvette, lying to, to leeward of her, who on my closing made all sail, and evinced every wish to avoid a contest with us."

" I immediately used means to enable me to bring her to close action ; and from our superior sailing I had in a few minutes the gratification to be within half a cable's length on her weather quarter. But I lament to state at this anxious crisis the ' Avon's' situation became most alarming ; she had commenced firing minute guns, and making every other signal of distress and of being in want of immediate assistance. I must here (as my pen can but inadequately describe) leave you, sir, to judge the feelings of myself, officers, and crew, as, from the confusion which evidently prevailed on board the enemy, the damage she had sustained, and her bad steerage, together with the cool and steady conduct of the officers and men I have the honor to command. I had no doubt of her falling an easy prey could we have persisted in attacking her, but which was not to be done without sacrificing the lives of the surviving gallant crew of our consort. Thus situated . . . I was obliged . . . to leave the flying enemy to escape ; but I feel somewhat gratified the situation of the ' Castilian' enabled me to give him a raking, and I doubt not from the closeness of the vessels a most destructive broadside, which he did not return even with a single gun, — a circumstance that, I trust, cannot fail to prove how destructive the ' Avon's' fire must have been."

Lieutenant Lloyd did not explain how his enemy was to bring guns to bear under the circumstances,

the " Castilian " tacking under the " Wasp's " stern
at half a cable's length distance, and immediately
standing in the opposite direction, nor did he say
what had become of the " Tartarus." Doubtless the
" Wasp " steered badly, her rigging being much damaged ; and Blakeley was chiefly intent on keeping off
till he could reeve new braces. The " Castilian's "
broadside cut the " Wasp's " rigging and sails, and
shot away a lower main cross-tree, but did no other
serious damage.

The " Avon " lost ten men killed and thirty-two
wounded, besides being reduced to a sinking condition in an hour of night action in a ten-knot wind,
with two more ships-of-war in sight and hearing.
The " Wasp " lost two men killed and one wounded,
four round shot in the hull, and the " rigging and
sails suffered a great deal." [1]

Blakeley had done enough, and could hardly do
more. Besides two eighteen-gun brigs, he made in
his cruise fourteen prizes, which he destroyed, several
of great value. In that year all the frigates in the
United States service had not done as much. With
a single-decked ship of five hundred tons, armed with
carronades, Blakeley blockaded the British Channel
for two months, capturing vessels in sight of ships-
of-the-line, and destroying two sloops-of-war in rapid
succession, without serious injury to himself, and to
the consternation of the British marine.

After sinking the " Avon," September 1, Blakeley

[1] Blakeley's Report, Sept. 11, 1814; Niles, vii. 191.

held on his course toward Madeira, and there, September 21, captured the brig "Atlanta," which he sent to Savannah. Still later, October 9, near the Cape de Verde Islands, he spoke a Swedish brig, which reported him. After that day no word of tidings was ever received from the " Wasp." Somewhere under the waters of the Atlantic, ship and crew found an unknown grave.

Besides the large sloops-of-war, three smaller vessels — the "Syren," "Enterprise," and "Rattlesnake" — went to sea in 1814. The " Syren " was captured after a chase of eleven hours, nearly on a wind, by the " Medway," seventy-four; her sixteen guns, and everything else that could be spared, were thrown overboard during the chase. The " Rattlesnake " and " Enterprise " cruised in company toward the West Indies, and made some prizes. The " Rattlesnake " was fast, the " Enterprise " a very dull sailer; but after repeated hairbreadth escapes, the " Rattlesnake " was caught, July 11, by the frigate " Leander," with Cape Sable to windward, and was obliged to surrender.[1] The " Enterprise," with her usual good fortune, was never taken, but became a guardship.

After November 1 the United States government had not a ship at sea. In port, three seventy-fours were building, and five forty-fours were building or blockaded. Three thirty-six-gun frigates were laid up or blockaded. Four sloops-of-war were also in port, the " Peacock " having just returned from her long

[1] Letter from the Purser, July 29, 1814; Niles, vi. 391.

cruise.  Such a result could not be called satisfactory.
The few war-vessels that existed proved rather what
the government might have done than what the British had to fear from any actual or probable American navy.  The result of private enterprise showed
also how much more might easily have been done
by government.

The year 1814 was marked by only one great and
perhaps decisive success on either side, except Macdonough's victory.  This single success was privateering.  Owners, captains, and crews had then learned to
build and sail their vessels, and to hunt their prey with
extraordinary skill.  A few rich prizes stimulated the
building of new vessels as the old were captured, and
the ship-yards turned them out as rapidly as they were
wanted.  In the neighborhood of Boston, in the summer of 1814, three companion ships were built, — the
" Reindeer," " Avon," and " Blakeley ; " and of these
the " Reindeer " was said to have been finished in
thirty-five working days, and all three vessels were
at sea in the following winter.  No blockade short
of actual siege could prevent such craft from running out and in.  Scores of them were constantly
on the ocean.

On the Atlantic privateers swarmed.  British merchantmen were captured, recaptured, and captured
again, until they despaired of ever reaching port.  One
British master who was three times taken and as
often retaken, reported that he had seen ten American
privateers crossing his course.  A letter from Halifax

printed in the London "Times" of December 19 said: "There are privateers off this harbor which plunder every vessel coming in or going out, notwithstanding we have three line-of-battle ships, six frigates, and four sloops here." The West Indies and the Canaries were haunted by privateers. The "Rambler," "Hyder Ali," and "Jacob Jones" of Boston penetrated even the Chinese seas, and carried prize-goods into Macao and Canton. Had these pests confined their ravages to the colonies or the ocean, the London clubs and the lobbies of Parliament would have thought little about them; but the privateer had discovered the weakness of Great Britain, and frequented by preference the narrow seas which England regarded as her own. The quasi-blockade of the British coasts which American cruisers maintained in 1813 became a real and serious blockade in 1814. Few days passed without bringing news of some inroad into British waters, until the Thames itself seemed hardly safe.

The list of privateers that hung about Great Britain and Ireland might be made long if the number were necessary to the story, but the character of the blockade was proved by other evidence than that of numbers. A few details were enough to satisfy even the English. The "Siren," a schooner of less than two hundred tons, with seven guns and seventy-five men,[1] had an engagement with her Majesty's cutter "Landrail" of four guns, as the cutter was crossing the British Channel with despatches. The "Landrail"

[1] James, p. 361.

was captured after a somewhat sharp action, and sent to America, but was recaptured on the way. The victory was not remarkable, but the place of capture was very significant; and it happened July 12, only a fortnight after Blakeley captured the " Reindeer " farther westward. The " Siren " was but one of many privateers in those waters. The " Governor Tompkins " burned fourteen vessels successively in the British Channel. The " Young Wasp " of Philadelphia cruised nearly six months about the coasts of England and Spain and in the course of West India commerce. The " Harpy " of Baltimore, another large vessel of some three hundred and fifty tons and fourteen guns, cruised nearly three months off the coast of Ireland, in the British Channel and in the Bay of Biscay, and returned safely to Boston filled with plunder, including, as was said, upward of £100,000 in British Treasury notes and bills of exchange. The " Leo," a Boston schooner of about two hundred tons, was famous for its exploits in these waters, but was captured at last by the frigate " Tiber " after a chase of eleven hours. The " Mammoth," a Baltimore schooner of nearly four hundred tons, was seventeen days off Cape Clear, the southernmost point of Ireland. The most mischievous of all was the " Prince of Neufchatel " of New York, which chose the Irish Channel as its favorite haunt, where during the summer it made ordinary coasting traffic impossible. The most impudent was probably the " Chasseur," commanded by Captain Boyle, who cruised three months, and amused himself, when off the British coast, by sending to be posted at Lloyd's a " Proclamation of Blockade " of " all the ports, harbors, bays, creeks, rivers, inlets, outlets, islands, and sea-coast of the United Kingdom." The jest at that moment was too sardonic to amuse the British public.

As the announcement of these annoyances, recurring day after day, became a practice of the press, the public began to grumble in louder and louder tones. " That the whole coast of Ireland, from Wexford round by Cape Clear to Carrickfergus," said the " Morning Chronicle" of August 31, " should have been for above a month under the unresisted dominion of a few petty ' fly-by-nights' from the blockaded ports of the United States, is a grievance equally intolerable and disgraceful." The Administration mouthpiece, the " Courier," admitted, August 22, that five brigs had been taken in two days between the Smalls and the Tuskar, and that insurance on vessels trading between Ireland and England had practically ceased. The " Annual Register " for 1814 recorded as " a most mortifying reflection," that with a navy of nearly a thousand ships of various sizes, and while at peace with all Europe, " it was not safe for a vessel to sail without convoy from one part of the English or Irish Channel to another." Such insecurity had not been known in the recent wars.

As early as August 12, the London Assurance Corporations urged the government to provide a naval force competent to cope with the privateers. In September the merchants of Glasgow, Liverpool, and Bristol held meetings, and addressed warm remonstrances to government on the want of protection given to British commerce. The situation was serious, and the British merchants did not yet know all. Till that time the East India and China trade had suffered little, but at last the American privateers had penetrated even the Chinese seas ; and while they were driving the British flag into port there, they attacked the East India Company's ships, which were really men-of-war, on their regular voyages. In August the "Countess of Harcourt" of more than five hundred tons, carrying six heavy guns and ninety men, was captured in the British Channel by the privateer "Sabine" of Baltimore, and sent safely to America. The number and value of the prizes stimulated new energy in seeking them, and British commerce must soon yield to that of neutral nations if the war continued.

The merchants showed that a great change had come over their minds since they incited or permitted the Tories to issue the Impressment Proclamation and the Orders in Council seven years before. More than any other class of persons, the ship-owners and West India merchants were responsible for the temper which caused the war, and they were first to admit their punishment. At the Liverpool meeting, where Mr. Gladstone, who took the chair, began by declaring that some ports, particularly Milford, were under

actual blockade,[1] a strong address was voted; and at
a very numerous meeting of merchants, manufactur-
ers, ship-owners, and underwriters at Glasgow, September 7, the Lord Provost presiding, resolutions were
unanimously passed —

" That the number of American privateers with which
our channels have been infested, the audacity with which
they have approached our coasts, and the success with
which their enterprise has been attended, have proved
injurious to our commerce, humbling to our pride, and
discreditable to the directors of the naval power of the
British nation, whose flag till of late waved over every
sea and triumphed over every rival.

" That there is reason to believe, in the short space of
twenty-four months, above eight hundred vessels have
been captured by the Power whose maritime strength we
have hitherto impolitically held in contempt."

The war was nearly at an end, and had effected
every possible purpose for the United States, when
such language was adopted by the chief commercial
interests of Great Britain. Yet the Glasgow meeting
expressed only a part of the common feeling. The
rates of insurance told the whole story. The press
averred that in August and September underwriters
at Lloyd's could scarcely be induced to insure at
any rate of premium, and that for the first time in
history a rate of thirteen per cent had been paid on
risks to cross the Irish Channel. Lloyd's list then
showed eight hundred and twenty-five prizes lost to

---

[1] Morning Chronicle, Sept. 6, 1814.

the Americans, and their value seemed to increase rather than diminish.

Weary as the merchants and ship-owners were of the war, their disgust was not so intense as that of the navy. John Wilson Croker, Secretary of the Admiralty Board, whose feelings toward America were at best unkind, showed a temper that passed the limits of his duties. When the London-underwriters made their remonstrance of August 12, Croker assured them, in a letter dated August 19,[1] that at the time referred to "there was a force adequate to the purpose of protecting the trade both in St. George's Channel and the Northern Sea." The news that arrived during the next two weeks threw ridicule on this assertion; and Croker was obliged to reply to a memorial from Bristol, September 16, in a different tone.[2] He admitted that the navy had not protected trade, and could not protect it; but he charged that the merchants were to blame for losing their own ships. His letter was a valuable evidence of the change in British sentiment: —

"Their Lordships take this opportunity of stating to you, for the information of the memorialists, that from the accounts which their Lordships have received of the description of vessels which had formed the largest proportion of the captures in the Irish and Bristol channels, it appears that if their masters had availed themselves of the convoys appointed for their protection from for-

[1] Niles, vii. 174.

[2] Croker to the Mayor of Bristol, Sept. 16, 1814; Niles, viii. Supplement, p. 186.

eign ports, or had not in other instances deserted from
the convoys under whose protection they had sailed, before the final conclusion of the voyage, many of the captures would not have been made.    It is their Lordships'
determination, as far as they may be enabled, to bring
the parties to punishment who may have been guilty
of such illegal acts, and which are attended with such
injurious consequences to the trade of the country."

Little by little the Americans had repaid every
item of the debt of insult they owed, and after Croker's letter the account could be considered settled.
Even the " Times " was not likely to repeat its sneer
of 1807, that the Americans could hardly cross to
Staten Island without British permission.    Croker's
official avowal that no vessel could safely enter or
leave one port in the British Islands for another except under guard of a man-of-war, was published on
the same page with the memorialists' assertion that
the rate of insurance had gradually risen till it exceeded twofold the usual rates prevailing during the
wars on the Continent.

The spirit of exasperation shown by Croker extended through the navy.    The conduct of Cochrane
and Cockburn has been already told.    That of Captain Hillyar at Valparaiso was equally significant.    Under the annoyance of their mortifications the British
commanders broke through ordinary rules.    Captain
Lloyd of the " Plantagenet," seventy-four, on arriving
in the harbor of Fayal, September 26, saw a large
brig in the roads, which he must have known to

be an American privateer. He was so informed by his pilot. It was the " General Armstrong," Captain Samuel C. Reid, a brig which for two years had fretted and escaped the British navy. The " Plantagenet," with two other ships-of-war, appeared at sunset. Reid dared not run out to sea, and the want of wind would in any case have prevented success. A little after dusk, Reid, seeing the suspicious movements of the enemy, began to warp his vessel close under the guns of the castle. While doing so, at about eight o'clock four boats filled with men left the ships and approached him. As they came near he repeatedly hailed and warned them off, and at last fired. His fire was returned, but the boats withdrew with the loss of a number of men.[1]

Captain Lloyd, in a somewhat elaborate report to explain the propriety of his conduct, enclosed affidavits to prove that the Americans had violated the neutrality of the port. The affidavits proved that, knowing the character of the vessel, he sent two boats from his own ship to assist the boats of the " Carnation " to " watch " the privateer. His report told the story as he wished it to be understood:[2]

" On the evening of the 26th instant I put into this port for refreshments, previous to my return to Jamaica. In shore was discovered a suspicious vessel at anchor. I ordered Captain Bentham of the ' Carnation ' to watch

---

[1] Letter of Consul Dabney, Oct. 5, 1814; Niles, vii. 253.

[2] Robert Lloyd to Rear-Admiral Brown, Sept. 28, 1814; MSS. British Archives.

her movements, and sent the pinnace and cutter of this
ship to assist him on that service; but on his perceiving
her under way, he sent Lieut. Robert Faussett in the
pinnace, about eight o'clock, to observe her proceedings.
On his approaching the schooner, he was ordered to keep
off or they would fire into him, upon which the boat was
immediately backed off; but to his astonishment he received a broadside of round, grape, and musketry, which
did considerable damage.   He then repeatedly requested
them to leave off firing, as he was not come to molest
them; but the enemy still continued his destructive fire
until they had killed two men and wounded seven, without a musket being returned by the boat."

Lieutenant Faussett's affidavit threw more light on
this curious story of British naval management.   He
deposed —

"That on Monday, the 26th instant, about eight
o'clock in the evening, he was ordered to go in the pinnace as guard-boat unarmed on board her Majesty's brig
'Carnation,' to know what armed vessel was at anchor in
the bay, when Captain Bentham of said brig ordered him
to go and inquire of said vessel (which by information
was said to be a privateer).   When said boat came
near the privateer, they hailed (to say, the Americans),
and desired the English boat to keep off or they would
fire into her: upon which said Mr. Faussett ordered his
men to back astern, and with a boat-hook was in the
act of so doing, when the Americans in the most wanton manner fired into said English boat, killed two
men and wounded seven, some of them mortally, — and
this notwithstanding said Faussett frequently called out
not to murder them, that they struck and called for

quarter. Said Faussett solemnly declares that no resistance of any kind was made, nor could they do it,
not having any arms, nor of course sent to attack said
vessel."

Lieutenant Faussett's affidavit proved that the
" General Armstrong" had good reason for firing
into the British boats. The "Carnation" had anchored within pistol-shot of the privateer; four boats
of the " Plantagenet " and " Carnation," filled with
men, were on the water watching her in the moonlight; every act of the British squadron pointed to
an attack, when Captain Bentham ordered the pinnace " to go and inquire " of the vessel, known to be
an American privateer, what armed vessel it was. If
Captain Bentham did not intend to provoke a shot
from the privateer, his order was wanting in intelligence. Lieutenant Faussett accordingly approached
in the pinnace, the other boats being not far behind.
That his men were unarmed was highly improbable
to the privateer, which affirmed that their fire killed
one of the American crew and wounded the first lieutenant;[1] but their armament had little to do with the
matter. They approached as enemies, in the night,
with a large armed force immediately behind them.
The privateer repeatedly warned them off. Instead of
obeying the order, Lieutenant Faussett came alongside. When he was fired on, he was so near that by
his own account he shoved off with the boat-hook.

[1] Letter of Captain Reid, Oct. 4, 1814; Niles, vii. Supplement, p. 167.

Considering who and where he was, he had reason to be thankful that any of his boat's-crew escaped.

Captain Lloyd's report continued : —

" This conduct, in violating the neutrality of this port, I conceive left me no alternative but that of destroying her. I therefore repeatedly ordered Captain Bentham to tow in the brig and take that step immediately. All the boats of this ship and the ' Rota ' were sent under his orders to tow him alongside or assist him in the attack, as circumstances might require ; but from continued light baffling winds and a lee tide he was not able, as he informed me, with his utmost exertions to put my orders in execution."

Meanwhile Captain Reid of the " General Armstrong" warped his vessel close to the beach, under the fort, and made all his preparations for the attack which he knew must come. The people of the town, with the governor among them, lined the shore, and witnessed the affair. Captain Lloyd's report told the result : —

" Finding the privateer was warping under the fort very fast, Captain Bentham judged it prudent to lose no time, and about twelve o'clock ordered the boats to make the attack. A more gallant, determined one never was made, led on by Lieutenants Matterface of the ' Rota ' and Bowerbank of this ship ; and every officer and man displayed the greatest courage in the face of a heavy discharge of great guns and musketry. But from her side being on the rocks (which was not known at the time), and every American in Fayal, exclusive of part of the crew, being armed and concealed in these rocks, which were immediately over the privateer, it unfortunately happened when these brave men gained the deck they were under the painful necessity of returning to their boats, from the very destructive fire kept up by those above them from the shore, who were in complete security, — and I am grieved to add, not before many lives were lost exclusive of the wounded."

As far as the accounts [1] agree, the boats were twelve in number, with about two hundred men. The privateersmen numbered ninety. As the boats approached, the guns opened on them; and when they came alongside the privateer they found the boarding-nettings up, with a desperate crew behind. So vigorously did the British seamen attack, that they gained the forecastle for a time. All three American lieutenants were killed or disabled, and Captain Reid fought his brig alone; but the deck was at last cleared, and the surviving assailants dropped into their boats or into the water.

Proverbially, an unsuccessful boat-attack was the most fatal of all services. The British loss was excessive. According to their report at the time, "Lieutenants Bowerbank, Coswell, and Rogers of the 'Rota' were killed, as well as thirty-eight seamen, and eighty-three wounded; the first, fourth, and fifth lieutenants of the 'Plantagenet' were wounded, and twenty-two seamen killed, and twenty-four wounded.[2]"

[1] Niles, vii. 255. James's Naval History, vi. 509. Cf. Letter from Fayal, Oct. 15, 1814. Cobbett's "Weekly Register," reprinted in Niles, vii. Supplement, p. 171.

[2] Niles, vii. 255.

According to the official report, thirty-four were killed
and eighty-six were wounded.  The " Guerriere" in
her battle with the " Constitution " lost only seventy-
eight men altogether.  The " Macedonian " lost only
one hundred and four.  The attack on the " General
Armstrong " was one of the bloodiest defeats suffered by the British navy in the war.  Not only was
the privateer untaken, but she lost few of her crew,
— nine in all, killed and wounded.

Captain Lloyd then declared that he would destroy
the privateer if he had to destroy Fayal in doing it,
and ordered Captain Bentham of the " Carnation "
to attack her with his guns.  Reid abandoned and
scuttled the " General Armstrong," taking his men
on shore.  The " Carnation's " shot inflicted some injury on the town, before the privateer was set on fire
by the " Carnation's " boats.[1]

If the British navy cared to pay such a price for
the shell of an old privateer brig, which had already
cost British commerce, as Captain Lloyd believed, a
million dollars,[2] the privateers were willing to gratify
the wish, as was shown a few days afterward when
the " Endymion " tried to carry the " Prince of Neufchatel " by boarding.  This privateer had made itself
peculiarly obnoxious to the British navy by the bold-
ness of its ravages in British waters.  It was coming

[1] Dabney's Letter; Niles, vii. 254.   Reid's Letter of Oct. 4,
1814 ; State Papers, Naval Affairs, p. 495.

[2] Report of Captain Lloyd, Oct. 4, 1814 ; MSS. British
Archives.

to America filled with plunder, and with a prize in company, when off Gay Head the "Endymion" was sighted, October 11, and gave chase.

Captain Hope of the "Endymion" made an official report, explaining with much detail that he chased the privateer till evening, when the wind failed, and he then sent out his boats : [1] —

"I sent all the boats under command of Lieutenants Hawkins, Ormond, and Fanshaw. In approaching the ship an alarm was fired. The boats had been previously rowing up under a shoal, and had not felt the effects of a rapid tide which they almost instantaneously became exposed to. The second barge in taking the station assigned by Lieutenant Hawkins on the schooner's starboard bow, having her larboard oars shot away, unfortunately was swept by the stream athwart the first barge ; thereby all the boats became entangled ; and it is with extreme concern I acquaint you that the attack was in consequence at this moment only partially made. Notwithstanding this disadvantage at the first onset, every exertion that human skill could devise was resorted to to renew the contest ; and they succeeded in again getting alongside, but not in the position intended. Their failure, therefore, is to be ascribed in the first instance to the velocity of the tide, the height of the vessel's side, not having channel plates to assist the men in getting on her deck, and her very superior force (a schooner of the largest dimensions, the 'Prince of Neufchatel,' three hundred and twenty tons, eighteen guns, long-nine and twelve-pounders, with a complement of one hundred and forty

[1] Captain Hope to Rear Admiral Hotham, Oct. 11, 1814 ; MSS. British Archives.

men of all nations, commanded by Mons. Jean Ordronaux). The boats' painters being now shot away, they
again fell astern without ever being able to repeat the
attack, and with great difficulty regained the ship, with
the exception of the second barge."

Captain Ordronaux of the privateer had a crew of
less than forty men then at quarters, and they suffered severely, only nine men escaping injury. The
boarders gained the deck, but were killed as fast as
they mounted; and at last more than half the British party were killed or captured. According to
the British account, twenty-eight men, including the
first lieutenant of the " Endymion," were killed; and
thirty-seven men, including the second lieutenant,
were wounded.[1] This report did not quite agree
with that of the privateer, which claimed also twenty-
eight prisoners, including the second lieutenant, who
was unhurt. In any case, more than seventy men
of the " Endymion's " crew, besides her first and second lieutenant, were killed, wounded, or captured;
and the " Prince of Neufchatel " arrived in safety
in Boston.

In the want of adjacent rocks lined with armed
Americans, such as Captain Lloyd alleged at Fayal,
Captain Hope was reduced to plead the tides as the
cause of his defeat. These reports, better than any
other evidence, showed the feelings of the British
naval service in admitting discomfiture in the last
resort of its pride. Successively obliged to plead

[1] James's Naval History, vi. 527.

inferiority at the guns, inferiority in sailing qualities, inferiority in equipment, the British service saw itself compelled by these repeated and bloody repulses to admit that its supposed pre-eminence in hand-to-hand fighting was a delusion. Within a single fortnight two petty privateers, with crews whose united force did not amount to one hundred and fifty men, succeeded in repulsing attacks made by twice their number of the best British seamen, inflicting a loss, in killed and wounded, officially reported at one hundred and eighty-five.

Such mortifying and bloody experiences made even the British navy weary of the war. Valuable prizes were few, and the service, especially in winter, was severe. Undoubtedly the British cruisers caught privateers by dozens, and were as successful in the performance of their duties as ever they had been in any war in Europe. Their blockade of American ports was real and ruinous, and nothing pretended to resist them. Yet after catching scores of swift cruisers, they saw scores of faster and better vessels issue from the blockaded ports and harry British commerce in every sea. Scolded by the press, worried by the Admiralty, and mortified by their own want of success, the British navy was obliged to hear language altogether strange to its experience.

" The American cruisers daily enter in among our convoys," said the " Times " of February 11, 1815, " seize prizes in sight of those that should afford protection, and if pursued ' put on their sea-wings ' and

laugh at the clumsy English pursuers.  To what is this
owing?  Cannot we build ships? . . . It must indeed
be encouraging to Mr. Madison to read the logs of his
cruisers.  If they fight, they are sure to conquer ; if they
fly, they are sure to escape."

## CHAPTER VIII.

In the tempest of war that raged over land and ocean during the months of August and September, 1814, bystanders could not trust their own judgment of the future; yet shrewd observers, little affected either by emotion or by interest, inclined to the belief that the United States government was near exhaustion. The immediate military danger on Lake Champlain was escaped, and Baltimore was saved; but the symptoms of approaching failure in government were not to be mistaken, and the capture of Washington, which was intended to hurry the collapse, produced its intended effect.

From the first day of the war the two instruments necessary for military success were wanting to Madison, — money and men. After three campaigns, the time came when both these wants must be supplied, or the national government must devolve its duties on the States. When the President, preparing his Annual Message, asked his Cabinet officers what were the prospects of supplying money and men for another campaign, he received answers discouraging in the extreme.

First, in regard to money. In July, Secretary Campbell advertised a second loan, of only six million dollars. He obtained but two and a half millions at eighty. His acceptance of this trifling sum obliged him to give the same terms to the contractors who had taken the nine millions subscribed in the spring at eighty-eight. Barker found difficulty in making his payments, and from both loans the Treasury could expect to obtain only $10,400,000, owing to the contractors' failures.[1] The authorized loan was twenty-five millions. The secretary could suggest no expedient, except Treasury notes, for filling the deficit.

Bad as this failure was, — though it showed Secretary Campbell's incapacity so clearly as to compel his retirement, and obliged the President to call a special session of Congress, — the Treasury might regard it as the least of its embarrassments. Commonly governments had begun their most desperate efforts only after ordinary resources failed; but the United States government in 1814 had so inextricably involved its finances that without dictatorial powers of seizing property its functions could not much longer be continued. The general bankruptcy, long foreseen, at length occurred.

The panic caused by the capture of Washington, August 24, obliged the tottering banks of Philadelphia and Baltimore to suspend specie payments. The

[1] Report of Secretary Campbell, Sept. 26, 1814; State Papers, Finance, ii. 840.

banks of Philadelphia formally announced their suspension, August 31, by a circular explaining the causes and necessity of their decision.[1]   The banks of New York immediately followed, September 1; and thenceforward no bank between New Orleans and Albany paid its obligations except in notes.   Only the banks of New England maintained specie payments, with the exception of those in least credit, which took the opportunity to pay or not pay as they pleased.   The suspension was admitted to be permanent.   Until the blockade should be raised and domestic produce could find a foreign market, the course of exchange was fixed, and specie payments could not be resumed.   The British navy and the Boston Federalists held the country firmly bound, and peace alone could bring relief.

Suspension mattered little, and had the National Bank been in existence the failure might have been an advantage to the government; but without a central authority the currency instantly fell into confusion.   No medium of exchange existed outside of New England.   Boston gave the specie standard, and soon the exchanges showed wide differences.   New York money stood at twenty per cent discount, Philadelphia at twenty-four per cent, Baltimore at thirty per cent.   Treasury notes were sold in Boston at twenty-five per cent discount, and United States six-per-cents stood at sixty in coin.[2]   The Treasury

[1] Niles, vii.; Supplement, p. 176.
[2] Niles, vii.; Supplement, p. 176.

had no means of transferring its bank deposits from one part of the country to another. Unless it paid its debts in Treasury notes, it was unable to pay them at all. No other money than the notes of suspended banks came into the Treasury. Even in New England, taxes, customs-duties, and loans were paid in Treasury notes, and rarely in local currency. Thus, while the government collected in the Middle and Southern States millions in bank-notes, it was obliged to leave them in deposit at the local banks where the collection was made, while its debts in Boston and New York remained unpaid. The source of revenue was destroyed. The whole South and West, and the Middle States as far north as New York, could contribute in no considerable degree to the support of government.

The situation was unusual. The government might possess immense resources in one State and be totally bankrupt in another; it might levy taxes to the amount of the whole circulating medium, and yet have only its own notes available for payment of debt; it might borrow hundreds of millions and be none the better for the loan. All the private bank-notes of Pennsylvania and the Southern country were useless in New York and New England where they must chiefly be used. An attempt to transfer such deposits in any quantity would have made them quite worthless. The Treasury already admitted bankruptcy. The interest on the national obligations could not be paid.

The President's second inquiry regarded men. The new Secretary of War, Monroe, gave him such information as the Department possessed on the numbers of the army. A comparative account showed that in June, 1813, the regular troops numbered 27,609 ; in December, 34,325. In January, 1814, the number was nominally 33,822 ;[1] in July the aggregate was 31,503, the effectives being 27,010.[2] Since July the recruits had declined in numbers. The three months of March, April, and May produced 6,996 recruits ; the three months of July, August, and September were reported as furnishing 4,477.[3] The general return of September 30 reported the strength of the army at 34,029 men.[4] The government was not able to provide the money necessary to pay bounties due for the last three months' recruiting.[5] The Secretary of War admitted the failure of the recruiting service, and attributed it to the high bounties given for substitutes in the militia detached for United States service.[6]

[1] Armstrong to Eppes, Feb. 10, 1814; Niles, vi. 94. See *ante*, vol. vii. p. 381.

[2] Report; State Papers, Military Affairs, i. 535.

[3] Return of Enlistments, Nov. 2, 1814; State Papers, Military Affairs, i. 521. Letter of Assistant Inspector-General, Oct. 22, 1814; State Papers, Military Affairs, p. 518.

[4] The Inspector-General's Letter of Nov. 2, 1814; State Papers, Military Affairs, p. 520.

[5] Report of the Paymaster, Oct. 26, 1814; State Papers, Military Affairs, p. 519.

[6] Monroe to Giles, Oct. 26, 1814 ; State Papers, Military Affairs, p. 518.

The smallness of the armies in the field showed worse results than were indicated by the returns. Macomb at Plattsburg claimed to have only fifteen hundred effectives. Izard carried with him to Buffalo only four thousand men. Brown's effectives at Fort Erie numbered two thousand. Apparently these three corps included the entire force in the field on the Canada frontier, and their combined effective strength did not exceed eight thousand men. The year before, Wilkinson and Hampton commanded fully eleven thousand effectives in their movements against Montreal. Nothing showed that the victories at Niagara and Plattsburg had stimulated enlistments, or that the army could be raised above thirty thousand effectives even if the finances were in a condition to meet the expense.

Much was said of the zeal shown by the State militia in hastening to the defence of their soil, and the New England Federalists were as loud as the Kentucky and Tennessee Democrats in praise of the energy with which the militia rose to resist invasion; but in reality this symptom was the most alarming of the time. Both in the military and in the political point of view, the persistence in depending on militia threatened to ruin the national government.

The military experience of 1814 satisfied the stanchest war Democrats that the militia must not be their dependence. In Maine the militia allowed themselves with hardly a show of resistance to be made subjects of Great Britain. At Plattsburg volunteers collected in considerable numbers, but the victory was won by the sailors and the engineers. At Niagara, Brown never could induce more than a thousand volunteers to support him in his utmost straits. Porter's efforts failed to create a brigade respectable in numbers, and at Chippawa his Indians outnumbered his whites. Four days after the repulse of Drummond's assault on Fort Erie, at the most anxious moment of the Niagara campaign, Major-General Brown wrote to Secretary Armstrong,[1] —

" I very much doubt if a parallel can be found for the state of things existing on this frontier. A gallant little army struggling with the enemies of their country, and devoting their lives for its honor and its safety, left by that country to struggle alone, and that within sight and within hearing."

A month afterward Brown succeeded in obtaining a thousand volunteers, and by some quality of his own made them assault and carry works that old soldiers feared to touch. The feat was the most extraordinary that was performed on either side in the remarkably varied experience of the war; but it proved Brown's personal energy rather than the merits of a militia system. At Washington the militia were thoroughly tested; their rout proved chiefly the incompetence of their general, but the system was shown, before the battle, to be more defective

[1] Brown to Armstrong, July [August] 19, 1814; MSS. War Department Archives.

than the army it produced. At Baltimore the militia were again routed, and the town was saved chiefly by the engineers and sailors. In Virginia, where more than forty thousand militia were in the field, they protected nothing, and their service was more fatal to themselves than though they had fought severe battles. Nearly all the Virginia militia summoned for the defence of Norfolk suffered from sickness, and the mortality when compared with that of the regular service was enormous ; five militia-men sickened and died where one regular soldier suffered.[1] In Tennessee and Georgia the experience was equally unfortunate ; the Georgia militia could do nothing with the Creeks, and Andrew Jackson himself was helpless until he obtained one small regiment of regulars.

Besides its military disadvantages the militia service was tainted with fraud. Habitually and notoriously in New England and New York, the militia-men when called out attended muster, served a few days in order to get their names on the pay-roll, and then went home. The United States government wasted millions of dollars in pay and pensions for such men. Another source of waste was in the time required to place them in the field. The government struggled to avoid a call of militia, even though risking great disasters by the neglect.

The worst of all evils lay still further in the background. The militia began by rendering a proper

[1] Niles, vii.; Supplement, p. 188.

army impossible, and ended by making government
a form.   The object of Massachusetts in praising the
conduct of militia, and in maintaining its own at a
high state of efficiency, was notorious.   The Federalists knew that the national government must sooner
or later abandon the attempt to support an army.
When that time should come, the only resource
of the government would lie in State armies, and
Massachusetts was the best equipped State for that
object.   Her militia, seventy thousand strong, well-
armed, well-drilled, and as yet untouched by war,
could dictate to the Union.   Whenever Massachusetts should say the word, the war must stop ; and
Massachusetts meant to say the word when the
government fairly ceased to possess either money
or arms.

That moment, in the belief of the Massachusetts
Federalists, had come.   Their course in the summer
and autumn of 1814 left no doubt of their intentions.
No act of open rebellion could be more significant
than their conduct when Sherbrooke's expedition occupied Castine.   Then at last Governor Strong con-
sented to call out the militia, which he refused to do
two years before, because, he asserted, Castine and
the other coast towns were sufficiently defended ; [1]
but the governor was careful to avoid the suspicion
that these troops were in the national service.   He
acted independently of the national government in

[1] Strong to Eustis, Aug. 5, 1812 ; State Papers, Military
Affairs, i. 610.

the terms of his general order of September, 1814,[1] placing his militia under the command of a major-general of their own, and making only a bare inquiry of the Secretary of War whether their expenses would be reimbursed,[2] — an inquiry which Monroe at once answered in the negative.[3] The force was a State army, and could not fail to cause the President more anxiety than it was likely ever to cause the Prince Regent.

At the same time the governor of Connecticut withdrew from the command of Brigadier-General Cushing the brigade of State militia then in the national service, and placed it under a major-general of State militia, with injunctions to obey no orders except such as were issued by State authority.[4] The evil of these measures was greatly aggravated by coinciding with the crisis which stopped the course of national government. Connecticut withdrew her militia, August 24; Washington was captured the same day; the Philadelphia banks suspended payment August 29; Castine was taken August 31; and Governor Strong called out the Massachusetts militia September 6. The government was prostrate,

[1] General Orders, Sept. 6, 1814; State Papers, Military Affairs, p. 613.

[2] Strong to the Secretary of War, Sept. 7, 1814; State Papers, Military Affairs, p. 613.

[3] Monroe to Strong, Sept. 17, 1814; State Papers, Military Affairs, p. 614.

[4] Cushing to the Secretary of War, Sept. 12, 1814; State Papers, Military Affairs, p. 620.

and New England was practically independent when
Sir George Prevost crossed the frontier, September 3.
So complete was the paralysis that Governor Chittenden of Vermont, on receiving official notice [1] that
the British army and navy were advancing on Lake
Champlain, refused to call out the militia, because
neither the Constitution nor the laws gave him authority to order the militia out of the State.[2]    He
could only recommend that individuals should volunteer to assist in the defence of Plattsburg.    Chittenden's conduct was the more suggestive because of
his undoubted honesty and the absence of factious
motive for his refusal.

The full meaning of Governor Strong's course was
avowed a few days afterward.    Having called a special meeting of the State legislature for October 5,
he addressed to it a message narrating the steps he
had taken, and the refusal of the President to assume
the expenses of the militia called into service for the
defence of the State.

" The situation of this State is peculiarly dangerous
and perplexing," said Governor Strong; [3] " we have
been led by the terms of the Constitution to rely on the
government of the Union to provide for our defence.
We have resigned to that government the revenues of
the State with the expectation that this object would
not be neglected. . . . Let us then, relying on the sup-

[1] Macomb to Chittenden, Sept. 4, 1814; Niles, vii. 102.
[2] Chittenden to General Newell, Sept. 5, 1814; Niles, vii. 103.
[3] Message of Oct. 5, 1814; Niles, vii. 113.

port and direction of Providence, unite in such measures for our safety as the times demand and the principles of justice and the law of self-preservation will justify."

The sense which this invitation was intended to bear could be best understood by appreciating the temper of the body thus addressed and the time when the appeal was made. The national government had for practical purposes ceased. The Boston " Centinel," a newspaper of large circulation, said to reach six thousand copies, announced September 10, 1814, that the Union was already practically dissolved, and that the people must rise in their majesty, protect themselves, and compel their unworthy servants to obey their will. Governor Strong knew that the legislature was controlled by extreme partisans of the Pickering type, who wished, to use his phrase, to "let the ship run aground." Even Josiah Quincy, one of the most vehement Federalists, was aware that the members of the General Court stood in danger of doing too much rather than too little.[1]

Strong's message of October 5 was echoed by Pickering from Washington, October 12, in a letter which closed with the exhortation to seize the national revenues : —

" As, abandoned by the general government except for taxing us, we must defend ourselves, so we ought to secure and hold fast the revenues indispensable to main-

[1] Quincy's Life of Quincy, p. 357.

tain the force necessary for our protection against the foreign enemy and the still greater evil in prospect, — domestic tyranny." [1]

The Massachusetts legislature could not fail to understand Governor Strong's message as an invitation to resume the powers with which the State had parted in adopting the Constitution.

The legislature referred the message to a committee, which reported only three days afterward through its chairman, Harrison Gray Otis : [2] —

" The state of the national Treasury as exhibited by the proper officer requires an augmentation of existing taxes ; and if in addition to these the people of Massachusetts, deprived of their commerce and harassed by a formidable enemy, are compelled to provide for the indispensable duty of self-defence, it must soon become impossible for them to sustain this burden.    There remains to them therefore no alternative but submission to the enemy, or the control of their own resources to repel his aggressions.    It is impossible to hesitate in making the election.    This people are not ready for conquest or submission ; but being ready and determined to defend themselves, they have the greatest need of those resources derivable from themselves which the national government has hitherto thought proper to employ elsewhere."

The report further showed that the United States Constitution had failed to secure to New England

[1] Pickering to Strong, Oct. 12, 1814; New England Federalism, p. 394.

[2] Report of Oct. 8, 1814; Niles, vii. 149.

the rights and benefits expected from it, and required immediate change. The prescribed mode of amendment was insufficient : —

" When this deficiency becomes apparent, no reason can preclude the right of the whole people who were parties to it to adopt another. . . . But as a proposition for such a convention from a single State would probably be unsuccessful, and our danger admits not of delay, it is recommended by the committee that in the first instance a conference should be invited between those States the affinity of whose interests is closest."

Thus, after ten years' delay, the project of a New England Convention was brought forward by State authority, through the process of war with England, which George Cabot from the first declared to be the only means of producing it.[1] As Otis's committee presented the subject, the conference was in the first place to devise some mode of common defence ; and, in the second, " to lay the foundation for a radical reform in the national compact by inviting to a future convention a deputation from all the States in the Union." The report closed by offering seven Resolutions, recommending the enlistment of a State army of ten thousand men, a loan of a million dollars at six per cent, and the appointment of delegates " to meet and confer with delegates from the States of New England or any of them " on the defence of those States and the redress of their grievances.

[1] Cabot to Pickering, Feb. 14, 1804 ; Lodge's Cabot, p. 341. See *ante*, vol. ii. p. 166.

The Senate committee also made a strenuous argument against the President's decision that State militia were in State service unless called for by a United States officer and placed under his direction,[1] and recommended that the subject should be referred to the next session. To the proposition for a conference of the New England States, and to Otis's other Resolutions, the Senate and House assented, October 13, by large majorities, varying in numbers, but amounting to two hundred and sixty against ninety in the case of the proposed convention. The minority in both Houses presented protests, charging the majority with intending more than was avowed. "The reasoning of the report," said the Protest signed by seventy-six members of the House,[2] " is supported by the alarming assumption that the Constitution has failed in its objects, and the people of Massachusetts are absolved from their allegiance, and at liberty to adopt another. In debate it has been reiterated that the Constitution is no longer to be respected, and that revolution is not to be deprecated." The House refused to receive the Protest, as disrespectful. The minority withdrew from further share in these proceedings ; and the majority then, October 19, chose twelve delegates " to meet and confer on the 15th December next with such as may be chosen by any or all of the other New England States upon our public grievances and concerns." The choice was marked

[1] Senate Report of Oct. 18, 1814; Niles, vii. 151.

[2] Niles, vii. 154.

by a conservative spirit not altogether pleasing to Timothy Pickering. George Cabot and Harrison Gray Otis stood at the head of the delegation.

The remonstrances and threats of the minority made the majority cautious, but did not check them. The legislature of Connecticut immediately appointed seven delegates to meet those of Massachusetts at Hartford, December 15, for the purpose of recommending " such measures for the safety and welfare of these States as may consist with our obligations as members of the national Union." [1] In this clause the legislature intended to draw a distinction between obligations to the Union and obligations to the Constitution. To the former the people avowed no hostility ; to .the latter they thought the war had put an end. On that point the committee's report was clear.[2]

Besides Massachusetts and Connecticut the legislature of Rhode Island, by a vote of thirty-nine to twenty-three, appointed, November 5, four delegates to confer at Hartford upon the measures which might be in their power to adopt to restore their rights under the Constitution, " consistently with their obligations." [3] These three States alone chose delegates. The governor and legislature of New Hampshire would probably have joined them had not the Republican council stood in the way. The legislature of Vermont, including its Federalist minority, unanimously declined the invitation.

[1] Niles, vii. 165.    [2] Report; Niles, vii. 164.
[3] Niles, vii. 181.

Immediately after these steps were taken, the autumn elections occurred. Members of Congress were to be chosen, and the people were obliged to vote for or against the Hartford Convention as the issue expressly avowed. President Madison might safely assume that no man voted for Federalist Congressmen in November, 1814, unless he favored the project of a New England Convention. The result was emphatic. Massachusetts chose eighteen Federalists and two Republicans ; Vermont, New Hampshire, Rhode Island, and Connecticut chose only Federalists. In all, New England chose thirty-nine Federalist Congressmen and two Republicans [1] for the Fourteenth Congress. In the Thirteenth Congress, chosen in 1812, when the feeling against the war was supposed to be strongest, the Federalist members from New England numbered thirty, the Republicans eleven.[2]

Beyond New England the autumn elections were less significant, but were still unsatisfactory to the Administration. New Jersey returned to her true sympathies, and as far as her Congressmen expressed her opinions gave unanimous support to the war ; but Pennsylvania, owing to local quarrels, elected five Federalist members; and Maryland elected five Federalists and four Republicans. In spite of the great loss in Federalist members which had occurred in the spring elections in New York, the Federalists numbered sixty-five in the Fourteenth

[1] Niles, ix. 281.          [2] Niles, iv. 268.

Congress ; in the Thirteenth they numbered sixty-eight. The Administration had hoped, and freely asserted, that a strong reaction in favor of the war had followed the burning of Washington and the avowal of England's designs against Maine and the Northwestern territory. The elections showed no such reaction. The war was no more popular than before.

The public apathy was the more alarming because, whatever was the true object of the Hartford Convention, all Republicans believed it to be intended as a step to dissolve the Union, and they supported the Administration chiefly because Madison represented the Union. Federalists might deceive themselves. Probably the men who voted for the Hartford Convention saw its necessary consequences less clearly than they were seen by the men who voted against it. The Republican vote represented the strength of Union sentiment more closely than the disunion sentiment was represented by the Federalist vote. Yet the States from Maryland to Maine chose a majority of Congressmen who were not Republicans. The New England States, New York, New Jersey, Pennsylvania, Delaware, and Maryland returned much more than half the members of Congress, — one hundred and eight in one hundred and eighty-two ; and of these fifty-seven were Federalists, while only fifty-one were Republicans. The unpopularity of the Administration was not easily overestimated when Madison could win no more support than this, at a

time when the public believed a vote for Federalism
to be a vote for disunion.

" I give you the most serious assurance," wrote Randolph in an open letter to James Lloyd, of Massachusetts,[1] remonstrating against the Convention, " that
nothing less than the shameful conduct of the enemy and
the complection of certain occurrences to the eastward
could have sustained Mr. Madison after the disgraceful
affair at Washington.    The public indignation would
have overwhelmed in one common ruin himself and his
hireling newspapers."

Randolph's political judgments were commonly
mistaken, but in this instance he proved himself to
be at least partially right; for at the next election,
six months later, when the current had turned decidedly in Madison's favor, Randolph after a sharp
contest defeated Eppes and recovered control· of his
district.    Virginia could hardly have chosen a representative less calculated to please Madison.

The President himself betrayed unusual signs of
distress.    Nothing in Madison's character was more
remarkable than the placidity with which he commonly met anxieties that would have crushed a
sensitive man ; but the shock of defeat at Bladensburg, the flight from Washington, and the anxieties that followed broke him down.    William Wirt
visited Washington October 14, before the action
of the Massachusetts legislature was yet completed.
After viewing the ruins of the White House, a

[1] Randolph's Letter to Lloyd, Dec. 15, 1814; Niles, vii. 258.

" mournful monument of American imbecility and improvidence," he called upon the President at Colonel Tayloe's Octagon House, which Serurier had occupied, but which Madison took for his residence after his return.

" P—— and I called on the President," wrote Wirt in a private letter.[1]  " He looks miserably shattered and woe-begone.  In short, he looked heart-broken.  His mind is full of the New England sedition.  He introduced the subject and continued to press it, painful as it obviously was to him.  I denied the probability, even the possibility, that the yeomanry of the North could be induced to place themselves under the power and protection of England, and diverted the conversation to another topic ; but he took the first opportunity to return to it, and convinced me that his heart and mind were painfully full of the subject."

No misconduct of New England alone would have so unmanned a Virginia President.  Madison's worst troubles lay nearer home ; Massachusetts made only the last straw in his burden.  Jefferson, with his usual kindliness, tried to console and encourage him ; but Jefferson's consolations proved only the difficulty of finding words or arguments to warrant satisfaction with the past or hope for the future.

" In the late events at Washington," wrote Jefferson, September 24,[2] " I have felt so much for you that I cannot withhold the expression of my sympathies.  For

---

[1] Kennedy's Life of Wirt, i. 339.
[2] Jefferson to Madison, Sept. 24, 1814 ; Works, vi. 385.

although every reasonable man must be sensible that all
you can do is to order, — that execution must depend on
others, and failures be imputed to them alone, — yet I
know that when such failures happen they affect even
those who have done everything they could to prevent
them. Had General Washington himself been now at
the head of our affairs, the same event would probably
have happened."

Jefferson's estimate of Washington's abilities was
lower than that commonly accepted; and his rule that
a President's responsibility ceased after giving an
order, besides ignoring the President's responsibility
for the selection of agents, seemed to destroy the
foundation of the public service. "I never doubted
that the plans of the President were wise and sufficient," wrote Jefferson to Monroe.[1] "Their failure
we all impute, (1) to the insubordinate temper of Armstrong, and (2) to the indecision of Winder." The
rule that an administrator might select any agent,
however incompetent, without incurring responsibility
for the agent's acts, was one which in private affairs
Jefferson would hardly have accepted.

Yet Jefferson's opinions probably expressed Republican sentiment in Virginia, and showed better than
any other evidence the course of thought among
Madison's friends. In that respect his expressions
retained permanent value. The Virginians were
willing to throw off responsibility for public disaster;
and they naturally threw it on New England, since

[1] Jefferson to Monroe, Jan. 1, 1815; Works, vi. 407.

New England challenged it. Writing to his friend William Short, Jefferson spoke of the threatening attitude of Massachusetts : [1] —

" Some apprehend danger from the defection of Massachusetts. It is a disagreeable circumstance, but not a dangerous one. If they become neutral, we are sufficient for one enemy without them, and in fact we get no aid from them now."

Probably most Virginians shared this belief, at least so far as concerned the aid rendered by Massachusetts to the war. In truth, Massachusetts gave little aid, and made a profession of her wish to give none at all; but the difficulty did not end there. Massachusetts and Virginia were States of the first class. The census of 1810 allotted to Massachusetts, including Maine, a population of about seven hundred thousand ; to Virginia, a white population of five hundred and fifty-one thousand, and a colored population of four hundred and twenty-three thousand, — nine hundred and seventy-four thousand in all. In the ratio of representation Massachusetts counted for twenty, Virginia for twenty-three. The quota of Massachusetts in the direct tax was \$316,000 ; that of Virginia was \$369,000. On the scale furnished by these data, Virginia should have contributed in support of the war about one eighth or one seventh more men and money than were required from Massachusetts. The actual result was different.

[1] Jefferson to Short, Nov. 28, 1814 ; Works, vi. 398.

The amount of money contributed by Massachusetts could not be compared with that contributed by Virginia, partly because of the severe blockade which closed the Virginian ports. The net revenue from customs derived from Virginia in 1814 was $4,000; that from Massachusetts was $1,600,000.[1] Unlike the customs revenue, the receipts from internal revenue were supposed to be reasonably equalized, so that each State should contribute in due proportion. According to the official return, dated Nov. 24, 1815, the total internal duties which had then been paid to the collectors for the year 1814 in Massachusetts was $198,400; in Virginia it was $193,500. The total amount then paid to the Treasury was $178,400 in Massachusetts, and $157,300 in Virginia.[2] The direct tax was fixed by Congress and was assumed by the State in Virginia, but regularly assessed in Massachusetts. One paid $316,000; the other, $369,000. The total revenue derived from Massachusetts was therefore $2,114,400 in the year 1814; that from Virginia, $566,500. Of the loans effected in the same year, Massachusetts took a small part considering her means, — hardly a million dollars. Virginia took still less, — only two hundred thousand.[3]

In money, Massachusetts contributed four times as much as Virginia to support the war, and her contributions were paid in Treasury notes or paper

[1] Seybert, p. 436 ; Pitkin, p. 415.

[2] Statement, etc. ; State Papers, Finance, iii. 44–48.

[3] State Papers ; Finance, ii. 846, 847.

equivalent to coin, — not in the notes of banks worthless beyond the State. In men, the estimate was affected by the inquiry whether the militia were to be considered as protecting the national government or the State. Owing to the presence of the British in the Chesapeake, Virginia kept a large force of militia on foot, some of which were in garrison at Norfolk, and a few were on the field of Bladensburg. Massachusetts also was obliged to call out a considerable force of militia to protect or garrison national posts.

The relative numbers of regular troops were also somewhat doubtful; but the paymaster of the army reported Oct. 26, 1814, that he had distributed in bounties during the year $237,400 for Massachusetts, and $160,962 for Virginia.[1] During the year, six regular regiments — the Ninth, Twenty-first, Thirty-third, Thirty-fourth, Fortieth, and Forty-fifth — recruited in Massachusetts. Three — the Twelfth, Twentieth, and Thirty-fifth — recruited in Virginia. Perhaps the military aid furnished by the different sections of the seaboard could be better understood by following the familiar divisions. New England furnished thirteen regiments. New York, New Jersey, and Pennsylvania furnished fifteen. The Southern States, from Delaware to South Carolina inclusive, furnished ten. Of all the States in the Union New York alone supplied more regular soldiers than Mas-

[1] Letter of Paymaster Brent, Oct. 26, 1814 ; State papers, Military Affairs, i. 519.

sachusetts, and Massachusetts supplied as many as were furnished by Virginia and the two Carolinas together.

Judged by these standards, either Massachusetts had done more than her share, or Virginia had done less than hers. The tests were material, and took no moral element in account; but in moral support the relative failure of Massachusetts was not beyond dispute. Public opinion in New England was almost equally divided, and the pronounced opposition to the war was much greater in the Eastern States than in the Southern; but in the serious work of fighting, New England claimed a share of credit. In the little army at Niagara New York supplied the Major-General, Virginia and Massachusetts the two brigadiers; but Winfield Scott's brigade was chiefly composed of New England men; and when, nearly half a century afterward, Scott in his old age was obliged to choose between his allegiance to his State and allegiance to the Union, the memory of the New England troops who had won for him his first renown had its influence in raising his mind above the local sympathies which controlled other Virginia officers. Without reflecting on Virginia courage or patriotism, the New England Republicans were warranted in claiming that not the Virginia regiments, but the Massachusetts Ninth, the Vermont Eleventh, the Massachusetts Twenty-first, and the Connecticut Twenty-fifth routed the Royal Scots at Chippawa, and bayoneted the British artillerymen at Lundy's Lane, and stormed

Drummond's intrenchments at Fort Erie. They could add that without their sailors the war might have been less successful than it was; and they would have been justified had they asked Jefferson to glance at his latest newspaper as he wrote that Massachusetts gave no aid to the war, and read the despatch of Johnston Blakeley reporting that the New England crew of the "Wasp" had sunk the "Avon" in the middle of a British fleet.[1] Virginians did not take kindly to the ocean; and on land, owing to the accidents of war, no Virginia regiment was offered a chance to win distinction.

These comparisons were of little weight to prove that New England was either better or worse than other parts of the Union, but they showed that the difficulties that depressed Madison's mind were not merely local. He might have disregarded the conduct of the State governments of Massachusetts and Connecticut had he enjoyed the full support of his own great Republican States, Pennsylvania, Virginia, and North Carolina. Except New York, Kentucky, Tennessee, and perhaps Ohio, no State gave to the war the full and earnest co-operation it needed. Again and again, from the beginning of the troubles with England, Madison had acted on the conviction that at last the people were aroused; but in every instance he had been disappointed. After the burning of Washington, he was more than ever convinced that the moment had come when the entire people would

[1] Niles's Register, Nov. 26, 1814.

rally in their self-respect; but he was met by the
Hartford Convention and the November elections.    If
the people would not come to the aid of their government at such a moment, Madison felt that nothing
could move them.    Peace was his last hope.

## CHAPTER IX.

CONGRESS was summoned to meet in extra session September 19, by a proclamation issued August 8, before the capture of Washington. On the appointed day the members appeared, but found their building in ashes, and met like vagrants, without a shelter they could call their own. The President caused the only public office that had been spared, to be fitted for their use. Partly owing to the exertions of Dr. Thornton, the head of the Bureau of Patents, partly owing to the tornado of August 25, the building used as Post and Patent Office was not burned. There Congress was obliged to hold its sessions, in such discomfort as it had never before known.

The President sent his Annual Message September 20, which informed Congress that it had been specially summoned to supply " any inadequacy in the existing provision for the wants of the Treasury," as well as to be ready for whatever result might be reached by the negotiation at Ghent. Two thirds of the Message related to the operations of war, and the President seemed rather disposed to suppress than to avow his difficulties, but the little he said of them

was heavy with anxiety. He announced that July 1
five million dollars remained in the Treasury, and
that " large sums " must be provided ; but he did
not add that the loan had failed, or that the banks
and Treasury had suspended specie payments. He
did not say that the regular army and the militia
system were inadequate to national defence ; but
he declared " the necessity of immediate measures
for filling the ranks of the regular army," and of
giving " the requisite energy and efficiency " to the
militia : —

" From this view of the national affairs Congress will
be urged to take up, without delay, as well the subject
of pecuniary supplies as that of military force, and on
a scale commensurate with the extent and the character
which the war has assumed. It is not to be disguised
that the situation of our country calls for its greatest
efforts. . . . From such an adversary, hostility in its
greatest force and in its worst forms may be looked
for."

The President threw on the Secretaries of the
Treasury and of War the ungrateful task of announcing the details of their need. Secretary Campbell
was first to address Congress, and the tone of his
report on the state of the finances received emphasis
from the resignation which he sent at the same
time to the President. Campbell's annual report of
September 23 was an admission of incompetence.
He had paid, he said, nearly twenty millions from
the Treasury between January and July ; twenty-

seven millions more were payable between July and the following January. For the year 1815 the Treasury would require at least as much as for 1814. Congress must therefore speedily provide at least seventy-four millions for the service between July 1, 1814, and Dec. 31, 1815. He ventured to suggest no means of obtaining this sum, or any amount approaching it.

July 1 the Treasury contained $4,722,000. From its various sources of revenue it could expect $4,840,000 during the remainder of the year; from loans already contracted, $4,320,000. In all, $13,822,000 might be considered as in hand, which was one half the sum immediately required. For the year 1815 the revenue in all its branches might produce $8,200,000, leaving $39,000,000 to be provided. Twenty-two millions were the extent of Campbell's resources, but fifty-two million dollars more must be raised merely to carry on the government as it had been administered in the past year.

The plan of finance adopted by Gallatin at the outset of the war assumed that all deficits could be covered by loans.

" The experience of the present year," said Campbell, " furnishes ground to doubt whether this be practicable, at least in the shape in which loans have hitherto been attempted. Nor is it even certain that the establishing and pledging of revenues adequate to the punctual payment of the interest and eventual reimbursement of the principal of the sums which will be required for the year 1815, would enable the Treasury to obtain them through the medium of loans effected in the ordinary way."

Loans being impracticable, Campbell discussed the possibility of using Treasury notes. Eight millions were already in issue, and of these more than four millions would fall due before December 31. Campbell considered that six millions in Treasury notes was about as large a sum as could easily be circulated, but by issuing notes of small denominations he hoped to raise the amount to ten millions.

From all sources Campbell hoped to obtain about twenty-four million dollars of the seventy-four millions required. For the remaining fifty millions he had no suggestion to offer. The means for new and extraordinary exertions, he said, "ought to be provided." He declared that the resources of the nation were ample, — which was true, but was also the most discouraging symptom of the time; for if the people, with ample resources, as he asserted, refused to come to the support of their own government on any terms, their decision must be accepted as final. Besides throwing upon Congress all these difficulties, without a suggestion of his own, Campbell added that Congress would be required to exert its powers to remedy the evils of the currency and the suspension of specie payments.

Congress on hearing this financial statement regarded the situation as desperate. " Tell Dr. Madison," Senator Lacock was reported [1] to have said to the President's private secretary, "that we are now willing to submit to his Philadelphia lawyer for head of the Treasury. The public patient is so very sick that we must swallow anything, however nauseous." Dallas was nominated October 5, and confirmed the next day without opposition, as Secretary of the Treasury. No stronger proof could have been given of the helplessness of Congress, for Dallas was a man who under no other circumstances could have obtained a ray of popular favor.

Dallas's character was high, his abilities undoubted, his experience large; but for ten years he had been one of the least popular men in Pennsylvania, the target of newspaper abuse and the champion of political independence. The people reasonably required that their leaders should more or less resemble some popular type, and if the result was monotonous the fault was in the society, not in its politics or its politicians; but Dallas was like no ordinary type in any people. His tone of intellectual and social superiority, his powdered hair, old-fashioned dress and refined manners, his free habits of expense, and the insubordination even more than the vivacity of his temper irritated the prejudices of his party.[2] He had little respect for Presidents, and none for Congress. For Jefferson and Virginia doctrines he felt distrust, which was returned. Earnest in temper and

---

[1] Ingersoll's History, ii. 253.
[2] Ingersoll's History, ii. 254, 257.

emphatic in tone, even to the point of tears and tropical excitability, Dallas came to Washington as though to lead a forlorn hope, — caring little for parties and less for ambition, but bent upon restoring to the government the powers that his friend Gallatin, too easily as he thought, had allowed to slip from its grasp.

The difficulties of the Treasury when Dallas took charge of it were not easily exaggerated. His own description,[1] given some six weeks afterward, made no disguise of them. " The Treasury," he said, " was suffering under every kind of embarrassment. The demands upon it were great in amount, while the means to satisfy them were comparatively small, precarious in collection, and difficult in their application. . . . The means consisted, first, of the fragment of an authority to borrow money when nobody was disposed to lend, and to issue Treasury notes which none but necessitous creditors or contractors in distress . . . seemed willing to accept;" second, of bank-credits, chiefly in the South and West, rendered largely useless by the suspension of specie payments; third, of the current receipts of taxes, also useless because paid chiefly in Treasury notes. The Treasury was bankrupt. The formal stoppage of payments in interest on the debt was announced, November 9, by an official letter from the secretary, notifying holders of government securities in Boston that the

[1] Dallas to William Lowndes, Nov. 27, 1814; State Papers, Finance, ii. 872.

Treasury could not meet its obligations, and that " the government was unable to avert or to control this course of events." [1] After that date the Treasury made no further pretence of solvency.

From this situation the government could be rescued only by a great effort; and obviously the currency must be first restored, for until some system of exchange could be established, every increase of taxation would merely increase unavailable bank deposits. Fifty millions of Southern bank-notes, locked in the vaults of Southern banks, would not pay the over-due interest on government bonds at Boston.

To this subject every one turned, but the schemes that seemed to have a chance of adoption were only two. The first came from President Jefferson, and was strongly pressed by the South. As Jefferson explained it, the plan seemed as simple as his plans were apt to be; he proposed to issue twenty millions in promissory notes every year as long as might be necessary. " Our experience," he told the President,[2] " has proved it [a paper currency] may be run up to two or three hundred millions without more than doubling what would be the prices of things under a sufficient medium, or say a metallic one." His plan included an increase of taxation by two million dollars every year to redeem the same amount of Treasury issues.

[1] Dallas to the Commissioner of Loans at Boston, Nov. 9, 1814; Niles, vii. 270.

[2] Jefferson to Madison, Oct. 15, 1814; Works, vi. 391.

Obviously the insuperable obstacle to this plan was the paper money of the State banks, which already stood at discounts varying from ten to fifty per cent in specie, and in any large quantity could not be discounted at all. Until private paper should be abolished, public or government paper could not be brought into common use. Jefferson's views on this, as on the whole subject, were interesting.

"The banks have discontinued themselves," he explained.[1]  "We are now without any medium; and necessity, as well as patriotism and confidence, will make us all eager to receive Treasury notes if founded on specific taxes. Congress may now borrow of the public, and without interest, all the money they may want, to the amount of a competent circulation, by merely issuing their own promissory notes of proper denominations for the larger purposes of circulation, but not for the small. Leave that door open for the entrance of metallic money. . . . The State legislatures should be immediately urged to relinquish the right of establishing banks of discount. Most of them will comply on patriotic principles, under the convictions of the moment; and the non-complying may be crowded into concurrence by legitimate devices."

Instead of "banks of discount," Jefferson probably meant to say banks of issue, although the Virginia school was hostile to all banks, and possibly he wished to destroy the whole system. If the scheme were adopted, twenty million dollars in paper money would not supply the wants of the Treasury, which required

[1] Jefferson to Thomas Cooper, Sept. 10, 1814; Works, vi. 375.

at least fifty millions within a year. The resource
was limited, even if the States could be compelled
to stop the issue of private notes, — which was extremely doubtful in the temper of Massachusetts and
with the leanings of Chief-Justice Marshall. Jefferson did not touch upon legal tender; but the assumption of power implied in the issue of paper money
seemed to require that the government should exercise the right of obliging its creditors to accept it.
The actual interest-bearing Treasury notes stood then
at a discount of about twenty per cent. The proposed
paper money could hardly circulate at a better rate,
and coin was not to be obtained. Under such conditions the notes must be a forced currency if they
were to circulate at all.

The scheme was reported to the House by the
Committee of Ways and Means through its chairman,
John W. Eppes, Jefferson's son-in-law.[1] For the report Eppes was alone responsible, and the plan in
his hands varied in some points from that of Jefferson. Starting from the admitted premise that loans
were not to be obtained, and that money could not
be transferred from one point to another in any existing medium at the disposition of government, Eppes
proposed to issue Treasury notes " in sums sufficiently small for the ordinary purposes of society,"
which were not to be made payable on demand in
coin, but might at any time be exchanged for eight
per cent bonds, and were to be received " in all pay-

[1] Report of Oct. 10, 1814; State Papers, Finance, ii. 854.

ments for public lands and taxes." Nothing was
said of legal tender, or of driving bank-notes from
circulation; but Eppes proposed to double the taxes
at one stroke.

Eppes's scheme lost the advantages of Jefferson's
without gaining any of its own. It abandoned the
hope of abolishing bank paper; and in want of such
a restraint on private issues, the proposed government paper would merely add one more element of
confusion to the chaos already existing. Eppes further altered Jefferson's plan by adding some ten
millions instead of two millions to the burden of
taxation; but even Jefferson protested that this part
of the scheme was impracticable.

" This is a dashing proposition," he wrote to Monroe;[1]
" but if Congress pass it, I shall consider it sufficient
evidence that their constituents generally can pay the
tax. No man has greater confidence than I have in the
spirit of the people to a rational extent. Whatever they
can, they will. But without either market or medium, I
know not how it is to be done. All markets abroad and
all at home are shut to us, so that we have been feeding
our horses on wheat. Before the day of collection, bank-
notes will be but as oak-leaves; and of specie there is
not within all the United States one half of the proposed
amount of the taxes."

This was the situation of the Virginia scheme
when Dallas took the matter in hand. Immediately
after entering into office, Dallas wrote to Eppes an

[1] Jefferson to Monroe, Oct. 16, 1814; Works, vi. 394.

official letter, dated October 17, expressing views wholly at variance with the Virginia plan.

" Under favorable circumstances and to a limited extent," he said,[1] " an emission of Treasury notes would probably afford relief ; but Treasury notes are an expensive and precarious substitute either for coin or for bank-notes, charged as they are with a growing interest, productive of no countervailing profit or emolument, and exposed to every breath of popular prejudice or alarm. The establishment of a national institution operating upon credit combined with capital, and regulated by prudence and good faith, is after all the only efficient remedy for the disordered condition of our circulating medium. While accomplishing that object, too, there will be found under the auspices of such an institution a safe depository for the public treasure and a constant auxiliary to the public credit. But whether the issues of a paper currency proceed from the national Treasury or from a national Bank, the acceptance of the paper in a course of payments and receipts must be forever optional with the citizens. The extremity of that day cannot be anticipated when any honest and enlightened statesman will again venture upon the desperate expedient of a tender-law."

Without a tender-law the Virginia scheme would hardly answer the purposes required, since the government must restrain the issue of paper within a limit too narrow for usefulness. Dallas did not press this point, but developed his own scheme, which required,

[1] Dallas to Eppes, Oct. 17, 1814 ; State Papers, Finance, ii. 866.

like that of Eppes, a duplication of taxes to produce twenty-one million dollars, and the creation of a
national Bank with a capital of fifty million dollars.

Either Eppes's or Dallas's plan might answer the
immediate object of providing a currency, and both
required the exercise of implied powers by Congress.
Apparently Congress had only to choose, but in truth
choice was most difficult.    The House readily adopted
Dallas's recommendation in principle, and voted, October 24, by sixty-six to forty, that it was expedient
to establish a national Bank; but the problem of
establishing a specie-paying bank without specie
passed its powers.    Dallas abandoned the attempt
at the outset.    He proposed a bank of fifty millions
capital, of which forty-four millions might be subscribed in government bonds and Treasury notes,
and six millions in coin.    The bank was at once to
lend to government thirty millions, — of course in
bank-notes, — and no one denied that an immediate
suspension of specie payments must follow such an
issue.    To any bank, strong or weak, the old Virginia influence represented by Eppes was hostile;
and to a bank insolvent from the start the Federalists also were opposed.

When the bill, reported November 7, was printed,
it was found to contain a provision authorizing the
suspension of specie payments at the President's discretion.    The discussion began November 14, and
every successive day revealed objections and increased
the opposition.    Calhoun complicated the subject

still further by bringing forward, November 16 a plan of his own, requiring the capital to consist " one tenth in specie, and the remainder in specie or in Treasury notes to be hereafter issued," and taking away all government control. Ingham of Pennsylvania, representing Dallas, combated Calhoun with force, but could not make his own measure agreeable to the House. His phrase in regard to the suspension of specie payments was significant. Congress, he said, would be to blame for " frantic enthusiasm " if it did not provide for the case. " It may happen, and probably will happen, that their specie payments cannot be continued, and what will then be the situation of the bank ? Failing to fulfil the purposes designed, its credit is blighted, its operations are stopped, and its charter violated ; and if this should take place before your Treasury notes are sold, the government will scarce obtain a moment's relief." That the new bank could not pay specie was obvious. The Bank of England itself could not pay specie, and had not attempted to do so for nearly twenty years.

The House in committee adopted Calhoun's amendment by a majority of about sixty, in spite of Ingham's opposition ; and thus substituted for Dallas's scheme a large private bank, over which the government was to exercise no control, with a capital of fifty millions, nine tenths of which were to be Treasury notes. The House then discovered so many unforeseen difficulties, that November 25 it recommitted the bill to a select committee, of which Lowndes, Calhoun, Ingham, Forsyth, and two Federalists were members.

Dallas was obliged openly to enter the lists against Calhoun, and wrote to the committee a letter, dated November 27,[1] sounding like a defiance : " The dividend on the funded debt has not been punctually paid ; a large amount of Treasury notes has already been dishonored ; and the hope of preventing further injury and reproach in transacting business with the Treasury is too visionary to afford a moment's consolation." Calhoun's scheme, he plainly intimated, was impracticable and mischievous.

The next day, November 28, Lowndes brought back Calhoun's bill to the House, together with Dallas's letter, and told the House that the committee could come to no agreement. Upon this admission of helplessness, Hanson addressed the House in a speech which seemed to carry Federalist exultation to the extremest point. Protesting his anxiety to defend the country, Hanson uttered a cry of triumph over the destruction of the government : —

" Not only had government bills been dishonored and the interest of the public debt remained unpaid, but . . . so completely empty was the Treasury and destitute of credit, that funds could not be obtained to defray the current ordinary expenses of the different Departments. Disgraceful, humiliating as the fact was, it ought not to be concealed from the nation, and he felt

[1] Dallas to Lowndes, Nov. 27, 1814 ; State Papers, ii. 872.

it his duty to state to the House that the Department of State was so bare of money as to be unable to pay even its stationery bill. The government was subsisting upon the drainings of unchartered banks in the District, which felt themselves compelled to contribute their means lest the rod *in terrorem* which was held over them should be applied, and an Act of incorporation refused."

No one contradicted or answered Hanson. The House wavered in incapacity that suggested dissolution. At last Richard M. Johnson, in order to force a decision right or wrong, moved the previous question and brought the House to a vote. Then the majority turned against Calhoun, as they had before turned against Dallas, and rejected the bill by a vote of one hundred and four to forty-nine.

The Southern preference for government paper currency lay at the bottom of Calhoun's scheme as of Jefferson's, and seemed to Dallas to combine ignorance with dishonesty. Treasury notes bearing interest could not be made to serve as a currency, and were useless as a foundation for government paper. "What use is there," asked Ingersoll,[1] "in such a mass of banking machinery to give circulation to some millions of Treasury notes? Why not issue them at once without this unwieldy, this unnecessary medium?" Yet when Bolling Hall of Georgia, in pursuance of Macon's aphorism that "paper money never was beat," moved, November 12, Resolutions

[1] Annals of Congress, 1814-1815, p. 606.

authorizing the issue of Treasury notes as legal tender, the House refused to consider it by a vote of
ninety-five to forty-two.    Eppes did not vote; Calhoun voted against it, and of the twenty-five Southern members who supported it Macon and Stanford
were the most prominent.

Nothing could be plainer than that the House must
ultimately come to inconvertible government paper,
whether issued by the Treasury or by a Bank.    Dallas, Eppes, and Calhoun were all agreed on that
point, if on no other; but after Congress had sat
two months and a half, the House was no nearer a
decision than when it met.    The Federalists, voting
at one time with Calhoun, at another with Dallas,
were able to paralyze action.    Eppes wrote to Dallas,
December 2, inviting further information; and Dallas wrote back the same day, recounting the needs
of the Treasury for the current month, merely on
account of the national debt.    Dallas reported that
$5,726,000 in Treasury notes and dividends were due,
or would fall due by January 1; and that including
unavailable bank-credits, and subject to possible con-
tingencies, the Treasury might contain resources to
meet these demands to the amount of $3,972,000.[1]
Eppes could do no more for immediate relief than
report a bill for the issue of some ten millions more
of interest-bearing Treasury notes, which was passed
without debate and became law, December 26, without improving the situation.

[1] Dallas to Eppes, Dec. 2, 1814; State Papers, Finance, ii. 877.

The House also passed the heavy tax-bills without much opposition except from Federalists who wished to stop military operations on the part of the government. Between thirty and forty members, or about one half of the Federalists, carried their opposition to that point. The bill raising the direct tax to six million dollars passed the House, December 22, by a vote of one hundred and six to fifty-three, and passed the Senate, January 5, 1815, by twenty-three to seven. Dallas and Eppes hoped to raise about twenty million dollars through the new taxation, or twice what had been previously attempted. Jefferson held that these taxes could not be paid, and expressed his opinion without reserve.

" If anything could revolt our citizens against the war," wrote Jefferson, November 28,[1] " it would be the extravagance with which they are about to be taxed. . . . The taxes proposed cannot be paid. How can a people who cannot get fifty cents a bushel for their wheat, while they pay twelve dollars a bushel for their salt, pay five times the amount of taxes they ever paid before? Yet this will be the case in all the States south of the Potomac."

If any conclusion was intended to be drawn from the official return[2] sent to Congress, October 13, of internal taxes received to that date in each State, the evil predicted by Jefferson seemed already to exist. In Massachusetts, of taxes to the amount of

---

[1] Jefferson to Short, Nov. 28. 1814 ; Works, vi. 398.

[2] Statement, etc. ; State Papers, Finance, ii. 861.

$200,000, accrued for the first two quarters of the
year, $170,000 had been received before October 10.
In New York $393,000 had accrued, and $303,000 had
been received; thus New York was nearly one fourth
in arrears. Pennsylvania was worse; of $470,000
accrued the government had received $280,000, —
leaving two fifths in arrears. Virginia was in somewhat worse condition than Pennsylvania; of $247,000
accrued $136,000 had been paid, — leaving four ninths
in arrears.

Yet Pennsylvania and Virginia paid taxes in their
own depreciated bank paper, while New York and
New England paid chiefly in Treasury notes. The
new taxes were still to be paid in the same medium, although the laws gave no express authority
for it. In the next Congress, when the subject
was discussed, Wright of Maryland said: [1] " When
Congress passed the revenue laws and imposed the
six million and three million land tax, did they
contemplate the payment of specie? No! they knew
the people had it not, and of course could not
pay it. . . . Does any man doubt that Congress intended these taxes being paid in bank paper? Nay,
has not the Secretary of the Treasury . . . sealed
this construction of the law by taking the bank
paper in discharge for these taxes?" That the
bank paper was worth less than Treasury notes was
shown by the Southern States paying their taxes in
such paper, when they might equally well have paid

[1] Annals of Congress, 1815-1816, p. 1435.

them in Treasury notes except for the difference in value.

The medium of depreciated ·and depreciating bank paper in which the taxes were to be paid, secured the States outside of New England from intolerable pressure by giving the means of indefinite depreciation; but to the government such a resource meant merely a larger variety of bank-credits, which were of no certain value even in the towns where the banks existed, and were of no value at all elsewhere. The burden of taxation would be thrown chiefly on New England; and if the Hartford Convention did nothing else, it was sure to take measures for sequestering the proceeds of taxation in New England for military purposes. The hope of restoring the finances by taxation was faint. Until the currency could be established and exchanges made secure, the government was helpless.

The House having broken down November 28, the Senate next took the matter in hand. Rufus King reported, December 2, a bill to incorporate a bank, which was in effect the bill recommended by Dallas. After a week's consideration the Senate passed the bill, December 9, by the vote of seventeen to fourteen, — King and the Federalists, with four Republican senators, voting against it. The House referred it to the Committee of Ways and Means, which reported it, December 14, with amendments. The debate began December 23, and was cut short December 27 by C. J. Ingersoll, who by the close vote of seventy-two to seventy obliged the House to call for the previous question, and order the bill to its third reading. This energy was followed by a reaction; the bill was recommitted for amendment, again reported, and vehemently attacked.

Never had the House shown itself more feeble. The Federalists took the lead in debate; and January 2 Daniel Webster, in a speech that placed him at the head of the orators of the time, dictated the action of Congress: —

"What sort of an institution, sir, is this? It looks less like a bank than like a department of government. It will be properly the paper-money department. Its capital is government debts; the amount of issues will depend on government necessities; government in effect absolves itself from its own debts to the bank, and by way of compensation absolves the bank from its own contracts with others. This is indeed a wonderful scheme of finance. The government is to grow rich because it is to borrow without the obligation of repaying, and is to borrow of a bank which issues paper without the liability to redeem it. . . . They provide for an unlimited issue of paper in an entire exemption from payment. They found their bank in the first place on the discredit of government, and then hope to enrich government out of the insolvency of the bank."

Webster was a master of antithesis, and the proposed bank was in effect what he described; but had he been a member of the British Parliament he might have made the same objections, with little alteration, to the Bank of England. The Hartford Convention was in session while he spoke.  Every word of his speech was a shock to the government and the Union, for his only suggestion was equivalent to doing nothing.  He moved to instruct the committee to report a bill creating a bank with thirty millions of capital, composed one fourth of specie and three fourths of government securities ; without power to suspend specie payments, and without obligation to lend three fifths of its capital to the government.  To such a bank he would give his support, " not as a measure of temporary policy, or an expedient to find means of relief from the present poverty of the Treasury," but as an institution most useful in times of peace.

The House came to a vote the same day, and divided eighty-one to eighty.  Then the Speaker, Langdon Cheves, rose, and after denouncing the proposed bank as " a dangerous, unexampled, and he might almost say a desperate resort," gave his casting vote against the bill.

No sooner had the House struck this blow at Dallas than it shrank back.  The next day, amid complaints and objections, it reconsidered its matured decision by the sudden majority of one hundred and seven to fifty-four.  Once more the bill was recommitted, and once more reported, January 6, in the form that Webster proposed.  Weary of their own instability, the majority hastened to vote.  Most of the Federalists supported the bill ; but Grosvenor of New York, one of the ablest, frankly said what every one felt, that the proposed institution could not be a specie bank, or get a million of its notes into circulation. "The government relying on it would be disappointed, and ruin soon stare them in the face." With this understanding the House passed the bill, January 7, by a vote of one hundred and twenty to thirty-eight; and the Senate, after a struggle with the House, accepted it, January 20, by a vote of twenty to fourteen.

Dallas was not a man to be easily daunted even in so desperate a situation. After ten days deliberation, the President sent to Congress a veto message.

"The most the bank could effect," said Madison, "and the most it could be expected to aim at, would be to keep the institution alive by limited and local transactions . . . until a change from war to peace should enable it, by a flow of specie into its vaults and a removal of the external demand for it, to derive its contemplated emoluments from a safe and full extension of its operations."

"I hope this will satisfy our friends," wrote Webster to his brother,[1] "that it was not a bank likely to favor the Administration." Either with or without such a bank, the Administration was equally helpless. The veto left the Treasury, February 1, without a resource in prospect. The unsatisfied demands reached nearly twenty millions. The cash balance, chiefly in bank-credits, was little more than six millions. A further deficit of forty millions re-

[1] Letter to E. Webster, Jan. 30, 1814; Webster's Correspondence, i. 250, 251.

mained to be provided above the estimated revenue of 1815. United States six-per-cents commanded only a nominal price, between fifty and sixty cents on the dollar,[1] and were quoted in Boston at a discount of forty cents.[2] Treasury notes being in demand for taxes, were worth about seventy-five cents in the dollar. Dallas had no serious hope of carrying on the government. In a letter to the Committee of Ways and Means, dated January 17, he could only propose to add six millions more to the taxes, issue fifteen millions in Treasury notes, and borrow twenty-five millions on any terms that could be obtained. In making these recommendations he avowed in grave words his want of confidence in their result : [3] —

" In making the present communication I feel, sir, that I have performed my duty to the Legislature and to the country ; but when I perceive that more than forty millions of dollars must be raised for the service of the year 1815, by an appeal to public credit through the medium of the Treasury notes and loans, I am not without sensations of extreme solicitude."

Young George Ticknor of Boston happened to be in the gallery of the House of Representatives when Eppes read this letter, January 21, and the next day he wrote,[4] —

[1] Review of Dallas's Report; Boston " Advertiser," Dec. 1815.

[2] Niles, vii. ; Supplement, p. 176.

[3] Dallas to Eppes, Jan. 17, 1817 ; State Papers, Finance, ii. 885.

[4] Life of George Ticknor, i. 31.

" The last remarkable event in the history of this remarkable Congress is Dallas's report. You can imagine nothing like the dismay with which it has filled the Democratic party. All his former communications were but emollients and palliations compared with this final disclosure of the bankruptcy of the nation. Mr. Eppes as Chancellor of the Exchequer, or Chairman of the Committee of Ways and Means, read it in his place yesterday, and when he had finished, threw it upon the table with expressive violence, and turning round to Mr. Gaston, asked him with a bitter levity between jest and earnest, —

" ' Well, sir! will your party take the government if we will give it up to them?'

" ' No, sir!' said Gaston; . . . ' No, sir! Not unless you will give it to us as we gave it to you!'"

## CHAPTER X.

WHILE Dallas struggled with Congress to obtain the means of establishing a currency in order to pay the army, Monroe carried on a similar struggle in order to obtain an army to pay. On this point, as on the financial issue, Virginian ideas did not accord with the wishes of Government. The prejudice against a regular army was stimulated by the evident impossibility of raising or supporting it. Once more Jefferson expressed the common feeling of his Virginia neighbors.[1]

" We must prepare for interminable war," he wrote to Monroe, October 16. " To this end we should put our house in order by providing men and money to an indefinite extent. The former may be done by classing our militia, and assigning each class to the description of duties for which it is fit. It is nonsense to talk of regulars. They are not to be had among a people so easy and happy at home as ours. We might as well rely on calling down an army of angels from heaven."

As Jefferson lost the habits of power and became once more a Virginia planter, he reverted to the opinions and prejudices of his earlier life and of the

[1] Jefferson to Monroe, Oct. 16, 1814; Works, vi. 394.

society in which he lived. As Monroe grew accustomed to the exercise and the necessities of power, he threw aside Virginian ideas and accepted the responsibilities of government. On the same day when Jefferson wrote to Monroe that it was nonsense to talk of regulars, Monroe wrote to Congress that it was nonsense to talk of militia. The divergence between Monroe and Jefferson was even greater than between Dallas and Eppes.

"It may be stated with confidence," wrote Monroe to Congress,[1] "that at least three times the force in militia has been employed at our principal cities, along the coast and on the frontier, in marching to and returning thence, that would have been necessary in regular troops; and that the expense attending it has been more than proportionately augmented from the difficulty if not the impossibility of preserving the same degree of system in the militia as in the regular service."

In Monroe's opinion a regular force was an object "of the highest importance." He told the Senate committee that the army, which was only thirty-four thousand strong on the first of October, should be raised to its legal limit of sixty-two thousand, and that another permanent army of forty thousand men should be raised for strictly defensive service. In the face of Jefferson's warning that he might as well call down an army of angels from heaven, Monroe called for one hundred thousand regular troops, when

[1] Monroe to Giles, Oct. 17, 1814; State Papers, Military Affairs, i. 514.

no exertions had hitherto availed to keep thirty thousand effectives on the rolls.

The mere expression of such a demand carried with it the train of consequences which the people chiefly dreaded. One hundred thousand troops could be raised only by draft. Monroe affirmed the power as well as the need of drafting. " Congress have a right by the Constitution," he said, " to raise regular armies, and no restraint is imposed on the exercise of it. . . . It would be absurd to suppose that Congress could not carry this power into effect otherwise than by accepting the voluntary service of individuals." Absurd as it was, such had been the general impression, and Monroe was believed to have been one of the most emphatic in maintaining it. " Ask him," suggested Randolph, " what he would have done, while governor of Virginia and preparing to resist Federal usurpation, had such an attempt been made by Mr. Adams and his ministers, especially in 1800. He *can* give the answer." Doubtless the silence of the Constitution in respect to conscription was conclusive to some minds in favor of the power ; but the people preferred the contrary view, the more because militia service seemed to give more pay for less risk.

The chance of carrying such a measure through Congress was not great, yet Monroe recommended it as his first plan for raising men. He proposed to enroll the free male population between eighteen and forty-five years of age into classes of one hundred, each to furnish four men and to keep their places supplied.[1] The second plan varied from the first only in the classification, not in the absence of compulsion. The militia were to be divided into three sections according to age, with the obligation to serve, when required, for a term of two years. A third plan suggested the exemption from militia service of every five militia-men who could provide one man for the war. If none of these schemes should be approved by Congress, additional bounties must be given under the actual system. Of the four plans, the secretary preferred the first.

The Senate committee immediately summoned Monroe to an interview. They wished an explanation of the failure in the recruiting service, and were told by Monroe that the failure was chiefly due to the competition of the detached militia for substitutes.[2] The military committee of the House then joined with the military committee of the Senate in sounding the members of both bodies in order to ascertain the most rigorous measure that could be passed. According to the report of Troup of Georgia, chairman of the House committee,[3] they " found that no efficacious measure, calculated certainly and promptly to fill the regular army, could be effectually

[1] Explanatory Observations, State Papers, Military Affairs, i. 515.

[2] Monroe to Giles, Oct. 26, 1814; State Papers, Military Affairs, i. 518.

[3] Annals of Congress, Feb. 6, 1815, p. 1130.

resorted to. Measures were matured and proposed by the [House] committee, but were not pressed on the House, from the solemn conviction that there was no disposition in the Legislature to act finally on the subject."

Yet the issue was made at a moment of extreme anxiety and almost despair. In October, 1814, the result of the war was believed to depend on the establishment of an efficient draft. The price of United States six-per-cents showed better than any other evidence the opinion of the. public ; but the military situation, known to all the world, warranted deep depression. Sir George Prevost, about to be succeeded by an efficient commander, — Sir George Murray, — was then at Kingston organizing a campaign against Sackett's Harbor, with an army of twenty thousand regular troops and a fleet that controlled the Lake. Another great force, military and naval, was known to be on its way to New Orleans ; and the defences of New Orleans were no stronger than those of Washington. One half the province of Maine, from Eastport to Castine, was already in British possession.

To leave no doubt of England's intentions, despatches from Ghent, communicating the conditions on which the British government offered peace, arrived from the American commissioners and were sent, October 10, to Congress. These conditions assumed rights of conquest. The British negotiators demanded four territorial or proprietary concessions, and all were vital to the integrity of the Union. First, the whole Indian Territory of the Northwest, including about one third of the State of Ohio, two thirds of Indiana, and nearly the entire region from which the States of Illinois, Wisconsin, and Michigan were afterward created, was to be set aside forever as Indian country under British guaranty. Second, the United States were to be excluded from military or naval contact with the Lakes. Third, they had forfeited their rights in the fisheries. Fourth, they were to cede a portion of Maine to strengthen Canada.

These demands, following the unparalleled insult of burning Washington, foreshadowed a war carried to extremities, and military preparations such as the Union had no means ready to repel. Monroe's recommendations rested on the conviction that the nation must resort to extreme measures. Dallas's financial plan could not have been suggested except as a desperate resource. Congress understood as well as the Executive the impending peril, and stood in even more fear of it.

Under these circumstances, when Troup's committee refused to act, Giles reported, on behalf of the Senate committee, two military measures. The first, for filling the regular army, proposed to extend the age of enlistment from twenty-one to eighteen years; to double the land-bounty; and to exempt from militia duty every militia-man who should furnish a recruit for the regular service.

The second measure, reported the same day, November 5, purported to authorize the raising an army of eighty thousand militia-men by draft, to serve for two years within the limits of their own or an adjoining State.[1] The provisions of this measure were ill-conceived, ill-digested, and unlikely to answer their purpose. The moment the debate began, the bill was attacked so vigorously as to destroy whatever credit it might have otherwise possessed.

Of all the supporters of the war, Senator Varnum of Massachusetts was one of the steadiest. He was also the highest authority in the Senate on matters pertaining to the militia. When Giles's bill came under discussion November 16, Varnum began the debate by a speech vehemently hostile to the proposed legislation. He first objected that although the bill purported to call for an army of eighty thousand men, "yet in some of the subsequent sections of it we find that instead of realizing the pleasing prospect of seeing an ample force in the field, the force is to be reduced to an indefinite amount, — which contradiction in terms, inconsistency in principle, and uncertainty in effect, cannot fail to produce mortification and chagrin in every breast." Varnum objected to drafting men from the militia for two years' service because the principle of nine months' service was already established by the common law. If the nation wanted a regular force, why not make it a part of the regular army without a system of drafting militia "unneces-

[1] A Bill, etc.; Niles, vii. 181.

sary, unequal, and unjust?"  The machinery of classification and draft was "wholly impracticable."  The
limit of service to adjoining States abandoned the
objects for which the Union existed.  The proffered
bounties would ruin the recruiting service for the
regular army; the proffered exemptions and reduc-
tions in term of duty left no permanency to the service.  The bill inflicted no penalties and charged no
officers with the duty of making the draft.  "I consider the whole system as resolving into a recommendation upon the patriotism of the States and Territories and upon the patriotism of the classes."

The justice of Varnum's criticism could not fairly
be questioned.  The bill authorized the President "to
issue his orders to such officers of the militia as he
may think proper," and left the classification and
draft in the hands of these militia officers.  Every
drafted man who had performed any tour of duty
in the militia since the beginning of the war was
entitled to deduct a corresponding term from his
two years of service; and obviously the demand created for substitutes would stop recruiting for the
regular army.

Hardly had Varnum sat down when Senator Daggett of Connecticut spoke.

"The bill," said the Connecticut senator, "is incapable of being executed, as well as unconstitutional and
unjust.  It proceeds entirely upon the idea that the
State governments will lend their aid to carry it into
effect.  If they refuse, it becomes inoperative.  Now,

sir, will the Executives, who believe it a violation of the Constitution, assist in its execution? I tell you they will not."

Every member of the Senate who heard these words knew that they were meant to express the will of the convention which was to meet at Hartford within a month. The sentiment thus avowed was supported by another New England senator, whose State was not a party to the Convention. Jeremiah Mason of New Hampshire was second to no one in legal ability or in personal authority, and when he followed Daggett in the debate, he spoke with full knowledge of the effect his words would have on the action of the Hartford Convention and of the State executives.

" In my opinion," he said, " this system of military conscription thus recommended by the Secretary of War is not only inconsistent with the provisions and spirit of the Constitution, but also with all the principles of civil liberty. In atrocity it exceeds that adopted by the late Emperor of France for the subjugation of Europe. . . . Such a measure cannot, it ought not to be submitted to. If it could in no other way be averted, I not only believe, but I hope, it would be resisted."

Mason pointed to the alternative, — which Massachusetts was then adopting, as the necessary consequence of refusing power to the government, — that the States must resume the powers of sovereignty :

" Should the national defence be abandoned by the general government, I trust the people, if still retaining a good portion of their resources, may rally under their State governments against foreign invasion, and rely with confidence on their own courage and virtue."

At that time the State of Massachusetts was occupied for one hundred miles of its sea-coast by a British force, avowedly for purposes of permanent conquest; and the State legislature, October 18, refused to make an inquiry, or to consider any measure for regaining possession of its territory, or to cooperate with the national government for the purpose,[1] but voted to raise an army of ten thousand men. The object of this State army was suggested by Christopher Gore, the Federalist senator from Massachusetts who followed Mason in the debate. In personal and political influence Gore stood hardly second to Mason, and his opinions were likely to carry the utmost weight with the convention at Hartford. With this idea necessarily in his mind, Gore told the Senate, —

" This [bill] is the first step on the odious ground of conscription, — a plan, sir, which never will and never ought to be submitted to by this country while it retains one idea of civil freedom ; a plan, sir, which if attempted will be resisted by many States, and at every hazard. In my judgment, sir, it should be resisted by all who have any regard to public liberty or the rights of the several States."

These denunciations were not confined to New England. Senator Goldsborough of Maryland, also a

[1] Message of Governor Strong, with documents, Jan. 18, 1815.

Federalist, affirmed that the sentiment of abhorrence
for military duty was almost universal : —

" Sir, you dare not — at least I hope you dare not —
attempt a conscription to fill the ranks of your regular
army.    When the plan of the Secretary of War made its
appearance, it was gratifying to find that it met with the
abhorrence of almost every man in the nation ; and the
merit of the bill before you, if such a measure can be
supposed to have merit at all, is that it is little else, as
regards the militia, than a servile imitation of the secretary's plan."

Nevertheless, when Goldsborough took his seat the
Senate passed the Militia Bill by a vote of nineteen
to twelve, — Anderson of Tennessee and Varnum of
Massachusetts joining the Federalists in opposition.
The Regular Army Bill, which was in effect a bill to
sacrifice the regular army, passed November 11,
without a division.    Both measures then went to
the House and were committed, November 12, to the
Committee of the Whole.

Ordinarily such a measure would have been referred
to the Military Committee, but in this instance the
Military Committee would have nothing to do with
the Senate bill.    Troup, the chairman, began the debate by denouncing it.[1]    The measure, he said, was
inadequate to its object.    " It proposed to give you a
militia force when you wanted, not a militia, but a
regular force . . . You have a deficiency of twenty-

[1] Debate of Dec. 2, 1814 ; Annals of Congress, 1814–1815,
iii. 705.

odd thousand to supply. How will you supply it ?
Assuredly the [Regular Army] bill from the Senate
will not supply it. No, sir, the recruiting system
has failed." On the nature of the force necessary for
the next campaign Troup expressed his own opinion
and that of his committee, as well as that of the
Executive, in language as strong as he could use
at such a time and place. "If, after what has happened, I could for a moment believe there could be
any doubt or hesitation on this point, I would consider everything as lost; then indeed there would
be an end of hope and of confidence." Yet on precisely this point Congress showed most doubt. Nothing could induce it to accept Troup's view of the
necessity for providing a regular army. "The bill
from the Senate," remonstrated Troup, "instead of
proposing this, proposes to authorize the President
to call upon the States for eighty thousand raw militia; and this is to be our reliance for the successful prosecution of the war ! Take my word for it,
sir, that if you do rely upon it (the military power
of the enemy remaining undivided) defeat, disaster,
and disgrace, must follow."

The House refused to support Troup or the President. Calhoun was first to yield to the general unwillingness, and declared himself disposed to accept the
Senate bill as a matter of policy. Richard M. Johnson, though sympathizing with Troup, still preferred
to accept the bill as the only alternative to nothing:
"If it was rejected, they would have no dependence

for defence but on six months' militia."[1]  On the other hand, Thomas K. Harris of Tennessee protested that if the British government had it in their power to control the deliberations of Congress, they could not devise the adoption of a measure of a military character better calculated to serve their purposes.  The people, he said, were in his part of the country prepared to make every sacrifice, and expected Congress, after the news from Ghent, to do its share ; but Congress was about to adopt a measure of all others the best calculated to prolong the war.[2]

While the friends of the government spoke in terms of open discouragement and almost despair of the strongest military measure which Congress would consent to consider, the Federalists made no concealment of their wishes and intentions.  Daniel Webster used similar arguments to those of his friend Jeremiah Mason in the Senate, affirming that the same principle which authorized the enlistment of apprentices would equally authorize the freeing of slaves,[3] and echoing pathetic threats of disunion.[4]  Other Federalists made no professions of sadness over the approaching dissolution of government.  Artemas Ward of Massachusetts spoke December 14, the day before

[1] Annals of Congress, 1814–1815, iii. 974.

[2] Annals of Congress, 1814–1815, iii. 891, 895.

[3] Annals of Congress, 1814–1815, iii. 734.

[4] Speech of C. J. Ingersoll, Dec. 9, 1814 ; Annals, 1814–1815, iii. 809.

the Hartford Convention was to meet, and announced the course which events were to take : [1] —

" That the Treasury is empty I admit ; that the ranks of the regular army are thin I believe to be true ; and that our country must be defended in all events, I not only admit but affirm. But, sir, if all the parts of the United States are defended, of course the whole will be defended. If every State in the Union, with such aid as she can obtain from her neighbors, defends herself, our whole country will be defended. In my mind the resources of the States will be applied with more economy and with greater effect in defence of the country under the State governments than under the government of the United States."

Such avowals of the intent to throw aside Constitutional duties were not limited to members from New England. Morris S. Miller of New York made a vehement speech on the failure of national defence, and declared the inevitable result to be " that the States must and will take care of themselves ; and they will preserve the resources of the States for the defence of the States." [2] He also declared that conscription would be resisted, and echoed the well-remembered declamation of Edward Livingston against the Alien Bill in 1798, when the Republican orator prayed to God that the States would never acquiesce in obedience to the law.

" This House," replied Duvall of Kentucky, "has

[1] Annals of Congress, 1814–1815, iii. 907.
[2] Annals of Congress, 1814–1815, iii. 790, 791.

heard discord and rebellion encouraged and avowed from more than one quarter." Indeed, from fully one fourth of its members the House heard little else. Under the shadow of the Hartford Convention the Federalist members talked with entire frankness. "This great fabric seems nodding and tottering to its fall," said Z. R. Shipherd of New York, December 9;[1] "and Heaven only knows how long before the mighty ruin will take place." J. O. Moseley of Connecticut " meant no improper menace" by predicting to the House, "if they were determined to prosecute the war by a recourse to such measures as are provided in the present bill, that they would have no occasion for future committees of investigation into the causes of the failure of their arms."[2] The latest committee of investigation had recently made a long report on the capture of Washington, carefully abstaining from expressing opinions of its own, or imputing blame to any one, and Moseley's remark involved a double sneer. None of these utterances were resented. Richard Stockton of New Jersey was allowed unanswered to denounce in measured terms the mild Militia Bill then under debate, from which the committee had already struck the term of two years' service by substituting one year; and Stockton concluded his fine-drawn arguments by equally studied menace : [3] —

[1] Annals of Congress, 1814–1815, iii. 829.
[2] Annals of Congress, 1814–1815, iii. 833.
[3] Annals of Congress, 1814–1815, iii. 848.

" This bill also attacks the right and sovereignty of the State governments.   Congress is about to usurp their undoubted rights, — to take from them their militia.   By this bill we proclaim that we will have their men, as many as we please, when and where and for as long a time as we see fit, and for any service we see proper.   Do gentlemen of the majority seriously believe that the people and the State governments will submit to this claim?   Do they believe that all the States of this Union will submit to this usurpation?   Have you attended to the solemn and almost unanimous declaration of the legislature of Connecticut?   Have you examined the cloud arising in the East?   Do you perceive that it is black, alarming, portentous ? "

The Resolution of the Connecticut legislature to which Stockton referred was adopted in October, and authorized the governor in case of the passage of the Militia Bill to convoke the General Assembly forthwith, to consider measures " to secure and preserve the rights and liberties of the people of this State, and the freedom, sovereignty, and independence of the same." [1]   Stockton's speech was made December 10, and " the cloud arising in the East," as he figured the Hartford Convention, was to take form December 15. The Republican speakers almost as earnestly used the full influence of these national fears to rouse the energies of the House.   They neither denied nor disguised the helplessness of government.   All admitted dread of approaching disaster.   Perhaps C. J. Ingersoll was the only member who declared that the war

[1] Resolution ; Niles, vii.; Supplement, p. 107.

had been successful, and that Americans need no longer blush to be Americans; but Ingersoll disliked the Militia Bill as cordially as it was disliked by Troup or Varnum, and voted for it only because "something must be done."[1]

"When our army," said Samuel Hopkins of Kentucky, in closing the debate, "is composed of a mere handful of men, and our treasury empty so that it cannot provide for this gallant handful; when an enemy, powerful and active, is beating against our shores like the strong wave of the ocean; when everything is at stake, — . . . surely such is not the moment for parsimonious feelings in raising taxes, or for forced constructions to defeat the means for raising men."

Notwithstanding every effort of the war-leaders, the opposition steadily won control over the House. Daniel Webster during his entire lifetime remembered with satisfaction that he shared with Eppes the credit of overthrowing what he called Monroe's conscription.[2] December 10, at Eppes's motion, the House voted by a majority of sixty-two to fifty-seven to reduce the term of service from two years to one.[3] A motion made by Daniel Webster to reduce the term to six months was lost by only one voice, the vote standing seventy-eight to seventy-nine.[4] The bill passed at last, December 14, by a vote of eighty-four to seventy-two, in a House where the true war majority was

[1] Annals of Congress, 1814–1815, iii. 808.
[2] Curtis's Life of Webster, i. 139.
[8] Annals of Congress, 1814–1815, iii. 869.
[4] Annals of Congress, 1814–1815, iii. 882.

forty-six. When the Senate insisted on its provision
of two years' service, Troup, in conference committee,
compromised on eighteen months. Then the House,
December 27, by a vote of seventy-three to sixty-four,
rejected the report of its conference committee. The
next day, December 28, in the Senate, Rufus King
made an unpremeditated motion for indefinite post-
ponement. Some members were absent; no debate
occurred. The question was immediately put, and
carried by a vote of fourteen to thirteen.[1] The effect
of this action was to destroy the bill.

With this failure the attempt to supply an army
was abandoned, and Congress left the government
to conduct the war in 1815, as in 1814, with thirty
thousand regular troops and six months' militia.
Monroe's effort to fill the ranks of the army ended
in doubling the land-bounty; in authorizing the enlistment of minors, who had till then been enlisted
without authorization; and in exempting from militia
duty such persons as should furnish a recruit for the
regular army.[2] The prospect was remote that such
inducements could do more than repair the waste of
the actual force; but the government was unable to
pay a larger number even if the force could be raised,
and Monroe was obliged to prepare for the next campaign with such slight means of defence as remained
to him. The last effort to induce the House to consider a serious method of raising troops was made

[1] Curtis's Life of Webster, i. 139 *note.*

[2] Act of Dec. 10, 1814; Annals of Congress, 1814–1815, p. 1837.

February 6, and was referred to the Committee of the Whole, with a tacit understanding that the ordinary process of recruiting was not to be disturbed.[1] According to the returns in the adjutant-general's office, the whole number of men — non-commissioned officers, privates, musicians, and artificers, present or absent, sick or well — in the regular army Feb. 16, 1815, was thirty-two thousand one hundred and sixty. During the previous two months it had remained stationary, the returns of December, 1814, reporting thirty-two thousand three hundred and sixty men. Nothing showed a possibility of greatly increasing the force by the means prescribed by Congress.

The navy requiring little new legislation, readily obtained the little it asked. Almost the first Act of the session, approved Nov. 15, 1814, authorized the purchasing or building of twenty sixteen-gun sloops-of-war. Another Act of Feb. 7, 1815, created a Board of Commissioners for the navy to discharge all the ministerial duties of the secretary, under his superintendence.

This legislation, with the various tax-bills, comprised all that was accomplished by Congress between the months of September and February toward a vigorous prosecution of the war. For the navy the prospect of success in the coming year was sufficiently fair, and privateering promised to be more active than ever; but the army was threatened with many perils. The most serious of all dangers to

[1] Annals of Congress, 1814–1815, pp. 1125–1130.

the military service of the Union was supposed by
Federalists to be the establishment of armies by the
separate States. The attempt to establish such an
army by Massachusetts in time of peace had been
one of the causes which led to the Constitution of
1789 ;[1] and at the close of 1814, when Massachusetts
voted to raise an army of ten thousand men, the sig-
nificance of the step was more clearly evident than
in the time of the Confederation.

The State of Massachusetts might be supposed to
act in a spirit of hostility to the Constitution ; but
no such motive actuated States outside of New England. If they followed the same course, they did so
because the national government was believed to be
incompetent to the general defence. Of all the States
Massachusetts alone possessed considerable resources,
and could command both credit and specie ; yet the
creation of a State army of ten thousand men over-
burdened her finances, and obliged her to claim her
share of the national revenues. No other State could
expect to support an army without immediate financial trouble. Yet Governor Tompkins of New York
recommended to the legislature in September the
establishment of a State army of twenty thousand
men,[2] and the legislature passed Acts for the purpose.
The legislature of Pennsylvania took a similar measure into consideration. The legislature of Maryland
passed an Act for raising five thousand State troops.

[1] Madison's Debates, ii. 712.

[2] Message of Sept. 30, 1814 ; Niles, vii. 97.

Virginia decided also to create a State army, with two major-generals. South Carolina passed a law for raising a brigade of State troops, and appointed the officers. Kentucky took measures for raising a State army of ten thousand men.

The national government, unable to create an efficient army of its own, yielded to necessity, and looked already to the State armies as levies to be taken into the national service in case of need. The States, on their side, unable to bear the expense of separate armies, expected to be relieved of the burden by the national government. Yet for the moment the States, however deficient their means might be, seemed better able than the general government not only to raise men but to support them. In January, 1815, the financial resources of the government were exhausted, so that the Treasury could not meet the drafts drawn by Major-General Jackson and the pressing demands of the paymaster at New Orleans. The Secretary of War was obliged to go from bank to bank of Washington and Georgetown asking, as a personal favor, loans of their bank-notes already depreciated about fifty per cent. So desperate, according to Monroe's account, was the situation that his success depended on adding his own guaranty to that of the government.[1] At no time of his life were Monroe's means sufficient to supply his private needs, and nothing could express so strongly his sense of

[1] Monroe's Memoir; Deposition of Tench Ringgold, Feb. 14, 1826, pp. 13, 58.

national bankruptcy as the assertion that his credit was required to support that of the United States.[1]

The State armies were the natural result of such a situation. Congress could not resist the movement, and passed an Act, approved Jan. 27, 1815, authorizing the President to receive into the national service a certain proportion of the State troops, not exceeding forty thousand men in the aggregate. Little was said in debate on the bearings of the Act, which seemed to concede the demand of Massachusetts that the States should be allowed to raise troops at the expense of the United States. The Hartford Convention had then met, deliberated, and adjourned. Its report had been published, and among its demands was one that "these States might be allowed to assume their own defence." The Federalists considered the Act of Jan. 27, 1815, as a "full and ample" concession of the demand.[2] Senator Gore wrote to Governor Strong, January 22, while the measure was before the President, commenting on the financial and military expedients of Dallas and Monroe:[3]

"These appear to me the spasms of a dying government. . . . The bill authorizing the raising of State troops by the States, and at the expense of the United States, according to the plan sent you some time since, has passed both Houses. Thus one part of the recom-

[1] Eulogy of James Monroe by J. Q. Adams, p. 75.

[2] H. G. Otis's Letters in Defence of the Hartford Convention, 1824, pp. 38, 39.

[3] Lodge's Cabot, p. 561.

mendation of the Hartford Convention seems to be adopted. The other, — that to authorize the States to receive the taxes, — will probably be more difficult to be attained. The accession to this seems not to accord with Mr. Monroe's intimation in your letter, or rather in his letter to you. Indeed, if they have fears of the State governments, one can hardly account for this government's authorizing the States to raise and keep in pay, at the expense of the United States, troops which may be used for purposes hostile to, or not conformable with, the views of the paymaster."

The accession to the principle of State armies which surprised Gore could be explained only by the government's consciousness of helplessness. Gore was somewhat careful to express no opinion of the probable consequences, but other Federalists spoke with entire candor. Timothy Pickering expected a division of the Union.[1] Less extreme partisans looked only to a dissolution of government. A year afterward, in the calmer light of peace and union, Joseph Hopkinson, a very distinguished Federalist of Philadelphia, not deluded like the New Englanders by local pride or prejudice, declared publicly in Congress the common conviction of his party on the probable consequences of another year of war :[2]

"The federal government was at the last gasp of existence. But six months longer and it was no more.

[1] Pickering to John Lowell, Jan. 24, 1815; New England Federalism, p. 425.

[2] Debate of Jan. 29, 1816; Annals of Congress, 1815–1816, p. 795.

. . . The general government would have dissolved into its original elements; its powers would have returned to the States from which they were derived; and they doubtless would have been fully competent to their defence against any enemy. Does not everybody remember that all the great States, and I believe the small ones too, were preparing for this state of things, and organizing their own means for their own defence?"

Calhoun contradicted Hopkinson and denied his assertions; but on that subject Hopkinson was at least an equal authority. Calhoun knew well his own State, but he knew little of New England; and he had yet to learn, perhaps to his own surprise, how easily a section of the Union could be wrought to treason.

## CHAPTER XI.

THE Massachusetts legislature issued, October 17, its invitation to the New England States for a conference,[1] and on the same day the newspapers published the despatches from Ghent, to August 20, containing British conditions of peace, — which required, among greater sacrifices, a cession of Massachusetts territory, and an abandonment of fisheries and fishing rights conceded with American independence. Two counties of the State beyond the Penobscot were then in British military possession, and a third, Nantucket, was a British naval station. Yet even under these circumstances the British demands did not shock the Federalist leaders. Governor Strong, after reading the Ghent documents October 17, wrote to Pickering at Washington,[2] —

" If Great Britain had discovered a haughty or grasping spirit, it might naturally have excited irritation ; but I am persuaded that in the present case there is not a member of Congress who, if he was a member of Parliament, would have thought that more moderate terms ought in the first instance to have been offered."

[1] Letter of Invitation, Oct. 17, 1814; Niles, vii. 179

[2] Lodge's Memoir of Strong; Proceedings of Massachusetts Historical Society, 1879.

The argument seemed to prove only that members of Congress could also be haughty and grasping; but Governor Strong thought the British demands reasonable, and began at once to sound his friends in regard to the proposed concessions. The following day he wrote [1] that the Essex people expected to lose the fisheries, but were ready to give up a portion of Maine to retain them.

Pickering wrote in reply, acquiescing in the proposed barter of territory for fisheries, and also in the more extravagant British demands for the Indians and the Lakes. " I was gratified," said Pickering,[2] " to find my own sentiments corresponding with yours." The leading Federalists united with Pickering and Strong in blaming the American negotiators and the government for rejecting the British offers. The same view was taken by the chief Federalist newspaper of the State, the Boston " Centinel." [3]

Thus in the November election, a few weeks later, two issues were impressed on the people of New England. In regard to neither issue did the Federalist leaders attempt concealment. The people were invited, as far as the press of both parties could decide the points of dispute, to express their opinion, — first, whether the British conditions of peace should

[1] Lodge's Memoir of Strong; Proceedings of Massachusetts Historical Society, 1879.

[2] Pickering to Strong, Oct. 29, 1814; Lodge's Cabot, p. 535.

[3] Boston Centinel, Oct. 19, 1814.

have been taken into consideration ; second, whether the States should be represented at the Hartford Convention. The popular response was emphatic. Everywhere in New England the Republican candidates were defeated ; and the Federalists, encouraged by the result, — believing the Hartford Convention to be the most popular action taken by Massachusetts since the State adopted the Federal Constitution,[1] — prepared to support measures, looking to the restoration of peace and to the establishment of a new Federal compact comprising either the whole or a portion of the actual Union.

However varied the wishes of the majority might be, they agreed in requiring a radical change in the organic law. This intention was their chief claim to popularity. The Boston "Centinel," announcing November 9 the adhesion of Connecticut and Rhode Island to the Hartford Convention, placed over the announcement the head-line, "Second and third Pillars of a new Federal Edifice reared." During November and December, almost every day, the newspapers discussed the question what the convention should do; and the chief divergence of opinion seemed to regard rather the immediate than the ultimate resort to forcible means of stopping the war. The extremists, represented in the press by John Lowell, asked for immediate action.

"Throwing off all connection with this wasteful war," — wrote "A New England Man" in the "Centinel," if

[1] Otis's Letters in Defence of the Hartford Convention, p.

December 17, — "making peace with our enemy and opening once more our commerce with the world, would be a
wise and manly course.    The occasion demands it of us,
and the people at large are ready to meet it."

Apparently Lowell was right.    The people showed
no sign of unwillingness to meet any decision that
might be recommended by the convention.    As the
moment approached, the country waited with increasing anxiety for the result.    The Republican press —
the "National Intelligencer" as well as the Boston
"Patriot" — at first ridiculed the convention, then
grew irritable, and at last betrayed signs of despair.
On both sides threats were openly made and openly
defied; but in Massachusetts the United States government had not five hundred effective troops, and
if the convention chose to recommend that the State
should declare itself neutral and open its ports, no
one pretended that any national power existed in
Massachusetts capable of preventing the legislature
from carrying the recommendation into effect if it
pleased.

From immediate extravagance Massachusetts was
saved by the leaders who, knowing the popular excitement, feared lest the convention should be carried
too fast into disorder, and for that reason selected
representatives who could be trusted to resist emotion.    When George Cabot was chosen as the head
of the State delegation, the character of the body was
fixed.    The selection of Cabot did not please the
advocates of action.    Pickering wrote to Lowell sug-

gesting doubts whether Cabot was the fittest choice.[1]
Lowell replied that he shared these doubts, and that
in consequence he had been led to oppose the convention altogether, because it would not withdraw
the State resources from the general government.[2]
Cabot, he said, was " most reluctantly dragged in like
a conscript to the duty of a delegate;" he had always
been despondent as to the course of public affairs,
and felt no confidence in the possibility of awaken-
ing the people to their true disease, — which was not
the war or the Union, but democracy. Lowell did
not know " a single bold and ardent man " among
the Massachusetts or Connecticut delegates. In the
" Centinel " of December 7 he described Cabot's ten-
dencies in language evidently intended as a warning
to Cabot himself : —

"There are men who know that our troubles are not
the offspring of this war alone, and will not die with it.
But they despair of relief, and think resistance unavailing.
They consider the people in their very nature democratic,
and that nothing but the severity of their sufferings has
driven them from those men and that system out of
which have grown all our evils ; that should they be
restored to that state of prosperity which they once enjoyed, the same passions and opinions would diffuse
themselves through the country, and the same course
of conduct be again followed out."

Cabot shocked Pickering by expressing all his
favorite political views in one brief question: " Why

[1] Pickering to Lowell, Nov. 7, 1814; Lodge's Cabot, p. 541.
[2] Lowell to Pickering, Dec. 3, 1814; Lodge's Cabot, p. 545.

can't you and I let the world ruin itself its own
way?"[1]   Such a turn of mind was commonly the
mark of a sceptical spirit, which doubted whether
the world at best was worth the trouble of saving;
and against this inert and indifferent view of human
affairs New England offered a constant protest.   Yet
the Massachusetts delegation to Hartford was in sympathy with Cabot, while the Massachusetts legislature
seemed to sympathize with Pickering.   William Pres-
cott, another member of the delegation, was chiefly
remarkable for prudence and caution; Nathan Dane
bore the same stamp; Harrison Gray Otis took character and color from his surroundings.   The Connecticut delegation — James Hillhouse, Chauncey
Goodrich, Roger M. Sherman, and others — were little likely to recommend " effectual measures."   The
convention consisted of men supposed to be inclined
to resist popular pressure, and Cabot was probably
serious in replying to a young friend who asked
him what he was to do at Hartford : " We are going to keep you young hot-heads from getting into
mischief."[2]

In the Council Chamber of the State House at
Hartford the delegates assembled, December 15, and
gave instant evidence of their intention to discourage
appeals to popular emotion.   Their earliest steps decided their whole course.   They chose George Cabot
as their President, and they made their sessions se-

[1] Lodge's Cabot, p. 541.
[2] Lodge's Cabot, p. 519.

cret. Under no circumstances could the convention
have regarded itself as a popular body, for the delegates numbered only twenty-three persons, mostly
cautious and elderly men, who detested democracy,
but disliked enthusiasm almost as much. Two new
members, appointed by popular meetings in New
Hampshire, were next admitted ; and toward the
close of the sessions another member, representing
the county of Windham in Vermont, was given a
seat. Thus enlarged, the convention over which
George Cabot presided numbered twenty-six members besides the secretary, Theodore Dwight.

Excess of caution helped to give the convention an
air of conspiracy, which warned future conspirators
to prefer acting, or appearing to act, in public. The
secrecy of the Hartford conference was chiefly intended to secure freedom for the exchange of opinion, and also in some degree to prevent premature
excitement and intrusion of popular feeling ; but the
secrecy created a belief that the debates would not
bear publicity. Possibly much was said which verged
on treasonable conspiracy ; but the members were
not men of a class likely to act beyond their instructions, and they adhered strictly to the practical task
imposed on them. Some years afterward, Harrison
Gray Otis, laboring to clear his political reputation
from the stigma of membership, caused the official
journal of the convention to be published ; and the
record, though revealing nothing of what was said,
proved that nothing was formally done or proposed

which contradicted the grave and restrained attitude maintained in its public expressions.

On the first day of its meeting the convention appointed a committee to consider and report upon the business to be done. Chauncey Goodrich, Otis, and three other members formed this committee, which reported the next day the points in dispute between the States and the national government, — the militia power, conscription power, duty and means of defence, and matters of a like nature. After two days of discussion, the convention appointed another committee to frame a general project of measures, and again placed a Connecticut man — Nathaniel Smith — at its head, with Otis second. Still another committee was appointed, December 21, to prepare a report showing the reasons which guided the con. vention to its results ; and of that committee Otis was chairman.

Clearly, Otis took the chief burden of business ; and the result could scarcely fail to reflect in some degree the character of the man as well as of the body for which he was acting. Though ambitious of leading, Otis never led. John Lowell described his character, as it was understood in Boston, perhaps somewhat harshly, for Otis was no favorite with any class of men who held fixed opinions : [1] —

" Mr. Otis is naturally timid and frequently wavering, — to-day bold, and to-morrow like a hare trembling at every breeze. It would seem by his language that he is

[1] Lodge's Cabot, p. 548.

prepared for the very boldest measures, but he receives anonymous letters every day or two threatening him with bodily harm. It seems the other party suspect his firmness. He is sincere in wishing thorough measures, but a thousand fears restrain him."

Otis was the probable author of the report, adopted December 24, recommending a course to the convention; and he was chairman of the larger committee to which that report was referred, and within which the final report — after a discussion lasting from December 24 to December 30 — was framed. The discussions, both in committee and in convention, took much time and caused some difficulties; but nothing was ever known of the speeches made, or of the motions proposed, or of the amendments offered. All the reports were finally adopted by the convention; and all proposed business then having been finished, January 5 the convention adjourned without day, authorizing Cabot to call another meeting at Boston if he should at any time see occasion for it.

The report, therefore, contained all the information which the convention intended to make public, and only from that document could the ultimate object of the members be inferred. It was immediately published in Connecticut, and at the meeting of the legislatures of Massachusetts and Connecticut in January it was laid before them for approval.

Considering the conservative temper of the delegates and their dislike for extreme measures, the report bore striking evidence of the popular passion

which urged them forward.   A few paragraphs in
its first pages showed the spirit of its recommendations, and a few more showed the effect expected
from them : —

> " It is a truth not to be concealed that a sentiment
> prevails to no inconsiderable extent . . . that the time
> for a change is at hand. . . . This opinion may ulti-
> mately prove to be correct ; but as the evidence on which
> it rests is not yet conclusive, . . . some general con-
> siderations are submitted in the hope of reconciling all
> to a course of moderation and firmness which may . . .
> probably avert the evil, or at least insure consolation and
> success in the last resort. . . . A severance of the Union
> by one or more States against the will of the rest, and
> especially in time of war, can be justified only by abso-
> lute necessity."

Having thus discouraged precipitation, and argued
in favor of firm and moderate measures as a probable
means of preserving the Union, the report sketched
the limits of the Union that was to be preserved.
In a paragraph closely following the precedent of the
Virginia Resolutions of 1798, the report asserted the
right and duty of a State to " interpose its authority "
for the protection of its citizens from infractions of
the Constitution by the general government.   In the
immediate crisis, this interposition should take the
form of State laws to protect the militia or citizens
from conscriptions and drafts ; of an arrangement
with the general government authorizing the States
to assume their own defence, and to retain " a reason-

able portion of the taxes collected within the said
States" for the purpose; and of State armies to be
held in readiness to serve for the defence of the New
England States upon the request of the governor of
the State invaded.

Such measures involved the establishment of a
New England Confederation. The proposed union
of the New England States for their own defence
ignored any share to be taken by the general government in the defence of the national territory, and reduced that government to helplessness. What could
be done by New England might be done by all; and
the Federalists assumed that all would be obliged to
do it.

If the general government should reject the request
for the proposed arrangement, the ultimate emergency must arise; but with the measures to be then
taken the convention would not interfere.

"It would be inexpedient for this convention to
diminish the hope of a successful issue to such an application by recommending, upon supposition of a contrary
event, ulterior proceedings. Nor is it indeed within their
province. In a state of things so solemn and trying as
may then arise, the legislatures of the States, or conven-
tions of the whole people, or delegates appointed by
them for the express purpose in another convention, must
act as such urgent circumstances may then require."

Besides the measures of urgency which must be
immediately accepted by the national government,
the convention recommended seven amendments to

the Constitution ; but on these no immediate action
was required.  The single issue forced on the government by the convention was that of surrendering to
Massachusetts, Connecticut, and Rhode Island " a
reasonable portion of the taxes collected within said
States," and consenting to some arrangement " whereby the said States may, separately or in concert, be
empowered to assume upon themselves the defence
of their territory against the enemy."  If the United
States government should decline such an arrangement, the State legislatures were to send delegates
to another convention to meet at Boston, June 15,
" with such powers and instructions as the exigency
of a crisis so momentous may require."

While the convention was preparing its report,
from December 15 to January 5, the public waited
with the utmost curiosity for the result.  Major
Jesup, famous at Chippawa and Lundy's Lane, was
then recruiting for the Twenty-fifth United States
Infantry at Hartford, and reported constantly to the
President and War Department ; but he could tell
nothing of the convention that was not notorious.
His letters were mere surmises or unmilitary comments on the treasonable intentions of the meeting.[1]
The Federalists knew no more than was known to
the Republicans ; but while they waited, they expressed
fear only lest the convention should fall short of
their wishes.

[1] Ingersoll's History, ii. 232–238; MSS. War Department
Archives.

" I care nothing more for your actings and doings," wrote Gouverneur Morris to Pickering in Congress.[1] " Your decree of conscriptions and your levy of contributions are alike indifferent to one whose eyes are fixed on a star in the East, which he believes to be the dayspring of freedom and glory. The traitors and madmen assembled at Hartford will, I believe, if not too tame and timid, be hailed hereafter as the patriots and sages of their day and generation."

As far as newspapers reflected public opinion, the people of New England held the same views as those expressed by Gouverneur Morris. The Boston " Centinel" contained, December 28, an address to the Hartford Convention announcing that the once venerable Constitution had expired: " At your hands, therefore, we demand deliverance. New England is unanimous. And we announce our irrevocable decree that the tyrannical oppression of those who at present usurp the powers of the Constitution is beyond endurance. And we will resist it." A meeting at Reading in Massachusetts, January 5, pledged itself to make no more returns for taxation and to pay no more national taxes until the State should have made its decision known.

A newspaper paragraph copied by the Federalist press[2] advised the President to provide himself with a swifter horse than he had at Bladensburg if he meant to attempt to subjugate the Eastern States.

[1] Morris to Pickering, Dec. 22, 1814; Morris's Works, iii. 324.
[2] Boston Gazette, Jan. 5, 1815.

" He must be able to escape at a greater rate than
forty miles a day, or the swift vengeance of New England will overtake the wretched miscreant in his
flight." Such expressions of the press on either side
were of little authority, and deserved no great attention ; but the language of responsible and representative bodies could not be denied weight. Opposition to
the convention seemed cowed. Apparently the State
was ready for immediate action ; and the convention, in recommending a delay of six months, risked
general disapproval.

While the public was in this temper, the convention adjourned, and its report was given to the press.
No one doubted that moderate men would approve
it. The only persons whose approval was in question
were " bold and ardent " partisans, like Gouverneur
Morris, Pickering, and John Lowell, who wanted instant action. Chiefly for the sake of unanimity, these
men gave in their adhesion. John Lowell hastened
to publish his acquiescence in the convention's report.[1] Pickering also approved it, although Pickering's approval was partly founded on the belief that
the Union was already dissolved, and no further effort
in that direction need be made.

" If the British succeed in their expedition against
New Orleans," Pickering wrote to Lowell,[2] — " and if
they have tolerable leaders I see no reason to doubt of
their success, — I shall consider the Union as severed.

[1] Boston Centinel, Jan. 14, 1815.
[2] Pickering to Lowell, Jan. 23, 1815 ; Lodge's Cabot, p. 561.

This consequence I deem inevitable. I do not expect to see a single representative in the next Congress from the Western States."

Governor Strong and Senator Gore also approved the convention's report. On receiving it at Washington, January 14, Gore wrote to Strong: "The result of the Hartford Convention is here, and affords satisfaction to most if not to all, — to some because they see not the point nor consequence of the recommendation as relates to taxes." The point and consequence of that recommendation were clear to Gore, and he approved of both.

If any leading Federalist disapproved the convention's report, he left no record of the disapproval. In such a case, at such a moment, silence was acquiescence. As far as could be inferred from any speeches made or letters written at the time, the Federalist party was unanimous in acquiescing in the recommendations of the Hartford Convention.

In Massachusetts and Connecticut the acquiescence was express. The legislature, convened at Boston, January 18, hastened to refer the convention's report to a joint committee, which reported, January 24, Resolutions that the legislature "do highly approve" the proceedings of the convention, and that State commissioners should immediately proceed to Washington to effect the arrangement proposed.[1] By a very large majority of three to one, the legislature adopted the Resolutions, making the acts of

[1] Report of Committee, Jan. 24, 1815; Niles, vii. 372.

the convention their own.    Three commissioners
were quickly appointed, — Harrison Gray Otis at
their head, — and in the early days of February
started for Washington.

Massachusetts was then more than ever convinced
that it must peremptorily insist on taking its share
of the national revenue into its own hands.    Already the first step toward providing a State army
had plunged the State treasury into financial difficulties, and measures for defence were stopped until
new resources could be obtained.    To the surprise of
Governor Strong, the Massachusetts banks, restrained
by their charters, applied to the State government
the same rigorous refusal of credit which they had
applied to the national government, and Strong
found himself unable to obtain even the loan of one
million dollars authorized by the legislature at its
autumn session.    The miscarriage cast a shade of
ridicule on the character of the State which criticised
so severely the failure of the national government
to defend it, and found itself unable to take the first
step toward defence without the aid of the national
government, bankrupt and impotent though it was.
Governor Strong sent to the legislature on the first
day of its winter session a message [1] that might
have been sent by Madison to Congress.    He re-
minded the legislature that it had, by a Resolution
of Oct. 11, 1814, authorized a loan of a million
dollars from the banks.

[1] Niles, vii. ; Supplement, p. 97.

" At that time," continued Strong's message, " it was supposed that there would be no difficulty in procuring the requisite sums from that source, and the treasurer soon obtained loans to a considerable amount; but the directors of some of the banks declared themselves unable to lend, and others have expressed such reluctance as forbids an expectation that the whole amount can be obtained in that way during the continuance of the present cautious operations of the banks."

The treasurer had obtained $631,000, and with the expenditure of that sum the work of defence and the organization of the State army ceased. " The efforts of defensive preparation which were made in this State the last year," Governor Strong declared, " will, if continued at the expense of the Commonwealth, be fatal to our finances." The necessary consequence followed, that the State must take the national revenues. Accordingly the committee of both Houses, to which the subject was referred, reported [1] an approval of suspending the organization of State troops " until in virtue of some arrangement to be made with the national government sufficient funds can be provided for their pay and support, without recourse to additional taxes." Under such circumstances the national government was little likely to surrender its resources, and every symptom showed that the State then meant to seize them.

The same committee formally approved the gover-

[1] Boston Centinel, Feb. 4, 1815.

nor's course in declining to co-operate with the
national government in expelling the enemy from
Maine. The public excuse for the refusal was
founded on the condition of the Treasury. In Federalist society the weightier motive was supposed to
be the wish to leave on the national government
the odium of failure to defend the State.[1]

While Massachusetts sustained the Hartford Convention, and pressed to an issue the quarrel with the
national government, Connecticut acted with equal
zeal in the same sense. The governor, John Cotton
Smith, was an old man, and neither his opinions nor
his passions were extreme; but as far as concerned
the Hartford Convention, his views differed little from
those of Pickering and Lowell. He called a special
session of the legislature for January 25, to act on
the delegates' report; and his speech at the opening
of the session would have been taken for irony, had
his moderation of character not been known.[2] "The
temperate and magnanimous course proposed for
our adoption cannot fail to allay the apprehensions
which many have professed to entertain, and to
enliven the hopes of all who cherish our national
Union, and are disposed to place it on a solid and
durable basis." The legislature without delay approved the measures recommended by the convention, and appointed delegates to accompany those

[1] Sumner's East Boston, p. 739.

[2] Speech to the Connecticut Legislature; Niles, vii.; Supplement, p. 95.

sent from Massachusetts to effect the proposed arrangement with the government at Washington.

In later times the Hartford Convention was often and vigorously defended by writers whose works were friendly to the national government, and whose influence was popular.[1] The wisdom, loyalty, and patriotism of George Cabot and his associates became the theme of authors whose authority was above dispute. Nearly always the defence rested on the argument that popular opinion went beyond the convention's report, and that the convention risked its credit by refusing to advise instant withdrawal from the Union.[2] This view was apparently correct. The efforts of the moderate Federalists to praise the moderation of the report, and the labored protests of the extremists against the possible suspicion that they objected to its moderation,[3] showed that the convention was then believed to have offered resistance to what Governor Smith stigmatized as " rash councils or precipitate measures." The tone of the press and the elections bore out the belief that a popular majority would have supported an abrupt and violent course.

The tone of the minority at the time showed a similar belief that Massachusetts favored disunion. During all the proceedings of the State legislatures

---

[1] Lodge's Cabot, pp. 504–526; Lossing, p. 1015 ; Goodrich's Recollections, ii. pp. 9–61.

[2] Lodge's Cabot, p. 518.

[3] Pickering to Lowell, Jan. 23, 1815; Lodge's Cabot, p. 561.

and the convention, the loyal press and citizens never
ceased to point out the dangerous, treasonable, and absurd results to be expected from the course pursued.
In the Massachusetts Senate John Holmes of Maine
attacked the convention and its doings in a speech
that gave him wide reputation.[1]    Threats of civil war
were freely uttered and defied.    Among the least violent of Federalists was James Lloyd, recently United
States senator from Massachusetts ; and to him as a
man of known patriotism John Randolph addressed a
letter, Dec. 15, 1814, remonstrating against the Hartford Convention that day to meet.    Lloyd replied in
a letter also published, advising Randolph and the
Virginians to coerce Madison into retirement, and to
place Rufus King in the Presidency as the alternative to a fatal issue.[2]    The assertion of such an
alternative showed how desperate the situation was
believed by the moderate Federalists to be.

A long letter of a similar kind was written, Nov.
26, 1814, by Jonathan Mason to Wilson Cary Nicholas.[3]    The opinion of the men among whom Mason
lived was expressly declared by Mason to the effect
that " Great Britain will not treat with Mr. Madison.
He must retire, or the country and the Union are at
an end. . . . This is plain language, but in my soul
I believe it true.    We shall not be destroyed to-day

[1] Niles, vii.; Supplement, pp. 49–53.

[2] Palladium, Jan. 24, 1815.   Cf. Pickering to Lowell, Jan. 24,
1815; New England Federalism, p. 426.

[3] Mason to Nicholas, Nov. 26, 1814; Nicholas MSS.

or to-morrow, but it will come; and the end of these measures [of the Administration] will be disunion and disgrace."

In the Republican party the belief was universal that the Hartford Convention could lead only to a New England Confederation; and the belief was not confined to partisans. An anecdote that George Ticknor delighted in telling, illustrated the emotion that then agitated men far beyond the passing and fitful excitements of party politics. Ticknor, a young Federalist twenty-three years old, wished for letters of introduction to Virginia, and asked them from John Adams, then a man of eighty, whose support of the war made him an object of antipathy to the party he had led.

"When I visited him in Quincy to receive these letters," related Ticknor,[1] "I had a remarkable interview with him, which at the time disturbed me not a little. . . . Soon after I was seated in Mr. Adams's parlor, — where was no one but himself and Mrs. Adams, who was knitting, — he began to talk of the condition of the country with great earnestness. I said not a word; Mrs. Adams was equally silent; but Mr. Adams, who was a man of strong and prompt passions, went on more and more vehemently. He was dressed in a single-breasted dark-green coat, buttoned tightly by very large white metal buttons over his somewhat rotund person. As he grew more and more excited in his discourse, he impatiently endeavored to thrust his hand into the breast of his coat. The buttons did not yield readily; at last he *forced* his

[1] Life of Ticknor, i. 12.

hand in, saying, as he did so, in a very loud voice and most excited manner: 'Thank God! thank God! George Cabot's close-buttoned ambition has broke out at last: he wants to be President of New England, sir!'"

Whether George Cabot wanted it or not, he was in danger of becoming what John Adams predicted. He was far from being the first man who had unwillingly allowed himself to be drawn into a position from which escape was impossible. After going so far, neither leaders nor people could retreat. The next and easy step of sequestrating the direct and indirect taxes was one to which the State stood pledged in the event of a refusal by President Madison and Congress to surrender them. After such an act, the establishment of a New England Confederation could hardly be matter of choice.

If so considerable a mass of concurrent testimony did not prove the gravity of the occasion, as it was understood by the most intelligent and best-informed men of the time, ample evidence could be drawn from other sources. William Wirt described the painful anxiety of Madison as early as the month of October. Throughout Virginia the depression was akin to despair. John Randolph and Wilson Cary Nicholas gave expression to it in letters to prominent New Englanders; but Jefferson in private was still more pronounced in his fears. "The war, had it proceeded, would have upset our government," he wrote to Gallatin a year later,[1] "and a new one, whenever tried,

[1] Jefferson to Gallatin; Works, vi. 498.

will do it." George Ticknor, after obtaining at Quincy his letter of introduction from John Adams to Jefferson, delivered it at Monticello at a time when the anxiety for the safety of New Orleans was acute. He found Jefferson convinced that the city must fall, and Jefferson expressed the expectation that the British would hold it indefinitely.[1] Pickering felt the same conviction, and regarded the event as a dissolution of the Union.

The " Federal Republican " of Baltimore published, January 5, the day when the Hartford Convention adjourned, a letter from Washington announcing " an explosion at hand ; that the President would be called on to resign ; and there must be peace by that or a future Administration." The fall of New Orleans was to be the signal for a general demand that Madison should resign, and the Federalist press already prepared the ground by insisting that " Mr. Madison has scarcely raised his little finger to preserve New Orleans," and would finally determine to abandon the State of Louisiana.[2] That Madison's authority could survive two such blows as the capture of Washington and the loss of Louisiana seemed improbable ; but that he should resign was impossible, though the alternative was a collapse of government.

When the month of February arrived, government and people were waiting with keen apprehension for some new disaster, and the least probable solution

[1] Life of Ticknor, i. 37.
[2] The Federal Republican, Jan. 14 and 16, 1815.

was that England knowing the situation would consent to any tolerable peace. The "Federal Republican" of January 28, commenting on the expected bank veto, summed up the consequences, not unfairly from its point of view, in few words : —

"It is impossible, as Mr. Giles said in his luminous and eloquent argument upon the measure [of a national bank], that the government can stand these reiterated shocks. . . . The interest upon the public debt remains unpaid, and there exists not the means, without making the most ruinous sacrifices, to pay it. The government is in arrears to the army upward of nine million dollars ; to the navy, about four millions. . . . The condition of our finances is known to the enemy ; and is it possible he will be such a fool as to give us peace, after the mortal blow we aimed at him, when he knows we cannot pay the interest on the public debt, that we cannot pay our army or our navy, and when he finds us unable to defend any part of the country at which he strikes?"

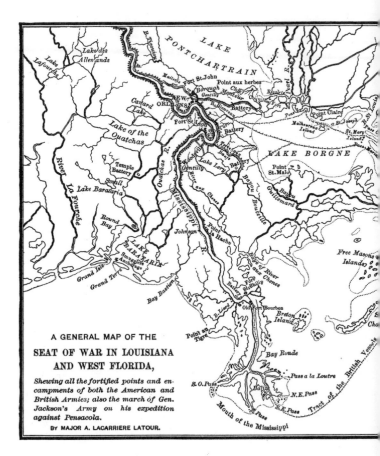

A GENERAL MAP OF THE

SEAT OF WAR IN LOUISIANA
AND WEST FLORIDA,

*Shewing all the fortified points and en-
campments of both the American and
British Armies; also the march of Gen.
Jackson's Army on his expedition
against Pensacola.*

BY MAJOR A. LACARRIERE LATOUR.

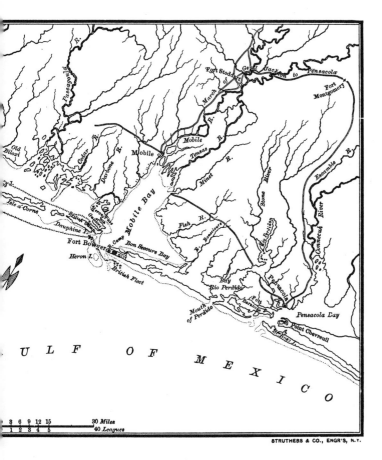

## CHAPTER XII.

A DESPATCH from Lord Bathurst, marked " most secret," and dated July 30, 1814, informed Major-General Ross that, after finishing his operations in Chesapeake Bay, he was to sail with his whole force to Jamaica, where he would join an expedition then preparing in England to rendezvous at Cape Negril on the west coast of Jamaica about November 20. Lieutenant-General Lord Hill was to command the combined land-forces.[1] These orders were given before the arrival of a long report from Vice-Admiral Cochrane concerning the military condition of the American territories on the Gulf of Mexico, which Cochrane considered such " that he had no doubt in his mind that three thousand British troops landed at Mobile, where they would be joined by all the Indians, with the disaffected French and Spaniards, would drive the Americans entirely out of Louisiana and the Floridas." [2]

Circumstances induced the British government to defer sending Lord Hill, with a large force, to the

[1] Bathurst to Ross, July 30, 1814; MSS. British Archives.
[2] Cochrane to Croker, June 20, 1814 ; MSS. British Archives.

Gulf; and Cochrane was informed by a despatch, dated August 10, that Major-General Ross was directed to carry out the Vice-Admiral's plans, which required fewer men.[1] Orders were sent to Ross, of the same date, informing him that reinforcements amounting to more than twenty-one hundred rank-and-file were preparing to sail from England, which with the Fifth West India regiment and two hundred black pioneers from Jamaica would enable Ross to carry more than five thousand effective rank-and-file to the theatre of his operations.[2]

Ross's detailed instructions were dated September 6.[3] They began by recounting the force which was intended to act against New Orleans. The brigade from the Gironde which Ross took to the Chesapeake was estimated at about twenty-three hundred effectives, and a battalion which he had taken from Bermuda was supposed to have raised his rank-and-file to thirty-four hundred men. In addition to this force, a brigade under Major-General Keane, numbering twenty-one hundred and fifty men, was under orders for Jamaica, which with the black troops would enable Ross to proceed to his destination "with near six thousand men, exclusive of the marines and seamen. . . . About the same time you will be joined by the First West India regiment from Guadeloupe."

[1] Croker to Cochrane, Aug. 10, 1814; MSS. British Archives.
[2] Bathurst to Ross, Aug. 10, 1814 ; MSS. British Archives.
[3] Bathurst to Ross, Sept. 6, 1814; MSS. British Archives.

The objects which rendered the success of the expedition " extremely important " were two : first, the command of the mouth of the Mississippi, so as to deprive the back settlements of America of their communication with the sea ; second, " to occupy some important and valuable possession by the restoration of which we may improve the conditions of peace, or which may entitle us to exact its cession as the price of peace."

The point of attack was left to the discretion of Cochrane and Ross. They might proceed directly against New Orleans, or move in the first instance into the back parts of Georgia and the country of the friendly Indians. In either case, the second object in view could not be attained against the will of the inhabitants. " With their favor and co-operation, on the other hand, we may expect to rescue the whole province of Louisiana from the United States."

" If therefore you shall find in the inhabitants a general and decided disposition to withdraw from their recent connection with the United States, either with the view of establishing themselves as an independent people or of returning under the dominion of the Spanish Crown, you will give them every support in your power ; you will furnish them with arms and clothing, and assist in forming and disciplining the several levies, provided you are fully satisfied of the loyalty of their intentions, which will be best evinced by their committing themselves in some act of decided hostility against the United States. . . . You will discountenance any proposition of the inhabitants to place themselves under the dominion

of Great Britain; and you will direct their disposition
toward returning under the protection of the Spanish
Crown rather than to the attempting to maintain what it
will be much more difficult to secure substantially, — their
independence as a separate State; and you must give
them clearly to understand that Great Britain cannot
pledge herself to make the independence of Louisiana,
or its restoration to the Spanish Crown, a *sine qua non*
of peace with the United States."

After occupying New Orleans, Ross and Cochrane
were to decide whether any further military operations could be carried on; and if nothing of material
importance could be attempted, they were to send the
disposable part of their force to Bermuda.

Ross's report of the capture of Washington reached
Lord Bathurst September 27, and caused so much
satisfaction that the British government decided to
show its approval by placing another major-general,
Lambert, with a brigade numbering twenty-two hundred rank-and-file, under Ross's command, to be used
without restriction, either in the Middle or the Southern States.[1] The Prince Regent highly applauded the
ability with which Ross had conducted the capture
of Washington, " an enterprise so creditable to his
Majesty's arms, and so well calculated to humble
the presumption of the American government, which
contrary to the real interests, and as it is believed
contrary to the prevailing wish, of the nation has
involved that country in an unnecessary and unjust

[1] Bathurst to Ross, Sept. 28, 1814; MSS. British Archives.

war against his Majesty." [1]  Only in one respect did
Bathurst hint a criticism on the course pursued by
Ross. While informing him, September 29, that reinforcements were on their way which would place
upward of ten thousand men under his command,
to be used very much at his discretion, Bathurst
added, [2] —

" You and your troops have gained great credit in the
discipline you observed at Washington. It is no dispar-
agement of your merit to say that it was prudent as well
as merciful to show such forbearance. If, however, you
should attack Baltimore, and could, consistent with that
discipline *which it is essential for you not to relax*, make
its inhabitants *feel* a little more the effects of your visit
than what has been experienced at Washington, you
would make that portion of the American people experience the consequences of the war who have most contributed to its existence."

When this despatch was written, Ross had made
his attack on Baltimore, and had failed. The report
of his failure and death was received by the War
Department in London October 17, and Bathurst as
soon as possible selected a new commander for the
expedition to New Orleans. Orders, dated October
24, were sent to Major-Generals Sir Edward Pakenham and Gibbs to join Vice-Admiral Cochrane forthwith, detailing the force at their command. Pakenham was to follow the instructions already given to

[1] Bathurst to Ross, Sept. 29, 1814; MSS. British Archives.
[2] Bathurst to Ross, Sept. 29, 1814; MSS. British Archives.

Ross, and was especially enjoined to conciliate the
people of Louisiana : —

" You will for that purpose cause the force under your
command to observe the strictest discipline ; to respect
the lives and the property of all those who are inclined to
a peaceable deportment, and by no means to excite the
black population to rise against their masters."

The " Statira " received orders, October 28, to convey Major-Generals Pakenham and Gibbs to the rendezvous at Negril Bay in Jamaica, whither the large
force intended for New Orleans was already moving from several distant quarters. The day for beginning the movement on New Orleans was already
fixed for November 20, and Pakenham could at that
season hardly expect to reach Jamaica in time to sail
with his troops. Meanwhile the English press talked
openly of the expedition and its object.

Military District No. 7, in which New Orleans and
Mobile were situated, had not been neglected by the
United States government. The regular force assigned by Secretary Armstrong for its defence consisted of five regiments of United States Infantry, —
the Second, Third, Seventh, Thirty-ninth, and Forty-
fourth, with three hundred and fifty artillerists, — an
aggregate of two thousand three hundred and seventy-
eight men. The provision was relatively liberal.
District No. 5, on Chesapeake Bay, contained an aggregate of two thousand two hundred and eight regular troops ; District No. 6, including North and
South Carolina and Georgia, was allotted two thou-

sand two hundred and forty-four men. One half the regular army was employed in such garrison duty, and a greater number could not have been allotted consistently with retaining an army in the field. Indeed, the only means by which Armstrong could provide so strong a defence, aggregating nearly eight thousand men, for the Southern States was by stripping Massachusetts. District No. 1, including Massachusetts and Maine, contained only six hundred and fifty-five regular troops; and District No. 2, including Rhode Island and Connecticut, contained only seven hundred and fourteen. Besides the regular troops, New Orleans enjoyed the protection of gunboats and one or two larger armed vessels. The city needed only an efficient commander to defy any ordinary attack.

Armstrong supplied a commander who might, as he believed, be safely considered efficient. In the month of May Andrew Jackson was appointed to the command of Military District No. 7, with headquarters at Mobile. At that moment Jackson, having finished the Creek war, was about to make the necessary arrangements for the future control of the Creek nation, and he did not take immediate command of his district. No occasion for haste existed. During the summer of 1814 no British force of consequence approached the Gulf of Mexico, or was likely to approach it until the frosts began. Jackson was detained in the centre of Alabama, undisturbed by fears for New Orleans, until the so-called Treaty or

Capitulation of August 9 with the Creeks released
him from further duties in that region.  He left the
Creek country August 11, with his regular troops,
going by water down the Alabama River, and arriving
at Mobile about August 15.

At the same moment government was brought to a
stand-still at Washington by the appearance of General Ross's army in the Patuxent, and the raids on
Washington and Baltimore.  Between August 20 and
September 25 the War Department could do little
more than attend to its own pressing dangers.  Jackson was left independent, substantially dictator over
the Southwest.  If New England carried out its intentions, and the government sank, as seemed probable, into helplessness, his dictatorship was likely to
be permanent.

When Jackson arrived at Mobile, August 15, the
defence of New Orleans was not in his mind.  The
people of Tennessee and Georgia had long been bent
on the seizure of the Floridas, and Jackson had been
one of the most ardent in favoring the step.  The
Creek war and the escape of the hostile Creeks to
East Florida strengthened his conviction that the
Spaniards must be expelled.  He had begun the war
with the idea of pushing his army directly through
the Creek country to Pensacola, which he meant to
hold.[1]  The instant he succeeded in destroying the
military power of the Creeks, he began preparations
for invading Florida.  As early as July he wrote

[1] Eaton's Jackson, p. 210.

to the War Department suggesting an attack on Pensacola : —

" Will you only say to me, Raise a few hundred militia (which can be quickly done), and with such a regular force as can be conveniently collected, make a descent upon Pensacola and reduce it? " [1]

At the same time Jackson entered, July 12, into an angry correspondence with the Spanish governor of Pensacola, and requested him to deliver up the Creek warriors who had taken refuge in East Florida, — a demand with which he knew that the Spaniard had no means of complying. August 10 he wrote to Armstrong announcing that he had given orders for the reoccupation of Mobile Point. " The United States in possession of Pensacola and Mobile, well defended, our whole coast and country in this quarter would be secure." [2] A direct attack by the British on New Orleans had not occurred to his mind.

Although Jackson received no answer from Washington to his suggestion, he came to Mobile, August 15, determined to pursue his object; and his decision was confirmed by the eccentric conduct of Major Nicholls, an Irish officer, who was sent to Pensacola, July 23, with the sloops-of-war " Hermes " and " Carron," with four officers, eleven non-commissioned officers, and ninety-seven privates of the Royal Marines, taking two howitzers, a field-piece, a thousand

[1] Eaton's Jackson, p. 212.
[2] Jackson to Armstrong, Aug. 10, 1814; MSS. War Department Archives.

stand of arms, and three hundred suits of clothing
for the Creek warriors.[1]  Nicholls landed his marines, seized Fort Barrancas, disembarked arms,
and began to collect the fugitive Creeks, commonly
known as Red Sticks, with a view to invading
Louisiana, while he spread extravagant stories of
his plans.

Had the British government sent Nicholls to Pensacola expressly to divert Jackson's attention from
New Orleans, he could not have used his means more
successfully for his purpose.  Jackson at Mobile,
some sixty miles away, learned within forty-eight
hours what Nicholls was doing at Pensacola, and
wrote instantly, August 27, to Governor Blount of
Tennessee,[2] calling out the whole quota of Tennessee
militia, twenty-five hundred men, who were to march
instantly to Mobile.  " It is currently reported in
Pensacola," he added, " that the Emperor of Russia
has offered his Britannic Majesty fifty thousand of
his best troops for the conquest of Louisiana, and
that this territory will fall a prey to the enemy before
the expiration of one month."

During the next three months Nicholls with a
mere handful of men distracted Jackson's whole
attention.  From Pensacola, August 29, Nicholls
issued a proclamation calling on the natives of Louisiana to assist him " in liberating from a faithless,

[1] Sir Alexander Cochrane to Croker, July 23, 1814; MSS.
British Archives.

[2] Jackson to Governor Blount, Aug. 27, 1814; Niles, vii. 47.

imbecile government" their paternal soil.[1]  A few
days afterward, September 3, a British sloop-of-war,
the "Sophie," appeared at Barataria, forty miles
south of New Orleans.   There for several years
smugglers and pirates had established a station, to
the scandal of society and with its connivance.[2]
Three Frenchmen, the brothers Laffite, — Jean, Pierre,
and Dominique, — ruled over this community, and
plundered impartially the commerce of England and
Spain, while defying the laws of the United States
and the power of the national government.[3]  The
British sloop-of-war brought to Jean Laffite a letter
from Major Nicholls asking him and his men, with
their vessels, to enter into British service, under penalty of destruction to their establishment.[4]  Laffite,
preferring to make terms with the United States, and
knowing that the authorities at New Orleans were
about to break up his establishment in any case, sent
to Governor Claiborne the letters he received from
Captain Lockyer of the "Sophie," and offered his
services to defend Barataria.

Nothing in these demonstrations suggested a direct
attack on New Orleans.   Nicholls constantly gave out
that he meant to attack Mobile, and from there " push
for New Orleans ; "[5] but his force was wholly inade-

---

[1] Military and Naval Letters, p. 407.
[2] Latour, p. 14.
[3] National Intelligencer, Oct. 22, 1814.
[4] Latour, Appendix, p. ix.
[5] Anonymous Letter of Aug. 8, 1814 ; Latour, Appendix, p. v.

quate, and his rank was much too low, to warrant
the belief that he intended a serious campaign.   Yet
such noisy and insulting conduct was adapted to irri-
tate a man of Jackson's temper, and to keep his attention fixed on Mobile and Pensacola.   Nicholls even
undertook to annoy Jackson in his headquarters.

On a bare sand-point at the entrance of Mobile Bay,
General Wilkinson, on taking possession of Mobile in
April, 1813, established a battery which he armed
with Spanish cannon.   The redoubt, which was called
Fort Bowyer, could not hold against a land attack
properly supported, and offered a temptation to the
enemy; but in the absence of a land force competent
to besiege it, the fortification was useful to close the
entrance of Mobile Bay against marauders.   In Fort
Bowyer Jackson placed one hundred and sixty men of
the Second United States Infantry, commanded by
Major William Lawrence.   Twenty guns were mounted
on the platforms, but according to the American account only two twenty-four pounders and six twelve-
pounders were likely to prove serviceable.[1]

The British force at Pensacola consisted chiefly of
four sloops, commanded by Captain W. H. Percy, —
the "Hermes," twenty-two guns, the "Carron,"
twenty, and the "Sophie" and "Childers" of eighteen guns each.   The usual armament of such vessels
consisted of thirty-two-pound carronades, with two
long-nines or sixes.   Apparently the British squadron
threw thirty-four thirty-two-pound shot, and four nine

[1] Latour, p. 34.

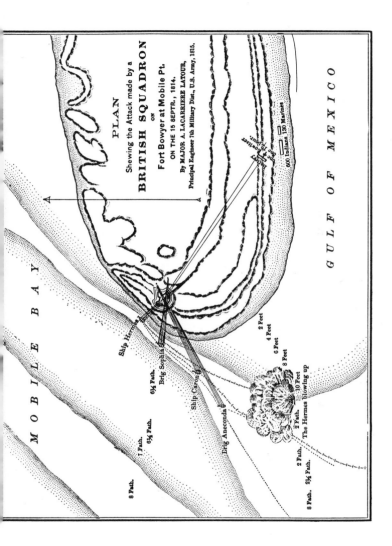

PLAN

Shewing the Attack made by a

**BRITISH SQUADRON**

ON

Fort Bowyer at Mobile Pt.,

ON THE 15 SEPTR., 1814.

By MAJOR. A. LACARRIERE LATOUR,

Principal Engineer 7th Military Dist., U.S. Army, 1815.

*M O B I L E   B A Y*

*G U L F   O F   M E X I C O*

8 Fath.

7 Fath.

6½ Fath.

6½ Fath.

Ship Hermes

Brig Sophia

Ship Carron

Brig Anaconda

8 Fath.  3½ Fath.

2 Fath.  2 Fath.

The Hermes blowing up

10 Feet

8 Feet

6 Feet

4 Feet

2 Feet

600 Indians  130 Marines

Battery
Bre. 20 Pounders.

or six pound balls at a broadside. Whether the armament was greater or smaller mattered little, for Captain Percy was unable to use with effect the batteries of either the " Carron " or the " Childers." With much difficulty, owing to the shoals, he brought his squadron within range of Fort Bowyer, and with more gallantry than discretion prepared for the attack.

According to the British account, the land force at Percy's command consisted of sixty marines and one hundred and twenty Indians, with one five-and-a-half-inch howitzer. According to the American account, a twelve-pound field-piece was placed ashore in battery with the howitzer. Such a force was insufficient to do more than intercept the garrison if it should be driven out of the fort. The brunt of the action fell on the ships, and experience did not warrant Percy in believing that his sloops, with their carronades, could silence a work like Fort Bowyer.

Nevertheless Percy gallantly made the attempt. At half-past four of the afternoon of September 15, he brought the " Hermes " close in, and opened fire within musket-shot of the fort. The " Sophie " came to anchor some distance astern, but within range. The " Carron " and the " Childers " anchored so far out that their carronades were useless, and apparently even the American twenty-four-pounders did not touch them. The " Hermes " and the " Sophie " alone sustained injury,[1] but their experience was decisive.

[1] James, ii. 344.

After an hour's action, the cable of the "Hermes" being cut, she became unmanageable, and at last grounded and was abandoned. Captain Percy set her on fire, and carried his crew, including the wounded, with much difficulty to his other vessels. The "Sophie" withdrew from fire, and the squadron returned at once to Pensacola.

Assuming that Captain Percy could use with effect only the twenty guns of the broadsides of the "Hermes" and "Sophie" against the twenty guns of the fort, the American gunnery was evidently superior to the British. The "Hermes" lost twenty-five men killed and twenty-four wounded, — a very severe loss in a crew which could not much have exceeded one hundred and fifty men. A better test of marksmanship was offered by the "Sophie," which received comparatively little attention from the fort, but lost six killed and sixteen wounded. The whole American loss was reported as four killed and five wounded,[1] under the combined fire of both ships at close range, the fort having no casemates, and parapets only on the front and flanks.[2] Three guns were dismounted.

Greatly pleased by this success, Jackson issued a counter-proclamation[3] to the people of Louisiana, somewhat in the style of that which Nicholls had issued three weeks before.

"The base, the perfidious Britons," it began, "have attempted to invade your country. They had the temer-

[1] General Orders of Sept. 17, 1814; Niles, vii. 95.
[2] Latour, p. 33.    [3] Latour, Appendix, p. xxix.

ity to attack Fort Bowyer with their incongruous horde of Indians and negro assassins. . . . The proud, vain-glorious boaster Colonel Nicholls, when he addressed you, Louisianians and Kentuckians, had forgotten that you were the votaries of freedom. . . . I ask you, Louisianians, can we place any confidence in the honor of men who have courted an alliance with pirates and robbers? Have not these noble Britons, these honorable men, Colonel Nicholls and the honorable Captain W. H. Percy, the true representatives of their royal master, done this? Have they not made offers to the pirates of Barataria to join them and their holy cause? And have they not dared to insult you by calling on you to associate as brethren with them and this hellish banditti?"

With the exception of this proclamation and another [1] of the same date to the free negroes of Louisiana, Jackson paid no attention to the defence of New Orleans, but left it entirely to Governor Claiborne. He disregarded a memorial from the citizens, dated September 18, urging his personal attention and presence. "My whole force would not satisfy the demands they make," he wrote to the War Department, October 10.[2] "As soon as security is given to this section of my district, which is first indispensably necessary, I shall hasten to New Orleans," he wrote from Mobile, October 14.[3] He entertained no doubt

[1] Latour, Appendix, p. xxxi.

[2] Jackson to Monroe, Oct. 10, 1814; MSS. War Department Archives.

[3] Jackson to Monroe, Oct. 14, 1814 ; MSS. War Department Archives.

that at Mobile he stood between the British and their object. " Unless Pensacola were reduced," said his confidential biographer [1] ten years afterward, " it was vain to think of defending the country. . . . The attack on Mobile Point was a confirmation of his previous conjectures as to the views of the enemy."

The Government at Washington became alarmed. While Jackson waited at Mobile for the arrival of General Coffee with his Tennesseeans to attack Pensacola, Monroe at Washington received warnings from Europe, Halifax, and Bermuda that the British force which had just laid Washington in ashes was but a division of a larger army on its way to attack New Orleans.   He wrote to Jackson, September 25,[2] —

" There is great cause to believe that the enemy have set on foot an expedition against Louisiana, through the Mobile, in the expectation that while so strong a pressure was made from Canada and in this quarter, whereby the force of the country and attention of the government would be much engaged, a favorable opportunity would be afforded them to take possession of the lower part of that State, and of all the country along the Mobile."

The President, he continued, had ordered five thousand additional troops from Tennessee to march to Jackson's aid, and had directed the governor of Georgia to hold twenty-five hundred more subject to Jackson's orders.   He had also sent one hundred thousand

[1] Eaton, pp. 239, 240.

[2] Monroe to Jackson, Sept. 25, 1814 ; MSS. War Department Records.   Monroe MSS.

dollars in Treasury notes to Governor Blount of Tennessee, to be applied to the necessary expenses of the
campaign, and Jackson could draw on him for the
necessary funds.    The orders to the governor of Tennessee were sent the same day, September 25.    A week
later, October 3, Monroe wrote to Governor Shelby of
Kentucky, requesting him to send twenty-five hundred
men to Jackson.    Again, October 10, Monroe wrote to
Jackson, informing him that not less than twelve
thousand five hundred men were already subject to
his orders, from Kentucky, Tennessee, and Georgia:

"There is strong reason to presume, from intelligence
just received from our ministers at Ghent, that a British
force consisting of twelve or fifteen thousand men sailed
from Ireland early in September for New Orleans and
the Mobile, with intention to take possession of that city
and of the country through which the great rivers on
which the whole of the United States westward of the
Alleghany Mountains so essentially depends."

When Monroe received a letter from Jackson, dated
September 9, indicating his intention of attacking
Pensacola, the secretary replied October 21,[1] forbid-
ding the step.    "I hasten to communicate to you the
directions of the President that you should at present
take no measures which would involve this government in a contest with Spain."    He reiterated the
warning that British forces would probably be directed
against Louisiana; but he did not order Jackson to

[1] Monroe to Jackson, Oct. 21, 1814; MSS. War Department
Records.

New Orleans, nor did he notify him that arms would be sent there. Not until November 2 were orders given that four thousand stand of arms should be sent from Pittsburg, and only November 11 and 15 were the arms shipped, not by steamer but by the ordinary flatboat.[1] Even then the arms were in advance of the men. The governor of Tennessee could not appoint an earlier day than November 13 for mustering the new levies, and on that day three thousand men assembled at Nashville, while two thousand collected at Knoxville. Not till November 20 did the Nashville division start down the river, to arrive a month later at New Orleans.

Jackson quietly waited at Mobile for the twenty-five hundred men he had summoned from Tennessee by his letter of August 27. Two months were consumed in this manner. The Tennessee brigade, under command of General Coffee, marched promptly, and passing through the Indian country arrived October 25 at Mobile. Coffee brought with him somewhat more than the number of men required by the call. His force was about twenty-eight hundred.[2] Jackson held at Mobile the Second, Third, Thirty-ninth, and Forty-fourth United States Infantry, besides some Mississippi troops and Choctaw Indians.[3] With the

[1] Monroe to Hugh L. White, Feb. 9, 1827 ; Monroe MSS., State Department Archives.

[2] Eaton, p. 243.

[3] Jackson to Governor Blount, Nov. 14, 1814 ; Official Letters, p. 451.

Tennesseeans he could dispose of more than four thousand troops.

Notwithstanding Monroe's warning letter of September 25, Jackson still paid no immediate attention to New Orleans. October 28 he wrote to Monroe, acknowledging a letter from him of September 27, and announcing that he was then organizing an attack on Pensacola. Having no authority for the act, and aware that the Government was anxious about New Orleans, he added : " I hope in a few weeks to place this quarter in perfect security, and to be able to move to New Orleans with General Coffee's mounted men." [1] October 31 Jackson wrote, apparently for the first time, that he needed arms, and that half the arms of the militia were not fit for use.[2]

Taking four thousand one hundred men,[3] without trains, Jackson marched November 3 against Pensacola, which he occupied, November 7, with little resistance, although " Spanish treachery," he said,[4] " kept us out of possession of the fort until nearly twelve o'clock at night." The next morning the British blew up Fort Barrancas, six miles below,

[1] Jackson to Monroe, Oct. 28, 1814; MSS. War Department Archives.

[2] Jackson to Monroe, Oct. 31, 1814 ; MSS. War Department Archives.

[3] Jackson to Monroe, Nov. 14, 1814 ; MSS. War Department Archives.

[4] Jackson to Monroe, Nov. 14, 1814 ; MSS. War Department Archives.

where they had established themselves, and Colonel Nicholls sailed away no farther than the Appalachicola River, leaving Jackson to do what he pleased with Pensacola, a position of no value to either party.

Even Armstrong, who favored Jackson against what he thought the ill-will of Madison and Monroe, afterward condemned the movement against Pensacola. "The general's attack and capture of the town on the 7th of November, 1814, was to say the least of it decidedly ill-judged, involving at once an offence to a neutral power, and a probable misapplication of both time and force as regarded the defence of New Orleans."[1] Jackson remained only two days at the place, and then returned to Mobile, where he arrived November 11 and remained until November 22, as though still in doubt. He detached Major Blue of the Thirty-ninth United States Infantry, with a thousand mounted men, to the Appalachicola to break up the depot established there for supplying assistance to the Red Stick Indians.[2] Nothing indicated that he felt anxiety for the safety of New Orleans, although the British expedition, comprising some fifty vessels, was then at Jamaica, and November 26 actually sailed for the Mississippi.[3]

Jackson's conduct greatly alarmed the President and the Secretary of War. When the despatches arrived at Washington announcing what was taking

[1] Armstrong's Notices, ii. 176.
[2] Eaton, p. 257.     [3] Subaltern, p. 101.

place at Mobile and Pensacola, Monroe hastened to order General Gaines to Mobile. He wrote to Jackson, December 7,[1] —

"General Gaines is ordered to join you and act under you in the defence of New Orleans and of the district under your command. Full confidence is entertained that this appointment of an officer of his merit will afford to you a very acceptable aid in the discharge of your highly important duties. . . . Much anxiety is felt lest you should remain too long on the Mobile. The city [New Orleans], it is presumed, is the principal object of the enemy, and it cannot be defended on either of the passes by which it may be approached, — one by the river Mississippi itself, another by the Fourche, the third by Lake Pontchartrain, — without occupying the ground bearing on these passes."

Three days afterward, December 10, Monroe wrote again in stronger terms : [2] —

"It is hoped that you will have long since taken a suitable position on the river to afford complete protection to that city. Mobile is a comparatively trifling object with the British government. Your presence at such a point on the river with the main body of your troops will be of vital importance."

Jackson left Mobile November 22, four days before the British expedition under Sir Edward Pakenham sailed from Jamaica. Both Jackson and Pakenham

[1] Monroe to Jackson, Dec. 7, 1814 ; MSS. War Department Records.

[2] Monroe to Jackson, Dec. 10, 1814 ; MSS. War Department Records.

were moving to New Orleans at the same time. Pakenham brought with him an immense fleet and a large army. Jackson, instead of taking, as Monroe hoped, " the main body " of his troops, left at Mobile the main body, consisting of the Second, Third, and Thirty-ninth regiments, about a thousand or twelve hundred men.

According to his friend's biography, probably founded on his own information, Jackson's " principal fears at present were that Mobile might fall, the left bank of the Mississippi be gained, all communication with the Western States cut off, and New Orleans be thus unavoidably reduced." [1] That the British should advance against the Mississippi by way of Mobile was improbable, as Monroe pointed out; but they could have taken no course which better suited the resources of Jackson. A march of near two hundred miles, through a barren and wooded country, with Jackson's whole force concentrated in their front, was an undertaking that promised little success.

Leaving at Mobile three regular regiments, Jackson ordered the Forty-fourth regiment to New Orleans, and directed Coffee with two thousand of his mounted brigade to march to Baton Rouge. He was himself ill and suffering, and made no excessive haste. " I leave this for New Orleans on the 22d instant," he wrote to Monroe, November 20,[2] " and if my health

---

[1] Eaton, pp. 261, 282.

[2] Jackson to Monroe, Nov. 20, 1814; MSS. War Department Archives.

permits, shall reach there in twelve days. I travel by land, to have a view of the points at which the enemy might effect a landing." Starting from Mobile November 22, he arrived at New Orleans, about one hundred and twenty-five miles, only December 2.[1] His troops were then much scattered. The main body was at Mobile. The Forty-fourth regiment was in march from Mobile to New Orleans, where the Seventh regiment was already stationed. A thousand volunteer horsemen, part of Coffee's brigade, under Major Blue of the Thirty-ninth Infantry, were scouring the Escambia, Yellow Water, and other remote Florida recesses. The remainder of Coffee's brigade was at Baton Rouge December 4, greatly reduced by various causes, and numbering only twelve hundred men.[2] A few Mississippi dragoons were near them. A division of Tennessee militia, twenty-five hundred strong, under General Carroll, had started from Nashville November 20, and might be expected at New Orleans about December 20. A division of Kentucky militia, also twenty-five hundred strong, was on its way, and might arrive about the new year. Meanwhile the British expedition was sailing, with much deliberation, past the shores of Cuba, toward Florida.[3]

At New Orleans nothing had yet been done for defence; but inaction was not the worst. Jackson found

[1] Jackson to Monroe, Dec. 2, 1814; MSS. War Department Archives.

[2] Eaton, p. 290.          [3] Subaltern, p. 193.

the people despondent and distrustful.[1]  The legislature showed incompetence and, as Jackson believed, indifference.  The whole population of Louisiana was but small, containing certainly not more than fifty thousand white inhabitants; while the city of New Orleans probably numbered hardly more than twenty thousand persons including slaves.  The State government supplied one thousand militia under the general requisition of the President.[2]  The city raised a battalion of volunteers nearly three hundred strong, a rifle company numbering sixty-two men when in the field, and a battalion of free mulattoes, chiefly refugees from St. Domingo, which produced two hundred and ten men, — in all, between five and six hundred troops. Jackson immediately reviewed the companies, December 2, and could expect no further aid from these sources.  No arms were in store, even if men could be found, and none of the necessary supplies of an army had been provided.

Jackson's first act after arriving at New Orleans showed no consciousness of danger.  Armstrong, criticising his measures, afterward said:[3]  " Had the general been better acquainted with military history, he would not have suffered a single day of the twenty he had for preparation to have passed without forming one or more intrenched camps for the protection of the city."  Instead of doing this, Jackson did what

[1] Eaton, p. 286; Latour, p. 53.
[2] General Orders of Aug. 6, 1814; Latour, Appendix, p. xvii.
[3] Notices, ii. 177.

had been done by Armstrong and Winder at Washington in August. Having arrived in the city December 2, he started two days afterward to inspect Fort St. Philip on the river sixty miles below. He returned to New Orleans December 11,[1] believing that the British would approach by the river, and prepared works to arrest their advance.[2] He then rode out to Chef Menteur and Lake Pontchartrain on the north, which he thought the next probable point of attack. He was still absent, December 15, examining the situation of different works northward of the city, when the British expedition struck its first blow.[3]

Six American gunboats, the whole force on the lakes, watched the entrance of Lake Borgne through which the British must pass if they attacked New Orleans by way of the lakes. They were stationed for observation rather than for resistance, — although for observation a few fishermen's boats would have been more useful. The British expedition, upward of fifty sail, made land December 10,[4] and was seen by the gunboats, which retired within the lake. The British land-forces were transferred from the heavy ships into the lighter vessels, and under convoy of sloops-of-war entered Lake Borgne December 13. The boats of the squadron, carrying about a thousand

---

[1] Jackson to Monroe, Dec. 12, 1814 ; MSS. War Department Archives.

[2] Eaton, p. 272.          [3] Eaton, p. 282.

[4] Sir Alexander Cochrane to J. W. Croker, Dec. 16, 1814; Latour, Appendix, p. cxxxviii.

seamen and marines,[1] left the ships during the night of December 12 in search of the American gunboats, which tried to escape, but were becalmed and obliged by the tide to anchor. After a tedious row of thirty-six hours the British boats overtook the gunboat flotilla December 14, and after a sharp struggle succeeded in capturing the whole, with a loss of seventeen men killed and seventy-seven wounded.[2] The American crews numbered one hundred and eighty-two men, and lost six killed and thirty-five wounded.

News of the capture of the gunboats, which occurred at noon December 14 about forty miles to the eastward of New Orleans, arrived on the evening of December 15, and produced the utmost consternation.[3] Jackson hurried back to the city, where his presence was no longer a matter of choice but necessity. Instantly on hearing the news he sent expresses to Coffee at Baton Rouge, and to Carroll and Thomas, wherever they might be found on the river, urging them to hasten with all possible speed to New Orleans. He issued a proclamation to the people of the city, in which he threatened them with punishment if they were not unanimous,[4] and at the same time he recommended the legislature to suspend the writ of habeas corpus. Finding the legislature hesitate, Jackson declared martial law by proclamation[5]

---

[1] James, ii. 349.

[2] Report of Captain Lockyer, Dec. 18, 1814 ; James, ii. 523.

[3] Letter of Dec. 16, 1814 ; Niles, vii. 316.

[4] General Orders, Dec. 16, 1814; Niles, vii. 316.

[5] General Orders, Dec. 16, 1814 ; Niles, vii. 317.

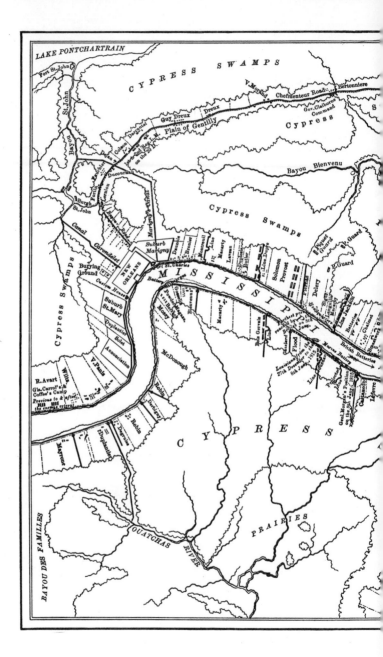

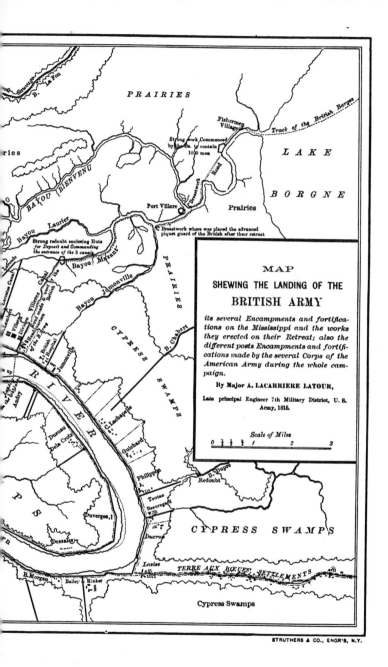

MAP

SHEWING THE LANDING OF THE

BRITISH ARMY

*its several Encampments and fortifications on the Mississippi and the works they erected on their Retreat; also the different posts Encampments and fortifications made by the several Corps of the American Army during the whole campaign.*

By Major A. LACARRIERE LATOUR,

Late principal Engineer 7th Military District, U. S.
Army, 1815.

Scale of Miles

0   ¼   ½   ¾   1        2        3

the same day, December 16, and assumed dictatorial powers.

Feverish activity followed. General Coffee above Baton Rouge received Jackson's summons on the evening of December 17, and marched the next morning with twelve hundred and fifty men. In two days he made one hundred and twenty miles, camping on the night of December 19 within fifteen miles of New Orleans, with eight hundred men.[1] Carroll, with the Tennessee brigade which left Nashville November 27, arrived at New Orleans December 21, and a squadron of mounted Mississippi volunteers hurried down. The British also lost no time. Their advance disembarked on the Isle aux Poix in Lake Borgne on the night of December 14, and during the following week all the boats and seamen of the fleet were occupied in transporting seven thousand men, with their equipment, thirty miles from the fleet to the island. During the night of December 18 two British officers reconnoitred the head of Lake Borgne.[2] At the mouth of Bayou Bienvenu, not fifteen miles from New Orleans, was a fishermen's village. The fishermen were Spaniards, with no love for the United States, and ready to accept British pay. They received the two British officers, and conveyed them in a canoe up the bayou to the Villeré plantation on the bank of the Mississippi only six miles from New

[1] Eaton, p. 290.

[2] Report of Major-General Keane, Dec. 26, 1814; James, ii. 529.

Orleans.[1] There, at their leisure, Lieutenant Peddie of the quartermaster's department and Captain Spencer of the "Carron" selected the line of advance for the British army, and returned, unmolested and unseen, through the bayou to the lake and the Isle aux Poix.

Only December 21, two days after the British reconnaissance, was an American picket of eight men and a sergeant placed at the fishermen's village,[2] where they remained thirty-six hours without learning that British officers had been on the spot, or that the fishermen were all away, acting as pilots for the approaching British boats. Meanwhile the troops at Isle aux Poix were ready to move almost as soon as Lieutenant Peddie could return to show them the way. At ten o'clock on the morning of December 22 the light brigade — sixteen hundred and eighty-eight rank-and-file,[3] under Colonel Thornton, who had led the advance at Bladensburg — embarked in boats, and after a day on the lake arrived the next morning, December 23, at daylight, without giving alarm, at the fishermen's village, where they surprised and captured the picket, and then passing up the bayou five miles, landed at a point about three miles from the Mississippi River. No attempt at concealment was made.[4] The troops

[1] Admiral Cochrane to Mr. Croker, Jan. 18, 1815; James, ii. 550.

[2] Latour, p. 77; Jackson's Report of Dec. 27, 1814; Latour, Appendix, p. xlv.

[3] James, ii. 355.   [4] Subaltern, p. 212.

were formed in column, and found no obstacles to their march except the soft ground and the ditches. Through reeds and cypress swamp they made their way about three miles, when their advance suddenly entered open fields skirted by an orange-grove, with the broad Mississippi beyond. They were on the Villeré plantation ; and they surprised and captured Major Villeré and his militia company, in his own house at noon-day, after a march of three miles with sixteen hundred men, from a point which had been recognized by Jackson as one of two or three necessary avenues of approach.

The record of American generalship offered many examples of misfortune, but none so complete as this. Neither Hull nor Harrison, neither Winder nor Samuel Smith, had allowed a large British army, heralded long in advance, to arrive within seven miles unseen and unsuspected, and without so much as an earthwork, a man, or a gun between them and their object. The disaster was unprecedented, and could be repaired only by desperate measures.

## CHAPTER XIII.

THE defence of New Orleans resembled the defence of Washington until the moment when in each case the British expedition came within sight. Jackson was even slower than Winder to see the point of danger or to concentrate his forces. At Washington, Winder took command July 1, and the British expedition arrived August 16; at Mobile, Jackson took command August 16, and the British expedition arrived December 14. In neither case was the interval seriously employed for defence. So much was Jackson misled that he collected no troops, and made no inquiry as to the military means at his disposal at New Orleans. Had he gone there September 1, he would have felt the want of arms and equipment, and would have been able to supply them. During the summer, while yet among the Creeks, he was said to have made requisition for a quantity of war material to be sent to New Orleans;[1] but he certainly showed no interest in its shipment or the causes for its delay in arrival. The arms should have reached New Orleans in October, when he would have had ample time to correct any failure or want

[1] Latour, p. 66.

of supply.   He could have used, in case of necessity, the steamboat "Enterprise," which was then
regularly plying on the Mississippi, and was not the
only steamboat on those waters.[1]   If New Orleans
was deficient in many articles of military necessity,
the fault was not wholly in the War Department.

A similar criticism applied to the political situation
at New Orleans.    Governor Claiborne wanted authority to control the factions in his legislature, and
the legislature wanted an impulse sufficiently ener-
getic to overcome its inertia.    Probably Jackson's
presence would at any time have given authority to
Claiborne and energy to the entire State government.
From the moment of his actual arrival, difficulties of
this kind seemed to cease.   "It is hardly possible,"
said the military historian of the campaign,[2] "to form
an idea of the change which his arrival produced on
the minds of the people."

When the British expedition was once known to
have appeared at the entrance of Lake Borgne, Jackson's task was perhaps simpler than Winder's, for
Winder might doubt whether the British meant to
attack Washington, and in fact General Ross took
the decision only at the last moment; but no one
could doubt that New Orleans was the object of
Pakenham's expedition.   Jackson had only to choose
his positions and collect his resources.   These were
small; but on the other hand the British were opposed
by natural difficulties much greater at New Orleans

[1] Eaton, p. 293, *note*.          [2] Latour, p. 53.

than at Washington. Even their greater numbers were a disadvantage when they were obliged to move in widely separated detachments, in open boats, from a point far distant from their column's head, and toward a point easily fortified.

If until the moment of the enemy's appearance Jackson showed no more military capacity than was shown by Winder, his conduct thenceforward offered a contrast the more striking because it proved how Washington might have been saved. Winder lost his head when he saw an enemy. Jackson needed to see his enemy in order to act; he thought rightly only at the moment when he struck. At noon, December 23, New Orleans was in greater danger than Washington on the afternoon of August 23, when the British advanced from the Patuxent. Had Colonel Thornton followed his impulses and marched directly on the city, he must have reached it before a gun could have been fired by the Americans ; his own muskets would have given the first news of his arrival. Major-General Keane, his commanding officer, preferred caution,[1] and his delay gave a few hours time for Jackson to show his qualities.

News that a British column had reached the Villeré plantation was brought to Jackson at headquarters in New Orleans, at about half-past one o'clock, much as the news was brought to Winder, August 24, that the British were marching on Bladensburg. The

[1] Subaltern, p. 215 (American edition, 1833).

distances were about the same. Winder and Jackson both allowed the enemy to approach within seven miles before anything had been done for defence. In one respect Jackson was more unfortunate than Winder, for his troops were not ready to march; they were not even collected. Jackson sent orders to the different corps, but several hours passed before the men could be brought down and posted between the city and the British.

Fortunately Major Latour, chief-engineer in Military District No. 7, had been sent that morning to examine the approaches from Lake Borgne, and as he rode down the road at noon he met persons flying toward town with news that the British had penetrated through the canal to Villeré's house. Latour was a trained French engineer, whose services were extremely valuable, not only during the campaign but afterward; for he subsequently wrote a " History of the War in West Florida and Louisiana," which was far the best military work published in the United States till long after that time, and furnished the only accurate maps and documents of the campaign at New Orleans.[1] On the morning of December 23 Latour approached within rifle-shot of the British force, and judged their number accurately as sixteen or eighteen hundred men.[2] Such exact information, which could not have been gained from any

[1] See Memoir of Latour in Cullum's Campaigns of the War of 1812–1815, p. 309.

[2] Latour, p. 88.

ordinary scout, was invaluable. Latour hastened to headquarters, and reported at two o'clock to Jackson the position and numbers of the enemy. The general, on that information, decided to attack.

For such a purpose Jackson's resources were ample. Four miles above the city his Tennessee militia were camped, — Carroll's brigade numbering probably about two thousand effectives, and the remnants of Coffee's mounted brigade numbering some seven hundred men in the field. The Mississippi and New Orleans volunteers could be reckoned at about seven hundred men,[1] besides three regiments of city militia. The Seventh United States Infantry produced four hundred and sixty-five men in the ranks; the Forty-fourth counted three hundred and thirty-one; while a detachment of artillerists, twenty-two in number, with two six-pound field-pieces, added greatly to the numerical strength of the Infantry.[2] Against Thornton's force, numbering one thousand six hundred and eighty-eight rank-and-file, or about nineteen hundred men all told, Jackson could oppose about five thousand Infantry with two field-pieces.

Besides these land forces Jackson was provided with another resource. In the river at New Orleans lay a war-schooner, the " Carolina," rated at fourteen guns, armed with one long twelve-pounder and six twelve-pound carronades on a broadside.[3] A sixteen-gun sloop-of-war, the " Louisiana," was also at New

---

[1] Latour, p. 105.        [2] Latour, p. 105.
[3] Captain Henley's Letter of Dec. 28, 1814 ; Niles, vii. 387.

Orleans, but not ready for immediate use. The " Carolina " could be brought instantly into action, and her broadside of seven twelve-pounders, added to the field-battery of two six-pounders, gave Jackson immense advantage over the British, who had no artillery except two three-pounders and rockets, and whose lines must be enfiladed by the " Carolina's " fire.

Jackson, aware of his superiority, expected with reason to destroy the British detachment. He did not even think more than half his force necessary for the purpose, but detached the whole of Carroll's brigade and the three regiments of city militia, — fully twenty-five hundred men, — to guard the town against an apprehended attack from the north. Without giving the reasons which led him to believe that the British could approach on that side without ample warning, his report said, —

" Apprehending a double attack by the way of Chef Menteur, I left General Carroll's force and the militia of the city posted on the Gentilly road, and at five o'clock P.M. marched to meet the enemy, whom I was resolved to attack in his first position, with Major Hind's dragoons, General Coffee's brigade, parts of the Seventh and Forty-fourth regiments, the uniformed companies of militia under the command of Major Plauché, two hundred men of color chiefly from St. Domingo, raised by Colonel Savary and acting under the command of Major Daquin, and a detachment of artillery under the direction of Colonel McRea, with two six-pounders under the command of Lieutenant Spots, — not exceeding in all fifteen hundred."

More exact returns showed that Jackson carried
with him eight hundred and eighty-four regular troops
and two field-pieces, five hundred and sixty-three
mounted riflemen of Coffee's brigade, five hundred
and fifty-nine Louisiana militia, one hundred and
seven Mississippians, and eighteen Choctaw Indians,
— in all, twenty-one hundred and thirty-one men
and two guns, besides the " Carolina," which dropped
down the river at four o'clock.[1]

Jackson did not, like Winder, pass the hours in
looking at his enemy, nor did he, like General Smith
at Baltimore, send out militia under militia officers,
to stand in close order on an open field and wait
attack. His chief difficulty was due to the ground,
which obliged him to make his main assault in a
narrow column along the road. To gain the advantage of his numbers, he detached Coffee with seven
hundred and thirty-two men, mostly armed with
rifles, to make a detour toward the left and fall on
the British flank and rear, while Jackson himself,
with fourteen hundred men and two guns, should
strike the British advance where it was posted on
the levee.

The signal for battle was to be given by the
" Carolina's " guns. Commodore Patterson in the
" Carolina " received his orders at half-past six, and
getting out sweeps, brought his vessel in a few minutes abreast of the British camp, where he anchored

[1] Latour, p. 104.    Parton, i. 617.    Commodore Patterson's
Report of Dec. 28, 1814; Latour, Appendix, p. xliii.

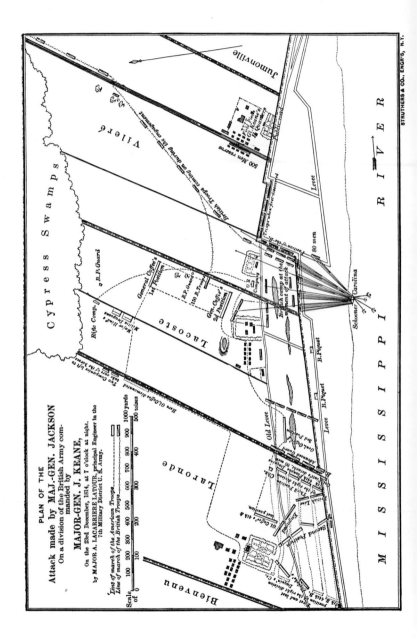

PLAN OF THE
Attack made by MAJ.-GEN. JACKSON
On a division of the British Army com-
manded by
MAJOR-GEN. J. KEANE,
On the 23d December, 1814, at 7 o'clock at night.
by MAJOR A. LACARRIERE LATOUR, principal Engineer in the
7th Military District U. S. Army.

Line of march of the American Troops.
Line of march of the British Troops.

Scale of 0  100 200 300 400 500 600 700 800 900 1000 yards
100 200 300 400 500 toises

STRUTHERS & CO., ENGR'S, N. Y.

close in shore and began a heavy fire,[1] soon after seven o'clock. Ten minutes later, Jackson, waiting about two miles above, ordered his men to advance, and moving down the road with his regulars and New Orleans companies struck the British outposts about a mile below his point of departure, at a few minutes before eight o'clock. At the same time Coffee, as he marched along the edge of the swamp, hearing the signal, wheeled to the right, and moved toward the British flank.

Night had then fallen. The weary British troops had lain down, when their sentries on the levee gave the alarm, and immediately afterward the roar of seven cannon close beside them threw their camp into confusion. About half an hour afterward, while the " Carolina " still swept the camp with its shot, the British sentries on the levee a mile above gave another alarm, and in a few moments the outposts were sharply attacked.

The accounts of the battle fought along the levee, under the command of Jackson in person, were both confused and contradictory. Thornton's brigade was composed of the Eighty-fifth and Ninety-fifth regiments, a company of rocketeers, one hundred sappers and miners, and the Fourth regiment as a support, — in all, sixteen hundred and eighty-eight rank-and-file.[2] At the point where the fighting began the

---

[1] Patterson's Report of Dec. 28, 1814 : Latour, Appendix, p. xliii.

[2] James, ii. 355.

British had merely an outpost, which was forced back by Jackson's attack, with some difficulty, about one hundred and fifty yards.[1] Colonel Thornton ordered two of his regiments — the Eighty-fifth and Ninety-fifth, eight hundred rank-and-file[2] — to support the outpost, and their arrival checked Jackson's advance. Indeed, the American line was driven back and lost ground, until the two field-pieces were in danger, and were hastily withdrawn.[3] Each party claimed that the other first withdrew from fire; but the American report admitted that the battle which began on the levee at eight ceased before nine, while Jackson seemed not to regard his attack as successful. His first brief report, written December 26,[4] said, —

" The heavy smoke occasioned by an excessive fire rendered it necessary that I should draw off my troops, after a severe conflict of upward of an hour."

Jackson's official report of December 27 said,[5] —

" There can be but little doubt that we should have succeeded on that occasion with our inferior force in destroying or capturing the enemy, had not a thick fog which arose about eight o'clock occasioned some confusion among the different corps. Fearing the consequences, under this circumstance, of the further prose-

[1] Latour's Plan.

[2] James, ii. 355.  Keane's Report of Dec, 26, 1814 ; James, ii. 529.

[3] Latour, pp. 96, 97.  Parton, ii. 90.

[4] Report of Dec. 26, 1815; Latour, Appendix, p. xliv.

[5] Report of Dec. 27, 1814; Niles, vii. 357.

cution of a night attack with troops then acting together for the first time, I contented myself with lying on the field that night."

Although the battle was severest where Jackson commanded, it was most successful where Coffee attacked. On hearing the "Carolina" open fire, Coffee turning to the right advanced on the British flank, striking it nearly opposite to the "Carolina's" position. The British, thus surrounded, were placed in a situation which none but the steadiest troops could have maintained. So great was the confusion that no organized corps opposed Coffee's men. Squads of twenty or thirty soldiers, collecting about any officer in their neighborhood, made head as they best could against Coffee's riflemen, and the whole British position seemed encircled by the American fire. Forced back toward the river, the British rallied behind an old levee which happened at that point to run parallel with the new levee, at a distance of about three hundred yards.[1] Knots of men, mixed in great disorder, here advancing, there retreating, carried on a desultory battle over the field, often fighting with clubbed weapons, knives, and fists. At last the British centre, finding a strong protection in the old levee which answered for an earthwork, held firm against Coffee's further advance, and were also sheltered by the new levee in their rear from the fire of the "Carolina's" guns. At about the same time several companies of the Twenty-first and

[1] Latour's Plan of the Battle of December 23; Peddie's Sketch.

Ninety-third regiments arrived from Lake Borgne, and raised the British force to two thousand and fifty rank-and-file.[1] Coffee then despaired of further success, and withdrew his men from the field.

"My brigade," wrote Coffee immediately afterward,[2] "met the enemy's line near four hundred yards from the river. The fire on both sides was kept up remarkably brisk until we drove them to the river-bank, where they gave a long, heavy fire, and finally the enemy fell behind the levee or river-bank that is thrown up. The battle had now lasted near two and a half hours. The regulars had ceased firing near one hour before I drew my men back."

The "Carolina" began firing soon after seven o'clock, and ceased at nine.[3] Jackson's attack with the regulars began at eight o'clock, and his force ceased firing before nine. Coffee withdrew his men at about half-past nine. The hope of destroying the British force was disappointed; and brilliant as the affair was, its moral effect was greater than the material injury it inflicted. Major-General Keane officially reported his loss as forty-six killed, one hundred and sixty-seven wounded, and sixty-four missing, — two hundred and sixty-seven in all.[4] Jackson reported twenty-four killed, one hundred and

---

[1] James, ii. 362. Keane's Report; James, ii. 530.

[2] Parton, ii. 100.

[3] Patterson to Secretary of Navy, Dec. 28, 1814; Latour, Appendix, p. xliii.

[4] Report of Major-General Keane, Dec. 26, 1814; James, ii. 529.

fifteen wounded, and seventy-four missing, — two hundred and thirteen in all. The two regular regiments suffered most, losing fifteen killed and fifty-four wounded. Coffee's Tennesseeans lost nine killed and forty-three wounded. The New Orleans volunteer corps and the colored volunteers lost seventeen wounded.

Compared with the night battle at Lundy's Lane, the night battle of December 23 was not severe. Brown's army, probably not more numerous than Jackson's, lost one hundred and seventy-one men killed, while Jackson lost twenty-four. Brown lost five hundred and seventy-one wounded, while Jackson lost one hundred and fifteen. Drummond at Lundy's Lane reported a British loss of eighty-four killed, while Keane reported forty-six. Drummond reported five hundred and fifty-nine wounded, while Keane reported one hundred and sixty-seven. The total British loss at Lundy's Lane was eight hundred and seventy-eight men; that of December 23 was two hundred and sixty-seven. Jackson's battle was comparatively short, lasting an hour and a half, while the fighting at Lundy's Lane continued some five hours. Lundy's Lane checked the enemy only for a day or two, and the battle of December 23 could hardly be expected to do more.

Conscious that the British army would advance as soon as its main body arrived, Jackson, like Brown, hastened to place his men under cover of works. Falling back the next morning about two miles, he took

position behind an old canal or ditch which crossed
the strip of cultivated ground where it was narrowest.
The canal offered no serious obstacle to an enemy,
for although ten feet wide it was shallow and dry,
and fully three quarters of a mile long.     Had the
British been able to advance in force at any time
the next day, December 24, directing their attack
toward the skirts of the swamp to avoid the "Carolina's" fire, they might have forced Jackson back
upon New Orleans; but they were in no disposition
to do on the 24th what they had not ventured to do
on the 23d, when they possessed every advantage.
Keane believed that Jackson's force in the night
battle amounted to five thousand men.[1]     Keane's
troops, weary, cold, without food, and exposed to the
"Carolina's" fire, which imprisoned them all day
between the two levees,[2] were glad to escape further
attack, and entertained no idea of advance.     The
day and night of December 24 were occupied by the
British in hurrying the main body of their troops
from the Isle aux Poix across Lake Borgne to the
Bayou Bienvenu.

By very great efforts the boats of the fleet trans
ported the whole remaining force across the lake,
until, on the morning of December 25, all were concentrated at the Villeré plantation.     With them
arrived Major-General Sir Edward Pakenham, and
took command.     Hitherto the frequent British dis-

[1] Keane's Report of December 26, 1814; James, ii. 531.
[2] Subaltern, pp. 228, 229.

asters at Plattsburg, Sackett's Harbor, Fort Erie, and the Moravian towns had been attributed to their generals. Sir George Prevost, Major-Generals Drummond and Riall, and Major-General Proctor were not officers of Wellington's army. The British government, in appointing Sir Edward Pakenham to command at New Orleans, meant to send the ablest officer at their disposal. Pakenham was not only one of Wellington's best generals, but stood in the close relation of his brother-in-law, Pakenham's sister being Wellington's wife. In every military respect Sir Edward Pakenham might consider himself the superior of Andrew Jackson. He was in the prime of life and strength, thirty-eight years of age, while Jackson, nearly ten years older, was broken in health and weak in strength. Pakenham had learned the art of war from Wellington, in the best school in Europe. He was supported by an efficient staff and a military system as perfect as experience and expenditure could make it, and he commanded as fine an army as England could produce, consisting largely of Peninsula veterans.

Their precise number, according to British authority, was five thousand and forty rank-and-file, on Christmas Day, when Pakenham took command.[1] Afterward many more arrived, until January 6, when ten regiments were in camp at Villeré's plantation, — Royal Artillery ; Fourteenth Light Dragoons ; Fourth, Seventh, Twenty-first, Forty-third,

[1] James, ii. 363.

Forty-fourth, Eighty-fifth, Ninety-third, and Ninety-fifth Infantry, — numbering, with sappers and miners and staff-corps, five thousand nine hundred and thirteen rank-and-file ; or with a moderate allowance of officers, an aggregate of at least sixty-five hundred Europeans. Two West India regiments of black troops accompanied the expedition, numbering ten hundred and forty-three rank-and-file. The navy provided about twelve hundred marines and seamen, perhaps the most efficient corps in the whole body. Deducting eight hundred men for camp-duty, Pakenham, according to British official reports, could put in the field a force of eight thousand disciplined troops, well-officered, well-equipped, and confident both in themselves and in their commander. More were on their way.

The Duke of Wellington believed such a force fully competent to capture New Orleans, or to rout any American army he ever heard of ; and his confidence would have been, if possible, still stronger, had he known his opponent's resources, which were no greater and not very much better than those so easily overcome by Ross at Bladensburg. The principal difference was that Jackson commanded.

Jackson's difficulties were very great, and were overcome only by the desperate energy which he infused even into the volatile creoles and sluggish negroes. When he retired from the field of the night battle, he withdrew, as has been told, only two miles. About five miles below New Orleans he halted his

troops. Between the river and the swamp, the strip
of open and cultivated land was there somewhat
narrower than elsewhere. A space of a thousand
yards, or about three fifths of a mile, alone required
strong defence. A shallow, dry canal, or ditch, ten
feet wide, crossed the plain and opened into the river
on one side and the swamp on the other. All day
the troops, with the negroes of the neighborhood,
worked, deepening the canal, and throwing up a
parapet behind it. The two six-pound field-pieces
commanded the road on the river-bank, and the
" Louisiana " descended the river to a point about
two miles below Jackson's line. A mile below the
" Louisiana " the " Carolina " remained in her old
position, opposite the British camp. By nightfall
the new lines were already formidable, and afforded
complete protection from musketry. For further security the parapet was continued five hundred yards,
and turned well on the flank in the swamp ; but this
task was not undertaken until December 28.[1]

The first act of Sir Edward Pakenham gave the
Americans at least three days for preparation. Even
veteran soldiers, who were accustomed to storming
mountain fortresses held by French armies, were annoyed at exposing their flank to the fire of fifteen or
twenty heavy guns, which hampered not only every
military movement but also every motion beyond
cover of the bank. Pakenham sent instantly to the
fleet for cannon to drive the ships away. In reality

[1] Latour, p. 121.

he could not so relieve himself, for the American commodore soon placed one twenty-four-pound gun and two twelve-pounders in battery on the opposite bank of the river, where they answered every purpose of annoyance, while the ships after December 28 took little part in action.[1]  Pakenham gained nothing by waiting ; but he would not advance without artillery, and the sailors, with much labor, brought up a number of light guns, — nine field-pieces, it was said,[2] two howitzers, and a mortar.  Pakenham passed two days, December 25 and 26, organizing his force and preparing the battery.    At daylight, December 27, the guns were ready.    Five pieces suddenly opened with hot shot and shell on the " Carolina," and in half an hour obliged the crew to abandon her.[3]    The " Louisiana," by extreme exertion, was hauled beyond range while the British battery was occupied in destroying the " Carolina."

Nothing then prevented Pakenham's advance, and the next morning, December 28, the whole army moved forward.

" On we went," said the Subaltern, " for about three miles, without any halt or hindrance, either from man or inanimate nature coming in our way.  But all at once a spectacle was presented to us, such indeed as we ought to have looked for, but such as manifestly took

[1] Patterson's Report of Jan. 2, 1815 ; Latour, Appendix, p. 1, no. xxviii.

[2] Gleig's Campaigns, p. 165.

[3] Report of J. D. Henley, Dec. 28, 1814; Niles, vii. 387.

our leaders by surprise. The enemy's army became
visible. It was posted about forty yards in rear of a
canal, and covered, though most imperfectly, by an unfinished breastwork."

The British left, coming under the fire of the
" Louisiana," was immediately halted and placed as
far as possible under cover. The skirmishers in the
swamp were recalled. In the evening the whole
army was ordered to retire beyond cannon-shot and
hut themselves.[1] They obeyed; but "there was not a
man among us who failed to experience both shame
and indignation." [2]

Beyond doubt, such caution was not expected from
Sir Edward Pakenham. Sir George Prevost at Sackett's Harbor and Plattsburg, and Colonel Brooke at
Baltimore had retired before American works ; but
those works had been finished forts, strongly held
and situated on elevated points. Even with such
excuses, and after suffering severe losses, Prevost
was discredited for his retreats. Pakenham did not
live to make a report, and his reasons remained un-
avowed ; but Admiral Cochrane reported that it was
" thought necessary to bring heavy artillery against
this work, and also against the ship which had can-
nonaded the army when advancing." [3] The decision implied that Pakenham considered the chances
unfavorable for storming the American line.

[1] Journal of Major Forrest; Latour, Appendix, p. cxlvii.
[2] Subaltern, p. 235.
[3] Cochrane's Report of Jan. 18, 1815; James, ii. 552.

In effect, Pakenham's withdrawal December 28 was equivalent to admitting weakness in his infantry, and to calling on the artillery as his strongest arm. The experiment showed little self-confidence. Not only must he sacrifice two or three days in establishing batteries, but he must challenge a contest with cannon, — weapons which the Americans were famous for using, both afloat and ashore, with especial skill.    Jackson could also mount heavy guns and allow Pakenham to batter indefinite lines. Sooner or later Pakenham must storm, unless he could turn the American position.

The seamen were once more set to work, and "with incredible labor" rowed their boats, laden with heavy guns, from the fleet to the bayou, and dragged the guns through three miles of bog to the British headquarters. The Americans also prepared batteries. From the lines one thirty-two-pounder, three twenty-four-pounders, and one eighteen-pounder commanded the plain in their front. Besides these heavy guns, three twelve-pounders, three six-pounders, a six-inch howitzer or mortar, and a brass carronade, useless from its bad condition,[1] — in all, twelve or thirteen guns, capable of replying to the British batteries, were mounted along the American lines. On the west bank of the river, three quarters of a mile away, Commodore Patterson established, December 30 and 31, a battery of one twenty-four-pounder and two long twelve-pounders, which took the British bat-

[1] Latour, pp. 147, 148.

# Sketch of the Position of the British and American Forces

## NEAR NEW ORLEANS, FROM THE 23rd OF DECEMBER TO THE 8th OF JANUARY, 1815.

*From original by John Peddie, D. A. Q. M. Genl., endorsed "Enclosure in M. Genl. Lambert's of 29 Jany., 1815."—British Archives.*

### REFERENCES.

- **A.** Enemy's position on the night of the 23rd of December when he attacked.
- **B.** Bivouac of the troops for the 23rd of December.
- **C.** Position on the night of the 23rd of December.
- **D.** Position on the night of the 24th of December.
- **E.** Position after the advance on the 28th of December.
- **F.** Col. Thornton's attack on the morning of the 8th of January.
- **G.** Col. Thornton's furthest advance.
- **1, 2, 3, 4, 5, 6, 7, 8.** Redoubt and batteries constructed after the advance of the 28th.
- **H.** The enemy retiring.

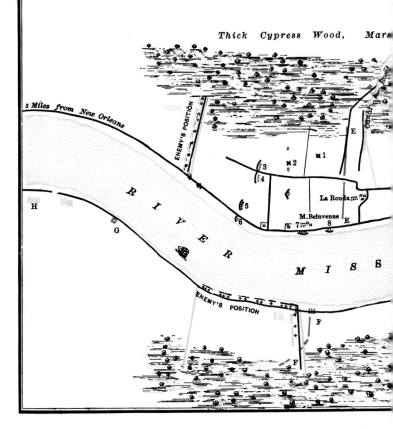

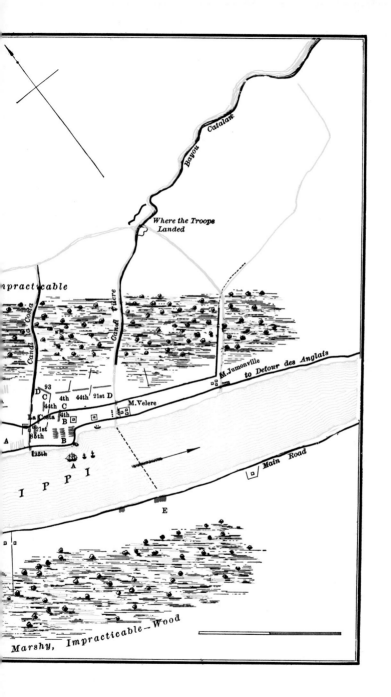

Bayou Catalan.

Where the Troops Landed

Impracticable

Canal la Costa

Canal Viere

M. Jumonville

to Detour des Anglais

D 93
C
4th   44th   21st D
44th   C
La Costa   4th
B
21st
86th   B
93th
A

M. Velere

Main Road

E

I P P I

Marshy, Impracticable—Wood

teries in flank.[1] Thus the Americans possessed fifteen effective guns, six of which were heavy pieces of long range. They were worked partly by regular artillerists, partly by sailors, partly by New Orleans militia, and partly by the "hellish banditti" of Barataria, who to the number of twenty or thirty were received by General Jackson into the service and given the care of two twenty-four-pounders.

The number and position of the British guns were given in Lieutenant Peddie's sketch of the field. Before the reconnaisance of December 28, field-pieces had been placed in battery on the river-side to destroy the "Carolina" and "Louisiana." Canon Gleig said that "nine field-pieces, two howitzers, and one mortar" were placed in battery on the river-side during the night of December 25.[2] Captain Henley of the "Carolina" reported that five guns opened upon him on the morning of December 26.[3] Captain Peddie's sketch marked seven pieces mounted in battery on the river-side, bearing on Commodore Patterson's battery opposite, besides four pieces in two batteries below. Their range was sufficient to destroy the "Carolina" and pierce the breastwork across the river,[4] and therefore they were probably twelve and nine pounders.

[1] Patterson's Report of Jan. 2, 1815; Latour, Appendix, p. l, no. xxviii.

[2] Campaigns, p. 166.

[3] Henley's Report of December 28; Niles, vii. 387.

[4] Latour, p. 136. Patterson's Report of Jan. 2, 1815; Latour, Appendix, p. l, no. xxviii.

Besides these lighter long-range guns, the British constructed three batteries in the night of December 31.

" Four eighteen-pounders," reported Major Forrest,[1] British assistant-quartermaster-general, " were placed in a battery formed of hogsheads of sugar, on the main road, to fire upon the ship if she dropped down. Preparations were also made to establish batteries, — one of six eighteen-pounders, and one of four twenty-four-pound carronades ; also batteries for the field-pieces and howitzers, the latter to keep the fire of the enemy under, while the troops were to be moved forward in readiness to storm the works as soon as a practicable breach was effected."

According to Peddie's sketch the Battery No. 6, on the road or new levee, contained not four but two guns. Battery No. 5, some fifty yards from No. 6, contained six guns, as Major Forrest reported. Battery No. 4, to the left of the old levee, contained four guns, probably the carronades. Battery No. 3, to the right of the old levee, contained five guns, probably the field-pieces and howitzers. In all, seventeen guns bore on the American lines, — besides seven, in Batteries No. 7 and No. 8, bearing on Commodore Patterson's three-gun battery across the river. According to Gleig,[2] the British had thirty guns ; but in any case they used not less than twenty-four guns, throwing a heavier weight of metal than was

[1] Journal of Major Forrest, Assistant-Quartermaster-General; MSS. British Archives. Latour, Appendix, p. cxlvii.

[2] Subaltern, p. 249. Gleig's Campaigns, p. 173.

thrown by the fifteen pieces used by the Americans. The British artillery was served by regular artillerists.

These details were particularly interesting, because the artillery battle of Jan. 1, 1815, offered the best test furnished during the war of relative skill in the use of that arm. The attack had every advantage over the defence. The British could concentrate their fire to effect a breach for their troops to enter; the Americans were obliged to disperse their fire on eight points. The American platforms being elevated, offered a better target than was afforded by the low British batteries, and certainly were no better protected. Three of the American guns were in battery across the river, three quarters of a mile from the main British battery of six eighteen-pounders, while the " Louisiana's " carronades were beyond range, and the " Louisiana " herself was not brought into action.[1] On the American side the battle was fought entirely by the guns in Jackson's lines and in Patterson's battery across the river, — one thirty-two-pounder, four twenty-four-pounders, one eighteen-pounder, five twelve-pounders, three six-pounders, and a howitzer, — fifteen American guns in all, matched against ten British eighteen-pounders, four twenty-four-pound carronades, and ten field-pieces and howitzers, — twenty-four guns in all. If the British field-pieces were twelves and nines, the

[1] Patterson's Report of Jan. 2, 1815; Latour, Appendix, p. 1, no. xxviii.

weight of metal was at least three hundred and fifty
pounds on the British side against two hundred and
twenty-four pounds on the American side, besides two
howitzers against one.

The main British batteries were about seven hundred yards distant from Jackson's line.  Opposite to
the battery of six eighteen-pounders were the American thirty-two and three twenty-four-pounders.  Behind the British batteries the British army waited
for the order to assault.  Toward eight o'clock on
the morning of Jan. 1, 1815, the British opened a
hot fire accompanied by a shower of rockets.  The
American guns answered, and the firing continued
without intermission until toward noon, when the
British fire slackened, and at one o'clock the British artillerists abandoned their batteries, leaving the
guns deserted.

During the entire war, no other battle was fought
in which the defeated party had not some excuse to
offer for inferiority.  Usually the excuse ascribed
greater force to the victor than to the vanquished,
or dwelt upon some accident or oversight which
affected the result.  For the defeat of the British
artillery, Jan. 1, 1815, no excuse was ever suggested.[1]
The British army and navy frankly admitted that
the misfortune was due to American superiority in
the use of artillery.  British evidence on that point
was ample, for their surprise and mortification were
extreme ; while the Americans seemed never fully

[1] James, ii. 369.

to appreciate the extraordinary character of the feat they performed. The most detailed British account was also the most outspoken.

" Never was any failure more remarkable or unlooked-for than this," said Gleig.[1] . . . " The sun, as if ashamed to shine upon our disgrace, was slow of making its appearance ; a heavy mist obscured him, and the morning was far advanced before it cleared away. At last, however, the American lines were visible, and then began a fire from our batteries, so brisk and so steadily kept up that we who were behind made not the smallest doubt of its effect. It was answered for a while faintly, and with seeming difficulty. By and by, however, the enemy's salutation became more spirited, till it gradually surpassed our own, both in rapidity and precision. We were a good deal alarmed at this, and the more that a rumor got abroad that our batteries were not proof against the amazing force of the American shot. We had, it may be stated, imprudently rolled into the parapets barrels filled with sugar, under the impression that sugar would prove as effectual as sand in checking the progress of cannon-balls. But the event showed that we had been completely mistaken. The enemy's shot penetrated these sugar-hogsheads as if they had been so many empty casks, dismounting our guns and killing our artillery-men in the very centre of their works. There could be small doubt, as soon as these facts were established, how the cannonading would end. Our fire slackened every moment ; that of the Americans became every moment more terrible, till at length, after not more than two hours and a half of firing, our batteries

[1] Subaltern, p. 249 (American edition, 1833).

were all silenced.    The American works, on the other
hand, remained as little injured as ever, and we were
completely foiled."

Admiral Codrington, writing from the British headquarters three days after the battle, expressed equal
astonishment and annoyance : [1] —

" On the 1st we had our batteries, by severe labor,
ready in situations from which the artillery people were,
as a matter of course, to destroy and silence the opposing
batteries, and give opportunity for a well-arranged storm.
But instead of so doing, not a gun of the enemy appeared
to suffer, and our firing too high was not made out until
we had expended too much of our hardly-collected ammunition to push the matter further.    Such a failure in
this boasted arm was not to be expected, and I think it a
blot in the artillery escutcheon."

Codrington somewhat under-estimated the effect of
the British fire.    Three of the American guns, including the thirty-two-pounder, were more or less
damaged, and the cotton-bales which formed the
cheeks of the embrasures proved to be as little serviceable as the hogsheads of sugar in the British river
battery.[2]    Two artillery caissons were exploded by
the British rockets.    Thirty-four men were killed or
wounded ; while the British reported a loss of seventy-
six killed and wounded between Jan. 1 and 5, 1815,
most of whom fell in the artillery battle.[3]

[1] Life of Codrington, i. 334.
[2] Latour, pp. 133, 134.
[3] Return of Casualties; James, ii. 543.

The British official reports said less, but their silence was equally significant.

" Our batteries made little impression upon the enemy's parapet," wrote Major Forrest.[1]  " The order for the assault was therefore not carried into effect.  The troops remained in this advanced position, and orders were given to retire the guns in the night.  The evening changed to wet, and the ground became in consequence so deep that it required the exertions of the whole army as a working-party, aided by the seamen, to retire the guns a short distance before daylight.  The army then fell back to the position it occupied on the 31st."

Admiral Cochrane's official report was still more brief, and best understood by the comments already quoted from his friend Admiral Codrington : —

" On the 1st instant batteries were opened ; but our fire not having the desired effect, the attack was deferred until the arrival of the troops under Major-General Lambert, which was daily expected."

If the Subaltern was right, the British defeat resulted in the loss of several guns.

" The enemy having made no attempt to carry off our heavy guns, which we abandoned to their fate," continued Gleig, " it was judged advisable to bring them into the camp as soon as circumstances would allow ; and for this purpose working parties were again sent out as soon as the darkness screened them.  It was my fortune to accompany them.  The labor of dragging a number of huge ship's guns out of the soft soil into which they

---

[1] Journal; Latour, Appendix, p. cxlvii.

had sunk, crippled too as most of them were in their carriages, was more extreme by far than any one expected to find it. Indeed, it was not till four o'clock in the morning that our task came to a conclusion, and even then it had been very imperfectly performed. Five guns were eventually left behind. These were rendered useless, it is true, by breaking their trunnions; but it cannot be said that in the course of the late operations the British army came off without the loss of some of its artillery."

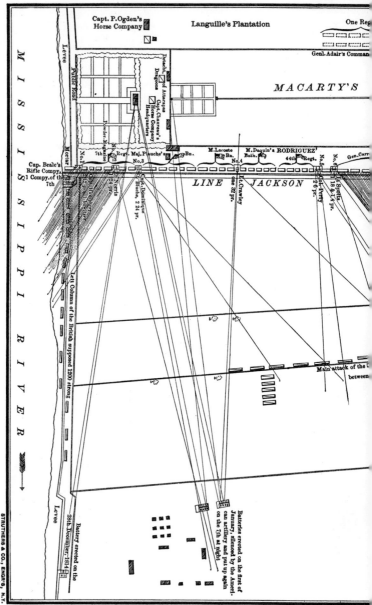

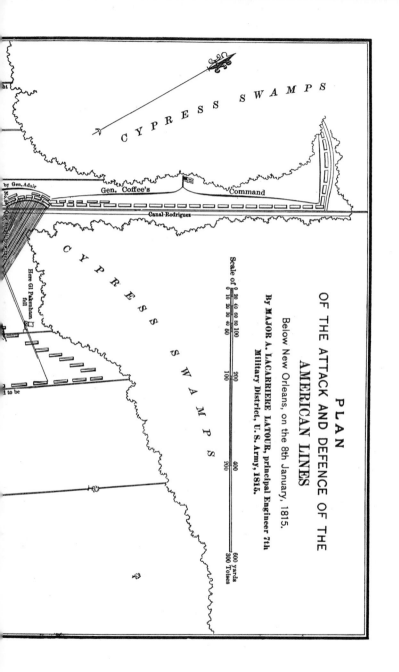

CYPRESS SWAMPS

Gen. Coffee's Command

Canal-Rodriguez

by Gen. Adair

CYPRESS SWAMPS

Here Gl Pakenham fell

CYPRESS SWAMPS

to be

# PLAN
## OF THE ATTACK AND DEFENCE OF THE
## AMERICAN LINES

Below New Orleans, on the 8th January, 1815.

By MAJOR A. LACARRIERE LATOUR, principal Engineer 7th Military District, U. S. Army, 1815.

Scale of
0 20 40 60 80 100    200    400    600 yards
0 10 20 30 40 60    100    200    300 Toises

## CHAPTER XIV.

EFFECTUALLY stopped by these repeated miscarriages, General Pakenham, with fully five thousand good soldiers at his command, decided to wait an entire week for Major-General Lambert, who was then on his way with two fresh regiments. In the meanwhile Pakenham adopted a suggestion made first by Vice-Admiral Cochrane,[1] to prepare for throwing a force across the river to turn Jackson's line from the opposite bank. The plan required that the Villeré canal should be extended through the levee to the river without the knowledge of the Americans. Perhaps Pakenham would have done better by dragging his boats across the intervening space; but he preferred to dig a canal, and the work, begun January 4, was done so successfully that until January 6, when it was completed, Jackson did not suspect the movement. On the same day Lambert's division arrived.

From this week of inaction the Americans gained little advantage. The lines were strengthened; but although the Kentucky reinforcements, more than

[1] Life of Codrington, i. 336. Lambert's Report of Jan. 28, 1815; Latour, Appendix, p. clxvi.

two thousand in number, under General Thomas and
John Adair, arrived January 4, they were ill provided
with arms, and Jackson could furnish them neither
with arms, clothing, nor equipment. The Louisiana
militia were in the same condition. Jackson did his
utmost to supply these wants; the people of New
Orleans did more, and lent at last the few hundred
muskets reserved against the danger of a slave in-
surrection,[1] until in the end, if Adair was correct,
a thousand of the Kentuckians were placed in the
line of battle. Yet after all the reinforcements had
been mustered, Jackson's main dependence was still
on his artillery and his intrenchments. In the open
field he could not meet the British force.

In his immediate front, Jackson had little to fear.
Three thousand marksmen, behind intrenchments
everywhere at least five feet high, defended by heavy
guns and supported by the "Louisiana" on the river
and a strong battery on the opposite shore, could defy
twice or three times their number advancing across
an open plain under fire of eight or ten heavy guns.
The result of the artillery battle of January 1, as
well as the reconnaissance of December 28, showed
what the British general and his staff thought of their
chances in a front attack. Twice they had refused
to attempt it when Jackson's lines were unfinished;
they were not likely to succeed when the lines were
strengthened by another week of labor.

[1] Adair's letters of Oct. 21, 1817 ; Letters of Adair and Jackson, Lexington, 1817.

In his direct front, therefore, Jackson had reason to think that the British did not intend serious attack. Their next attempt could hardly fail to be a flanking movement. Jackson had been surprised, December 23, by such a movement, and feared nothing so much as to be surprised again. For this reason he still kept a large body of troops, three regiments of Louisiana militia, on the north of the city.[1]  " His greatest fear, and hence his strongest defence next to the one occupied by himself, was on the Chef Menteur road, where Governor Claiborne, at the head of the Louisiana militia, was posted." He kept close watch on the bayous which extended on his immediate flank, and constructed other lines in his rear to which he could retreat in case his left flank should be turned through the swamp. Apparently the idea did not occur to him that the British might more easily turn his right flank by throwing a force across the river ; and when he learned, January 7, that the British were engaged in making this movement, the time had already passed when he could prevent it.

No means had been provided for transporting troops directly from one bank of the river to the other. If obliged to protect the batteries established by Commodore Patterson on the west bank, Jackson must march troops from his lines back five miles to New Orleans, cross them by the ferry, and march them down the other shore. Such a movement re-

[1] Eaton, p. 359.

quired a whole day, and divided the army in a manner hazarding the safety of both wings.

Practically the west bank was undefended when Jackson, January 7, first. heard that the British were about to occupy it.  Commodore Patterson had mounted there, as has been told, a number of heavy guns in battery, but these guns were not in position to cover their own bank against attack from below. Major Latour was engaged with negroes in laying out lines of defence, but nothing was completed.  In an advanced position, about a mile below the line of Jackson's works, a bastion had been raised close to the river, and near it a small redan, or salient, had been constructed.  This work, which was untenable in case of attack in flank or rear, was occupied by four hundred and fifty Louisiana militia, commanded by General David Morgan.  During the afternoon of January 7, after the British plan of attack was suspected, General Morgan caused three guns — one twelve-pounder and two six-pounders — to be mounted on his line.  Late the same evening General Jackson ordered four hundred men of the Kentucky division to New Orleans, where they were to obtain muskets, then to cross the river, and march down the opposite shore to reinforce Morgan.  The Kentuckians obeyed their orders, but they found only about seventy muskets at New Orleans ; and not more than two hundred and fifty armed men, weary with marching and faint from want of food, reached Morgan's quarters at four o'clock on the morning

of January 8.[1]  Adair, who should have known the
number best, declared that only one hundred and
seventy men were then in the ranks.[2]  They were
sent a mile farther and stationed as an advanced
line, with one hundred Louisiana militia.

Thus seven or eight hundred tired, ill-armed, and
unprotected militia, divided in two bodies a mile
apart, waited on the west bank to be attacked by a
British column which was then in the act of crossing
the river.  Their defeat was almost certain.  A
thousand British troops could easily drive them away,
capture all the batteries on the west bank, destroy
the " Louisiana " as they had destroyed the " Carolina," thus turning all Jackson's lines, and probably
rendering necessary the evacuation of New Orleans.
For this work Pakenham detached the Eighty-fifth
regiment, about three hundred strong, the Fifth
West India, two hundred seamen and two hundred marines, — about twelve hundred men in all,[3]
— under command of Colonel Thornton, who had
led the light brigade at Bladensburg and across
Lake Borgne to the Mississippi.  The movement
was ordered for the night of January 7, and was to
be made in boats already collected in the Villeré
canal.

[1] Latour, p. 170.

[2] Adair to Jackson, March 20, 1815; Letters of Adair and
Jackson, 1817 ; Latour, Appendix, p. cxxxii.

[3] Journal of Major Forrest, Assistant-Quartermaster-General;
MSS. British Archives.  Lambert's Report, Jan. 10, 1815 ; James,
ii. 543.

With some hesitation [1] Pakenham decided to make a simultaneous attack on Jackson. The arrangements for this assault were simple. The usual store of fascines and ladders was provided. Six of the eighteen-pound guns were once more mounted in battery about eight hundred yards from the American line, to cover the attack. The army, after detaching Thornton's corps, was organized in three divisions, — one, under Major-General Gibbs, to attack Jackson's left; another, under Major-General Keane, to attack along the river-side; a third, the reserve, to be commanded by Major-General Lambert.

" The principal attack was to be made by Major-General Gibbs," said the British official report.[2] The force assigned to Gibbs consisted of the Fourth, Twenty-first, and Forty-fourth regiments, with three companies of the Ninety-fifth, — about two thousand two hundred rank-and-file.[3] The force assigned to Keane consisted of " the Ninety-third, two companies of the Ninety-fifth, and two companies of the Fusileers and Forty-third," [4] — apparently about twelve hundred rank-and-file. " The first brigade, consisting of the Fusileers and Forty-third, formed the reserve " under Major-General Keane, apparently also twelve hundred strong. Adding two hundred artillerists and five hundred black troops of the First West India regi-

[1] Life of Codrington, i. 336.

[2] Lambert's Report of Jan. 10, 1815 ; Niles, viii. 177.

[3] James, ii. 373.

[4] Lambert's Report ; Niles, viii. 177.

ment, employed as skirmishers along the edge of the
swamp, the whole body of troops engaged on the
east bank in the assault, according to the official
report and returns of wounded,[1] numbered about
five thousand three hundred rank-and-file, consisting
of the Fourth, Seventh (Fusileers), Twenty-first,
Forty-third, Forty-fourth, Ninety-third, and Ninety-
fifth regiments, of whom twenty-two hundred were
to attack on the right, twelve hundred on the left,
and twelve hundred were to remain in reserve.

Thus of the whole British force, some eight thousand rank-and-file, fifty-three hundred were to assault
Jackson's line; twelve hundred were to cross the
river and assault Morgan; eight hundred and fifty
men were detailed for various duties; and the seamen, except two hundred with Colonel Thornton,
must have been in the boats.

To meet this assault, Jackson held an overwhelming force, in which his mere numbers were the smallest element. According to a detailed account given
by Jackson two years afterward, his left wing, near
the swamp, was held by Coffee's brigade of eight
hundred and four men; his centre, by Carroll's brigade of fourteen hundred and fourteen men; his right,
near the river, by thirteen hundred and twenty-seven
men, including all the regulars; while Adair's Kentucky brigade, numbering five hundred and twenty-
five men, were in reserve.[2] Adair claimed that the
Kentuckians numbered fully one thousand. The dis-

[1] Niles, viii. 180.      [2] Jackson to Adair, July 23, 1817.

pute mattered little, for barely one third of the entire force, whatever it was, discharged a gun.

Besides three thousand or thirty-five hundred men on the parapets and a thousand in reserve, Jackson had twelve pieces of artillery distributed along the line, covering every portion of the plain. The earth-wall behind which his men rested was in every part sufficiently high to require scaling, and the mud was so slippery as to afford little footing.[1]  Patterson's battery on the opposite shore increased in force till it contained three twenty-four-pounders and six twelve-pounders,[2] covered the levee by which the British left must advance.  The " Louisiana " took no part in the action, her men being engaged in working the guns on shore ; but without the " Louisiana's " broadside, Jackson had more than twenty cannon in position.  Such a force was sufficient to repel ten thousand men if the attack were made in open day.

Pakenham, aware of the probable consequences of attacking by daylight, arranged for moving before dawn ; but his plan required a simultaneous advance on both banks of the river, and such a combination was liable to many accidents.  According to the journal of Major Forrest, the British Assistant-Quartermaster-General,[3] forty-seven boats were brought up the bayou on the evening of January 7 :

[1] Latour, pp. 147–152.

[2] Patterson's Report of Jan. 13, 1815; Latour, Appendix, p. ix.

[3] Journal of Major Forrest, Assistant-Quartermaster-General; MSS. British Archives.

" As soon as it was dark, the boats commenced to be crossed over into the river. A dam erected below the sternmost boat had raised the water about two feet. Still there was a very considerable fall from the river; and through which, for an extent of two hundred and fifty yards, the boats were dragged with incredible labor by the seamen. It required the whole night to effect this, and the day had dawned before the first detachment of Colonel Thornton's corps (about six hundred men) had embarked; and they just reached the opposite bank when the main attack commenced on the enemy's line."

At six o'clock in broad dawn the columns of Gibbs and Keane moved forward toward Jackson's works, which were lined with American troops waiting for the expected attack. Gibbs's column came first under fire, advancing near the swamp in close ranks of about sixty men in front.[1] Three of the American batteries opened upon them. Coming within one hundred and fifty yards of the American line, the British column obliqued to the left to avoid the fire of the battery directly in face. As they came within musketry range the men faltered and halted, beginning a confused musketry fire. A few platoons advanced to the edge of the ditch, and then broke. Their officers tried in vain to rally them for another advance. Major-General Gibbs was mortally wounded, according to the official report, " within twenty yards of the glacis." [2] Pakenham himself rode forward to

[1] Latour, p. 154.

[2] Lambert's Report of Jan. 10, 1815; Latour, Appendix, p. cxlix.

rally Gibbs's column, and was instantly struck by a grape-shot and killed, nearly three hundred yards from the American line.[1]  " As I advanced with the reserve," said Lambert's report, " at about two hundred and fifty yards from the line, I had the mortification to observe the whole falling back upon me in the greatest confusion."

Keane's column on the left moved along the road and between the river and the levee.  Pressing rapidly forward, greatly annoyed by Patterson's battery on the west bank, the head of this column reached the American line, and stormed an unfinished redoubt outside the main work at the edge of the river. The concentrated fire of the whole American right almost immediately drove the column back in disorder ; the men who reached the redoubt were killed; Major-General Keane was severely wounded and carried off the field, while the casualties among officers of a lower grade were excessive.  The Ninety-third regiment in Keane's brigade lost its lieutenant-colonel and two captains killed, and four more captains severely wounded ; three hundred and forty-eight rank-and-file were wounded, ninety-nine were reported missing, and fifty-eight killed.  These losses amounted to five hundred and five in seven hundred and seventy-five rank-and-file.[2]

Lambert's report continued : [3] —

[1] Latour's Plan.

[2] Return of Casualties; James, ii 554

[3] James, ii. 373.

" In this situation, finding that no impression had been made ; that though many men had reached the ditch, they were either drowned or obliged to surrender, and that it was impossible to restore order in the regiments where they were, — I placed the reserve in position until I could obtain such information as to determine me how to act to the best of my judgment, and whether or not I should resume the attack ; and if so, I felt it could be done only by the reserve."

Just as the main attack ended, Colonel Thornton with his six hundred rank-and-file, having landed on the west bank, advanced against Morgan's line, routed it, turned the redoubt, and advanced on Patterson's heavy battery beyond. Patterson unable to use his guns had no choice but to spike his pieces and retreat. Thornton passed up the river a mile beyond Jackson's line,[1] and needed only a field-piece and some hot shot to burn the " Louisiana " and march opposite New Orleans.

From the eastern shore Jackson watched the progress of Thornton with alarm. His official report of January 9 gave an idea of his emotions.

" Simultaneously with his advance on my lines," Jackson said, " the enemy had thrown over in his boats a considerable force to the other side of the river. These having landed were hardy enough to advance against the works of General Morgan ; and what is strange and difficult to account for, at the very moment when their entire discomfiture was looked for with a confidence approaching to certainty, the Kentucky reinforcements in-

[1] Latour's Plan.

gloriously fled, drawing after them by their example the remainder of the forces, and thus yielding to the enemy that most formidable position. The batteries which had rendered me for many days the most important service, though bravely defended, were of course now abandoned, not however until the guns had been spiked. This unfortunate rout had totally changed the aspect of affairs. The enemy now occupied a position from which they might annoy us without hazard, and by means of which they might have been enabled to defeat in a great measure the effect of our success on this side the river."

John Adair, who was then in command of the Kentucky brigade, General Thomas being unwell, took great offence at Jackson's account of the battle on the west bank. " The detachment on the other side of the river," he reported to Governor Shelby,[1] " were obliged to retire before a superior force. They have been calumniated by those who ought to have fought with them, but did not." The tone of Jackson's report, and his language afterward, showed a willingness to load the Kentucky troops on the west bank with the responsibility for a military oversight with which they had nothing to do ; but the oversight was not the less serious, whoever was responsible for it. The Kentucky and Louisiana troops did not easily yield. The British returns of killed and wounded showed that Thornton's column suffered a considerable loss. Thornton himself was wounded : his regiment, the Eighty-fifth, numbering two hundred and ninety-

[1] Letter of Jan. 13, 1815; Niles, vii. 389.

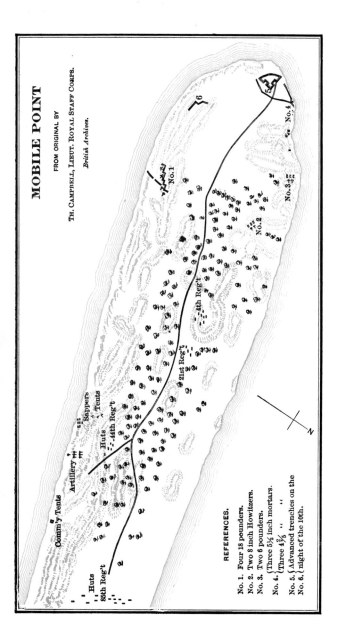

# MOBILE POINT

FROM ORIGINAL BY

TH. CAMPBELL, LIEUT. ROYAL STAFF CORPS.

*British Archives.*

Comm'y Tents

Artillery

Sappers

Huts — Tents

— 44th Reg't

4th Reg't

21st Reg't

4th Reg't

Huts
85th Reg't

No. 1

No. 2

No. 3

No. 4

No. 6

N

## REFERENCES.

No. 1. Four 18 pounders.
No. 2. Two 8 inch Howitzers.
No. 3. Two 6 pounders.
No. 4. {Three 5½ inch mortars.
       {Three 4⅖ " "
No. 5. Advanced trenches on the
No. 6. night of the 10th.

eight rank-and-file, reported a loss of forty-three men killed, wounded, and missing, besides their colonel. Of one hundred sailors employed in the attack [1] twenty were killed or wounded, besides Captain Money of the royal navy, " who, I am sorry to say, was severely wounded," said Thornton. The Americans made as good a resistance as could have been expected, and had they resisted longer they would merely have been captured when the next detachment of Thornton's column came up. The chief blame for the disaster did not rest on them.

Jackson was helpless to interpose. As he and his men, lining the river bank, watched the progress of Thornton's column on the opposite shore, Jackson could do nothing; but he ordered his men " that they should take off their hats, and give our troops on the right bank three cheers." Adair, who inclined to a severe judgment of Jackson's generalship, told the story more picturesquely : [2] —

" I was standing by him when he gave his order, and with a smile, not of approbation, observed I was afraid they could not hear us. The distance from us to them, on a straight line, was upward of one mile and a half : there was a thick fog, and I confess I could not see the troops of either army. All I could discover was the blaze from the guns ; and seeing that continue to progress up the river was the only knowledge we had that our men were retreating."

[1] Thornton's Report of Jan. 8, 1815; James, ii. 547.
[2] Letters of General Adair and General Jackson, 1817.

Jackson then ordered General Humbert, a French
officer acting as a volunteer, to take four hundred
men and cross the river at New Orleans to repulse
the enemy, cost what it might;[1] but had the enemy
pressed his advantage, no force at Jackson's command could have stopped their advance, without
causing the sacrifice of Jackson's lines.　Fortunately
the only remaining British general, Lambert, was not
disposed to make another effort.　The eight regiments of regular troops which made the bulk of Pakenham's army had suffered severely in the assault.
One of these regiments, the Eighty-fifth, was with
Thornton on the west shore.　Two, the Seventh and
Forty-third, had been in the reserve, and except two
companies had never approached the works within
musket-shot, yet had lost fifty-two killed, and about
one hundred wounded and missing, in an aggregate
of less than eighteen hundred.　The five remaining
regiments — the Fourth, Twenty-first, Forty-fourth,
Ninety-third, and Ninety-fifth — were nearly destroyed.　They went into battle probably about three
thousand strong:[2] they lost seventeen hundred and
fifty men killed, wounded, and missing.　The total
British loss was two thousand and thirty-six.[3]　The
American loss was seventy-one.　Even on the west
bank the American loss was much less than that of
the British.

The loss of three major-generals was almost as

[1] Latour, p. 175.　　　　[2] James, ii. 373.

[3] James, ii. 382.

serious as the loss of one third of the regular Infantry.  Lambert, the fourth major-general, weighed
down by responsibility and defeat, had no wish but
to escape.  He recalled Thornton's corps the same
evening from its position on the opposite bank, and
the next day, January 9, began preparations for his
difficult and hazardous retreat.[1]

Pakenham's assault on Jackson's lines at New
Orleans, January 8, repeated the assault made by
Drummond, August 15, at Fort Erie.  According to
the British account of that battle, Drummond's
engaged force numbered twenty-one hundred and
forty men ; the reserve, about one thousand.[2]  Drummond's direct attack, being made by night, was
more successful than Pakenham's ; his troops approached nearer and penetrated farther than those
of Gibbs and Keane ; but the consequences were
the same.   Of three thousand men, Drummond
lost nine hundred and five.   Of six thousand, engaged in the double action of Jan. 8, 1815, Pakenham lost two thousand and thirty-six.   In each
case the officers commanding the assaulting columns were killed or wounded, and the repulse was
complete.

After the battle General Lambert's position was
critical.   His withdrawal of Thornton's corps from
the west bank betrayed his intention of retiring, and
his line of retreat was exposed to attack from the

[1] Report of General Lambert, Jan. 28, 1815; James, ii. 565.

[2] James, ii. 179.

bayou which headed near Jackson's camp. Fortunately for him, Jackson was contented with checking his advance.

"Whether, after the severe loss he has sustained," wrote Jackson, five days after the battle,[1] "he is preparing to return to his shipping, or to make still mightier efforts to attain his first object, I do not pretend to determine. It becomes me to act as though the latter were his intention."

If Jackson's inaction allowed Lambert to escape, it was likely to hazard a renewal of the attack from some other quarter; but the armies remained for ten days in their old positions without further hostilities, except from artillery fire, until on the night of January 18, after making careful preparations, the whole British force silently withdrew to fortified positions at the mouth of the bayou, disappearing as suddenly and mysteriously as it came, and leaving behind it only eight or, according to the American report, fourteen [2] of the guns which had covered the river and held the "Louisiana" at a distance.[3] At the mouth of the bayou the army remained until January 27, when it was re-embarked in the ships off Chandeleur's Island.

On the day of the battle of January 8, a British

[1] Jackson to the Secretary of War, Jan. 13, 1815; Niles, vii. 374.

[2] Latour, p. 185.

[3] Lambert's Report of Jan. 28, 1815; Latour, Appendix, p. clxvi.

squadron appeared in the river below Fort St. Philip. Two bomb-vessels, under the protection of a sloop, a brig, and a schooner, bombarded the fort without effect until January 18, when they withdrew at the same time with the army above.

Notwithstanding the disastrous failure of the campaign before New Orleans, the British expedition, as it lay off Chandeleur Island February 1, still possessed nearly as much strength as when it appeared there December 11.  Reinforced by a thousand fresh soldiers, Lambert determined to attack Mobile.  " It was decided," reported Lambert,[1] "that a force should be sent against Fort Bowyer, situated on the eastern point of the entrance of the bay, and from every information that could be obtained it was considered that a brigade would be sufficient for this object, with a respectable force of artillery."  At daylight on the morning of February 8 a whole brigade and a heavy battering-train were disembarked in the rear of Fort Bowyer.

Jackson's determination to defend Mobile had already deprived him of the use of more than half the regular troops assigned to his military district, who remained inactive at Mobile during the months of December and January.  They were commanded by General Winchester, whose record as a military officer was not reassuring.  Although Fort Bowyer was known to be untenable against attack by land, Jackson not only retained Lieutenant-Colonel Law-

[1] Report of Feb. 14, 1815; Latour, Appendix, p. clxxii.

rence there, but increased his force until he had
three hundred and sixty men in his command, —
equal to the average strength of an entire regiment,
or half the force of regulars which Jackson commanded at New Orleans.    This garrison was only
large enough to attract, not to repel, an enemy.    The
obvious criticism on such a course was afterward
made by Armstrong : [1] —

" After the arrival of the British armament the garrison of Fort Bowyer was not only continued but increased, though from its locality wholly unable to aid
in any important purpose of the campaign.   Nor was
this the whole extent of the evil, for by the disposition
made of this gallant corps it was not only subjected to
present inaction, but ultimately . . . to the perils of a
siege and the humiliation of a surrender."

Colonel Lawrence had no choice but to capitulate,
which he did February 11.    He had not even the
opportunity to resist, for the British made regular
approaches, and could not be prevented from capturing the place without the necessity of assault.    Jackson reported to the Secretary of War [2] that this event
was one which he " little expected to happen but
after the most gallant resistance ; that it should have
taken place without even a fire from the enemy's
batteries is as astonishing as it is mortifying."    In
truth, the military arrangements, not Lawrence's de-

[1] Notices, ii. 176.

[2] Jackson's Report of Feb. 24, 1815; Latour, Appendix,
p. xcvii.

fence, were responsible for the result ; and Jackson had reason to fear that a greater disaster was at hand, for unless General Winchester should promptly evacuate Mobile, the disaster of the River Raisin was likely to be repeated on a larger scale.

END OF VOL. II.